BENT

Out of Shape

Reshaping Our
Emotional Lives

KAREN HENEIN

With Insights from Sam Henein, M.D.

Bent Out of Shape: Reshaping Our Emotional Lives

Copyright © 2008 Karen Henein

Unless otherwise indicated, Scripture quotations have been taken from The Living Bible, copyright © 1971 by Tyndale House Publishers, Wheaton, Illinois, 60189. Used by permission. All rights reserved.

Scripture quotations marked NIV are taken from the HOLY BIBLE, NEW INTERNATIONAL VERSION®. Copyright © 1973, 1978, 1984 by International Bible Society. Used by permission of Zondervan Publishing House. All rights reserved.

Scripture quotations marked NLT are taken from the *Holy Bible,* New Living Translation, copyright © 1996, 2004. Used by permission of Tyndale House Publishers, Inc., Wheaton, Illinois 60189. All rights reserved.

Scripture quotations marked NKJV are taken from the New King James Version, Copyright © 1979, 1980, 1982 by Thomas Nelson Inc., Publishers. Used by permission. All rights reserved.

Some words from Scripture have been *italicized* for emphasis by the author.

A few names have been changed to protect the privacy of the individual being referred to.

The views and opinions expressed by the author are not necessarily the opinions of any specific medical professional, except where a specific medical professional is directly footnoted, referred to, or quoted.

This book is not intended to take the place of medical advice from your personal physician or counseling advice from trained professionals. Readers are advised to consult their own doctors or other qualified health/counseling professionals regarding diagnosis and treatment of their physical, mental, and emotional health problems.

ISBN-10: 1-897373-44-9

ISBN-13: 978- 1-897373-44-6

WORD ALIVE PRESS

Published by:
Word Alive Press, 131 Cordite Road,
Winnipeg, MB, R3W 1S1

CONTENTS

THANK YOU NOTES

I express my deepest thanks to the many people who have journeyed with me as an author and helped to make this book possible.

First, I want to thank my husband, Sam, who encouraged me every step of the way and contributed wise insights to many chapters in this book. He spent a precious week with me on the seacoast of Maine, painstakingly critiquing the first draft of my manuscript, and later spent numerous late nights helping to polish the final draft.

I also thank my son, Darrin, and my daughter, Samantha, for their love and encouragement and for graciously granting me permission to use some stories from their lives. I am so proud of both of them.

I thank my mom, dad, sister, brothers, and sisters-in-law, for their interest, prayers, and support. I especially thank my brother, Dr. Darryl Milne, for taking the time to read my entire manuscript and for offering encouraging feedback.

I am also grateful to Shirley Hutchison for her helpful critique of an early draft and for her many prayers along the way.

Thanks to Jenny Morrison of Word Alive for her interest and support. Thanks to the rest of the staff at Word Alive Press for the parts they played in bringing this book to print, especially Caroline Schmidt, Larissa Bartos, and Nikki Braun.

So many others have helped and encouraged my ministry as an author: Bob and Hope Fitzgibbon of the Treasure House bookstores, Miranda, Sherif, and friends too numerous to name. I wish I could mention everyone who has prayed for me or contributed in some way to this book or to my journey as an author. I appreciate everyone who expressed their opinion and gave their input into title selection and cover design, especially Jill Goodman and my son, Darrin.

I thank every reader of my first book, particularly those who have taken the time to write, e-mail, phone, or speak with me in person, offering so many kind words. I pray that this second book is of some worth to many readers too.

Above all, I thank God for the time, energy, opportunity, knowledge, strength, inspiration, guidance, and help so generously granted to me. Without Him, I could not have brought this book to full fruition. May it be used for His purposes.

1
GRAFFITI
The Tangible Pain

...even the best years are filled with pain and trouble...
Psalm 90:10c (NLT)

...I am poor and needy, and my heart is full of pain.
Psalm 109:22 (NLT)

You have seen me tossing and turning through the night.
You have collected all my tears...
Psalm 56:8ab

A PSYCHIATRIST FRIEND named George practices in an urban neighborhood that is generally safe, clean, and prosperous. The quiet streets near his office are lined with comfortable homes and manicured gardens. On the surface, everything looks peaceful. How incongruent that so many people from these lovely homes need to spend time with George, downloading their various emotional problems.

George has confided how distressed he is about the rising number of his patients who are attempting to commit suicide. Some are so distraught that they slash their wrists in the washrooms of the medical building where George works, silently splattering the blood-red graffiti of their unbearable inner pain. George has to rise above his own discouragement to keep on treating his long roster of patients. The suicide attempts do not reflect on his professional abilities. They are, instead, a reflection of the society that we live in—and the growing pandemic of mental and emotional health problems in our present world.

Soul Dis-Ease

Pain inevitably shows up in everyone's life. So do problems, pressures, disappointments, stresses, and setbacks.

Many people in emotional turmoil do not know how to deal with their pain. To be honest, *all* of us need to learn more about how to handle our times of inner distress. Too often, we deal with our emotional discomfort in unhealthy ways.

Some cope by overeating, overspending, or over-indulging in alcohol. Others numb their feelings by watching hours of mindless television, robotically playing computer games, or aimlessly surfing the Net. Some turn to pornography, gambling, or drugs—whatever it takes to mask their persistent pain with the illusory relief of some soothing temporary pleasure. Emotional pain can be *distracted* and *dulled* by all of these strategies, but it is not eliminated—eventually the pain will burrow deep into the soul, becoming a powerful and primal force, causing all kinds of secondary problems.

Worldwide, one billion people are overweight. According to a 2006 United Nations study on drug abuse, about 200 million people (5% of the global population aged 15–64) use *illegal* drugs.[1] Millions more are hooked on prescription substances such as sleeping aids. For those who do not pop sleeping pills, insomnia holds further millions hostage at night. Close to half of Americans have a close family member (child, parent, spouse, or sibling) who is (or was) an alcoholic.[2]

Stress levels are skyrocketing off the charts. Billions of work-hours are lost to industry because of depression, chronic fatigue, and inability to concentrate. The opposite extreme also plagues our society—workaholics would rather work overtime at the office until exhaustion overtakes them than risk facing their inner selves at home in the evening.

---

[1] 2006 World Drug Report, published by the United Nations Office on Drugs and Crime.

[2] Statistics posted at www.alcoholism-information.com.

Edvard Munch's painting, *The Scream*, has achieved world-wide recognition—many people relate to the silent, naked agony on the contorted face that Munch painted. Reality television is wildly popular because we all like to know that other human beings feel the same messy emotions that we feel. Some chat rooms in cyberspace thrive for the same reason.

Doctor's offices cannot keep up with the long lines of patients, many of whom are seeking treatment for heartaches and headaches that originate at soul level. Waiting times for mental health professionals are especially long. (In my community, patients wait one year to see a psychiatrist.) Anorexia and bulimia cripple more and more young people. Violence is exploding all over the globe—not just *over there*, but in our own streets, parks, and college campuses.

All of this is not just happening to those *outside* the Christian faith. Any pastor will tell you that the Christian community also suffers from this pandemic of soul distress. Many sincere, committed Christians are poorly equipped to handle painful emotions in a healthy manner. They sometimes feel bent out of shape and don't know what to do about it. Like the rest of society, Christians are trying to cope with issues such as being unemployed, divorced, or diagnosed with a terminal illness—*and* all the uncomfortable feelings that follow. Even Christians who are highly successful in their careers and ministries, who are at the top of their games, who have great health and close circles of family and friends, sometimes quietly struggle with emotions such as anxiety or depression—and sadly, some succumb to alcoholism, pornography addiction, illicit affairs, career implosion, or other forms of needless self-destruction.

Kept busy with their parishioners' needs, pastors are often unable to process their own feelings. In a 2003 survey of over 1,200 clergy from United, Anglican, Presbyterian, Lutheran, Baptist, and Pentecostal churches, 62% agreed with the statement that sometimes their outward appearance conveys that they are happy and content while inside they are emotionally distressed.

Three quarters of them agreed with the statement that they are afraid to let their parishioners know how they *really* feel.[3]

Management Overload

This state of affairs has stealthily crept up on the Christian population. We are all so busy managing every *other* aspect of our overstressed, overstretched lives that we often do not have time or energy left to deal with our emotional dis-ease. Browse any bookstore and you will find shelves full of books on time management, money management, energy management, home management, lawn management, diet management—management of almost anything and everything under the sun. Recently, I read an article about cable management, offering tips on how to keep track of all the wires and cables in our home offices: the tangled mess of wires and cables connected to computer screens, hard-drives, keyboards, sound speakers, printers, scanners, telephones, and fax machines. At times, life can be a tangled mess on too many levels!

While we busily manage all the complex dimensions of modern life, we pay lesser attention to the endless stream of thoughts and emotions we experience each day. Our thoughts and feelings can sometimes become as chaotically tangled as all those interwoven wires and cables behind our desks. Too often, we allow ourselves to think *whatever* we think and feel *however* we feel while we focus much more faithfully on the management of car-pool schedules, grocery lists, career tasks, and credit card bills.

As you read this book, I invite you, for just a while, to forget about all those other lists, schedules, and tasks—and give yourself permission to focus and reflect on the *quality* of the thoughts and feelings you experience most days. I encourage you to give some prime time and attention to soul management.

---

[3] Survey results published on page L12 of the *Toronto Star* on September 15, 2007.

Secular Solutions Have Been Insufficient

Governments of wealthy countries are pouring billions of dollars into health care, including mental health care. Academics churn out study after study on human thought patterns and emotional functions. Pharmaceutical companies develop next-generation drugs that promise to elevate our moods or to chemically induce sleep. Television talk shows and popular magazines endlessly discuss emotional issues and supposed solutions. Yet the pandemic of soul distress continues. Secular help and media focus are of some use, of course, but clearly they have not stopped the tsunamic tide.

Many self-help books have been written on the subject of emotional management. But they offer only what they claim: self-help. If we could all help ourselves—*if it were only that simple!*—the world would already be a much saner, healthier, happier place. Alcohol, drugs, pornography, and other forms of pain relief would not be such big business. Self-help is of *some* worth, but it has not scratched the surface of the soul dis-ease that plagues our society. The latest psycho-babble can be as confusing as it is clarifying—yet these books continue to pile up on our bookshelves alongside the books on lawn management and diet management.

Perhaps it's time for us to stop relying so heavily on secular sources of help or on self-help. I believe there is a critical need for an entirely different source of help.

A "God-help" Book

I humbly submit that we need a lot more "God-help" in our emotional lives. That is what this book will attempt to deliver.

How *can* God help? What divine resources are available to us to help us turn the tide? What has God said about our feelings and how we should handle them? What does He expect us to do? What has He promised to do for us?

These are important questions to answer as we each struggle with a gamut of distressing, destructive emotions in these stress-crazed times. These critical questions intersect with some other common questions that Christians often ask, such as...

Where Is the Promised Love, Joy, and Peace?

Many years ago, when I was twenty years old, I had a perplexing conversation. As I tried to relax on a gorgeous summer day at a cottage on a Canadian lake, I chatted with an older woman about her life problems and her emotional stress. She had been a Christian for many years. I had only recently become a Christian. Her mood was out of sync with the exquisite beauty surrounding us. Her soul-baring did not fit comfortably with my youthful optimism and my freshly found spiritual enthusiasm.

As she described her low emotional state, this woman kept peppering me with questions like these: "Why don't Christians experience joy more often? Why is life such a struggle? Aren't we Christians promised love, joy, and peace?"

Barely into adulthood, I could not formulate a clear answer to those questions. I had recently finished an adventurous year of backpacking around Europe, during which I had decided to become a Christian. I was returning to university, excited about my studies and hopeful about a future in law. I did not bother to give these issues much thought that summer day. To be honest, I somewhat smugly wrote this older woman off as a bit of a whining misfit in the serene spiritual universe that seemed so tangible to *me* that day.

Some tough realities and tough feelings smack us all in the face sooner or later. Over time, I experienced my own share of hurts, failures, mistakes, problems, and disappointments—and all the messy emotions that accompanied them. I began to have more days when I felt discouraged, anxious, frustrated, or resentful.

At first, I fell into the trap of believing that I would be more consistently content and truly able to enjoy each day just as soon as I finished law school. Well, maybe it would happen after I finished the grueling exams of bar admission. Certainly I'd feel better once my career was firmly established. Surely I would find greater emotional satisfaction after I found a husband, settled into marriage, had children, set up a real home, and paid off the mortgage.

All of these milestones of life did not, however, *in and of themselves*, bring any consistently sustained emotional well-being—nor did the mere acts of attending church, teaching Sunday school, or serving on Christian Boards. I confess that I felt a little ripped off that my deepening Christian commitment did not guarantee the nirvana that I thought it should.

I don't want to paint too gloomy a picture. Over the years, I *have* felt joy, peace, and other wonderful emotions a lot of the time, especially when circumstances were great. But deep down, I have always believed that the *normal* Christian life should involve enjoying that kind of spiritual fruit *every* day—not just when the sun is shining and the sky is blue and the universe is as we think it should be.

So I found myself, from time to time, asking the same kinds of questions that my older friend had posed years before: Why *don't* we Christians experience love, joy, peace (and the other promised fruits of the Spirit) as our *normal* emotional state? Why do these desirable states of being sometimes seem so elusive? Are the promises in the Bible in this regard not genuine and trustworthy? As Christians, shouldn't we all be cheerful, radiant, and calm? Why do we sometimes feel as stressed, frustrated, beaten down, ticked off, and shaken up as the world around us? How should we deal with the plethora of unpleasant emotions that seem to be our human default setting?

Everyone Has Emotional Struggles

If we are honest, we all encounter some unpleasant emotions virtually every day. Some people primarily battle fear, worry, and anxiety. Others wrestle most often with anger, resentment, and bitterness. Many are disabled by discouragement, despair, and depression. A number feel unsettled by jealousy and discontentment. We *all* encounter these various feelings from time to time. No one sails along in unbroken bliss. We all have times when we feel bent out of shape.

Certain emotions eventually become more dominant in each of our lives. We can look at someone else's face, listen to the tone of their voice, absorb their words, observe their body language, watch their actions—and come away with an impression that they are an angry person, or a bitter person, or a sad person. Of course, it is much more difficult to see our own dominant emotions so clearly!

When we observe the lives of celebrities and high achievers—the rich, the beautiful, the brilliant, the talented, the anointed—we might imagine that they are exempt from this and that they are always satisfied, content, at ease, and well able to enjoy their lives. But if we look a little closer, we see that life deals some harsh blows to pretty much everyone, pummeling us all with unwelcome feelings.

Take, for example, Laura Bush, wife of American President George Bush. Photos of her usually show a smiling, serene, beautifully dressed, and dignified woman. She lives in a world of wealth, power, and privilege, surrounded by family and friends. Yet, even the most basic research into her life shows that she, too, has experienced her share of emotional pain and struggle.

As a seventeen-year-old teenager, for example, Laura drove past a stop sign at a country intersection, broad-siding a vehicle that was also crossing through the intersection. Her view of that other vehicle, as it had approached the fatal intersection, had been blocked by some trees. After the collision, the driver of the other vehicle died almost instantly. He was a popular star athlete at her high school *and* a close friend of hers. That single moment imploded her world.

Laura Bush was too distraught to go to the funeral. In fact, she stayed away from school for several weeks. The intensity and range of emotions she must have battled are beyond my comprehension. According to her, the pain and grief that she endured after that tragic accident were "crushing."[4]

Becoming a Christian does not protect us from tough circumstances or their attendant emotional trauma, turmoil, temptation, trials, and tempests. Even after becoming a Christian, we will still face times of guilt, fear, anger, worry, despair, and jealousy within our souls. It helps to frankly admit this.

And so, these interconnected questions face all Christians: What about the biblical promises that we will receive love, joy, peace, and other wonderful states of being? Why are so many Christians defeated, immobilized, unsettled, or chronically exhausted? Why *is* life such an emotional struggle so much of the time? How are Christians meant to find and maintain sound emotional health, wholeness, and well-being? Where *is* God in all of this?

In this book, I hope to show you that, with God's help, Christians *can* enjoy healthy emotional lives most moments of most days—that love, joy, peace, and other desirable states of being *can* permeate our normal lives, regardless of our ever-changing circumstances.

Presenting My Case

Let me share with you how my background has shaped the way that I will tackle the topic of soul management. I am not writing on this topic because I claim to be a spiritual giant with a perfectly-managed soul. If I tried to write this book on that basis, I would fall flat on my face! I am as human, fallible, and faltering as the next person, with my own share of frenzied feelings. Nor am I writing from the point of view of an expert on human emotions.

For twenty years, I practiced as a lawyer. It takes courage to admit this because I know that lawyers are not exactly popular—I

---

[4] Ann Gerhart, *The Perfect Wife: The Life and Choices of Laura Bush,* and various media reports.

have heard my share of nasty lawyer jokes. (What is the difference between a woman lawyer and a pitbull? Lipstick. You've got to agree that's nasty!) On the bright side, my training and experience as a trial lawyer has been useful in putting this kind of book together.

In each legal file I handled, I usually spent a few years building a case—reviewing germane documents, interviewing relevant witnesses, consulting the pertinent experts, and bringing to bear the proper laws and principles upon which everything else rested. All of this had to be organized, analyzed, and eventually presented to judges and juries—in simple layman's terms, understandable to all.

In the following pages, we will be discussing how Christians are meant to manage their emotional lives. I have approached researching and writing on this topic the same way I methodically assembled my legal cases. Like a well-prepared court case, this book will have some key components.

The Documents

The most important document that I will place into evidence to support the various points I make in this book is the Bible. I will present hundreds of Bible verses that shed light on what God has to say about our emotions. What I, the author, have to say to you is of limited value. What *God* has to say is life-changing.

The Bible offers tremendous insight into healthy emotional management. I do not want you to rely on *me*, nor on anyone else I refer to, to make you feel better. Remember, this is a "God-help" book. I want you to fundamentally turn to *Him* for the ultimate answers to your emotional dis-ease. Maybe you regard the Bible as the infallible word of God. If so, you will value the many Scripture verses I refer to. Maybe you're not convinced that the Bible is so special. I invite to read on anyway—you might be surprised at the insights you will receive from the verses I quote.

As a trial lawyer, I often had to read large briefs of written material before appearing in Court. As a committed Christian, I reasoned that I ought to know the Bible as well as I purposed to know my legal materials. Once that conviction hit me, I began reading the Bible daily with the same effort and diligence as I read my legal briefs.

Over the years, I have read the Bible from cover to cover a few dozen times. In recent years, as I worked on this book, I have made a point of specifically looking for stories and verses that involve the emotional dimension of human experience. If you are wondering what credentials I have for writing this "God-help" book, this is arguably my highest credential.

In preparing my points at the level of document review, I have also read numerous other books and articles. Some of them were written by experts who research emotions or who counsel those with emotional issues. Others were written by or about Christians who have battled tough emotions arising out of a range of life experiences such as rape, abuse, marital breakdown, unjust imprisonment, being held hostage, sustaining injuries in wartime hostilities, burying a murdered family member, and many other extremely difficult circumstances.

The Witnesses

Any case is brought to life by the testimony of witnesses—by the compelling stories of real people. In this book, several dozen well-known Christians will be my witnesses. Most of their lives will demonstrate God's partnership with them in getting a grip on some very brutal emotions. A few lives will serve as warnings of the dangers inherent in ignoring emotional dis-ease.

Friends and family members have given me permission to share some of their stories too. I have not been alone on my journey; how thankful I am for the many wonderful souls who have shared this life with me, messy emotions and all!

I have had my share of bumps and bruises. I will tell some of my own stories in the chapters ahead. You will read about how

God met with me in the toughest times, empowering me to keep moving forward, helping me to deal with unwanted emotions. Rest assured that I do not consider myself super-spiritual, nor do I hold myself out as the most exemplary role model to follow. I am *not* a perfectly-managed soul, nor am I on a pedestal looking down at you. I am simply a fellow Christian, struggling with my own human feelings and failings.

The Experts

Who are my experts? God is, of course, the most qualified Expert. He created our spirits and our souls. He knows how we are supposed to function at our best—spiritually, mentally, emotionally, relationally, and physically. He knows, with perfect understanding, how these dimensions of our lives ought to work together.

This book has also been enriched, to a degree, by the insights of Christian doctors, psychiatrists, psychologists, pastors, and other trained counselors. Some of them I know personally. Over the decades, I have heard many excellent sermons about emotions. As mentioned earlier, I have also read several books on the subject of healthy emotional management. My favorite books on this topic are listed in the Selected Bibliography at the end of this book. In addition, I have kept an eye on the opinions being expressed by secular experts and have foot-noted some of their books and articles.

From time to time, I will make specific reference to specific experts. Many of my comments, however, are undergirded with the blended opinions of multiple sources. After all, no single expert would profess to have nailed this whole subject down. Many of the points I will present are a synthesis of what I have learned from a variety of professionals and pastors as I have processed and applied their wise advice over my lifetime.

Let me tell you about my most special professional expert. His name is Sam and he has practiced medicine for nearly three decades. We married almost twenty-five years ago. As a doctor in general practice, Sam has counseled countless patients grappling with emotional traumas and issues. I have learned much from his deep insights and his compassionate understanding of human pain. By relational osmosis, I have absorbed some of his accumulated knowledge and perspective.

I have been interested to hear him say, time and again, that the majority of patients he sees on a daily basis are really there because of some underlying emotional difficulties. Of course, these patients usually come in initially complaining about some actual physical problem, such as insomnia or ulcers, high blood pressure or headaches. Sam does not usually have to scratch very deep below the surface, however, to discover that many patients (including his Christian patients) have issues with emotions such as anger, unforgiveness, anxiety, or despair.

I have consulted with my husband regarding parts of this book and have included some of his insights, which are based on his knowledge of studies in the fields of medicine and psychology, but also on his decades of experience as a primary care physician. He has helped me to understand how the mind, the emotions, and the body interact. He has given me insight into how particular feelings ultimately affect our physical health. He has discussed with me some of the best therapies available, particularly those compatible with Christian principles. I have learned so much from "Dr. Sam" and I know that you will too.

The Laws and Principles

What laws and principles will I be applying? First and foremost, everything I say is grounded upon the laws and life-principles that God has put into place regarding our spirit, soul, and body. On a secondary level, I will talk occasionally about the laws and principles of human fields of study.

Finding quality of emotional well-being does not have to be magical, mystical, or manufactured. Christians have the priceless privilege of having access to a host of biblical principles that teach us how to successfully manage our emotions.

Encountering God

Beyond the documents, witnesses, experts, and principles, you will hopefully have some fresh encounters with the living God in these pages—and you will be mightily impacted by any such encounters. I have no power to "fix" you, but I am acquainted with the living God who wants to keep each one of us on the path of ongoing emotional well-being.

This is not a theology textbook, a medical textbook, or a psychology textbook. This is ultimately a book about how God can be powerfully invited into the very depths of our souls and about how He wants to partner with us in overcoming our soul distress. God can help us to achieve emotionally healthy souls that no longer need to focus obsessively on self, but are instead free to love and bless others—even in the *midst* of the pain, problems, and pressures of this fallen world.

God has so much compassion for us in the area of emotional pain and struggle. He created us, emotions and all. Our heavenly Father is Himself an emotional Being. Even the most superficial read through the Bible reveals Him to be a God of love, anger, grief, sorrow, peace, and forgiveness. He *understands* our emotions.

Jesus, His Son, lived among us as a man so He could also fully relate to our feelings and our humanity.[5] Jesus experienced what it's like to enjoy people but also suffer emotional pain, rejection, criticism, and sorrow. He loved and He cared and He freely forgave. Jesus wept when He heard that Lazarus had died.[6] He was deeply distressed and troubled in the Garden of Gethsemane.[7] He is therefore able to personally identify with our human hurts and inner struggles.

Isaiah 61:1 tells us that one of the reasons Jesus came to live among us, and then to die for us, was so He could heal the

---

[5] Hebrews 4:14–15.

[6] John 11:35.

[7] Mark 14:32.

broken-hearted and bring good news to those who suffer. He wants to set us free from all harmful emotions.

God wants to partner with us in the management of our emotions. In this book, we will explore what part *we* are supposed to play, and what part *God* promises to play, in the development of a healthy emotional life.

Early in our Christian walk, there is a tendency to expect God to do everything—to pour out joy or peace on us just because we ask, or just because we have made a Christian commitment, or just because we go to church on Sunday. We naively expect to pray for love, joy, and peace and then be "zapped" with these wonderful states of being.

When this does not work, we often go to the other extreme and mostly rely on our own self-effort, trying in our own strength to feel how we believe Christians are supposed to feel.

I have personally tried both options: beseeching God to bestow upon me joy and peace as gifts from above and working hard at trying to create more joy and peace all on my own. Neither extreme works. Neither extreme is biblical.

Successful emotional management lies in an ongoing *partnership* between each one of us and God. We cannot always deal with powerful emotions on our own. We cannot expect God to do everything for us. If we do our part, He will do His.

The Invitation

Life will always have some problems and challenges. We cannot wait until life is perfect, settled, or under control before we seek joy, peace, and other attributes of emotional well-being. Life will never reach a steady state of being perfect, settled, or under control. Yet we *can* learn to enjoy our emotional lives every day, no matter what comes our way. We do not have to live with soul distress.

We do not need to be defeated by even the toughest of circumstances. Take, for example, Bethany Hamilton, a teenager whose life took an unexpected turn one October morning in

2003. She was just thirteen years old at the time and already such a highly ranked surfer that she was planning to turn pro. That morning, as she surfed off the coast of Hawaii, she was suddenly attacked by a large tiger shark. Within moments, she lost her left arm to the vicious shark.

Bethany could have spent her ensuing days, months, and years immobilized by anger, bitterness, self-pity, depression, and hopelessness. Instead, the vibrant young Christian used the attention of the international media to tell the world how her faith was helping her cope with her tragic circumstances. She invited God into her feelings as she coped with her circumstances. And He clearly responded. Both her physical and emotional recoveries were astounding. Within weeks she was back to surfing—in oceans still full of sharks—learning to balance with only one arm. She has high hopes of continuing with her surfing dreams.[8]

As you read many more incredible stories in the coming pages, I encourage you to invite God and His unlimited power into your circumstances and into your emotional responses to all that is happening in your life. He longs to comfort the broken-hearted and refresh the weary. He promises to respond when we call out for Him. He longs for us to live in love, forgiveness, peace, faith—with hope, joy, gratitude, and contentment. He can show us the way!

Come to me, all of you who are weary and carry heavy burdens,
and I will give you rest...Let me teach you
...and you will find rest for your souls.
Matthew 11:28–29 (NLT)

---

[8] www.bethanyhamilton.com and www.christianitytoday.com.

2
SPIRIT, SOUL, AND SYNERGY
Core Strength

FTER GIVING BIRTH to my second child, I began to experience a lot of back pain. I went to a doctor, expecting him to prescribe some medication to get rid of the pain. I wanted instant relief. Instead of prescribing pills, however, the doctor simply told me that I was out of shape. The only prescription he gave me was to get a lot more exercise—to work at developing core strength—strong and solid muscles in my back and abdomen to support the main trunk of my body.

This was not what I wanted to hear—who likes to hear that they are out of shape?—but I decided to take his advice. And it turned out he was right; once I developed that core strength, all the physical discomfort went away. I could comfortably stand straight again.

Just as we need to develop physical core strength, to function at our best, we also need to develop core strength in our interior world. Our lives will never be lived to their fullest potential if we fail to develop strength in our innermost core.

Our Inner Core: Spirit and Soul

Each individual has a body, a spirit, and a soul. This view derives from verses (such as 1 Thessalonians 5:23) which refer to the body, spirit, and soul as distinct parts of our beings. The body is obviously our outer self. The spirit and soul form the deepest inner core. This book will discuss how the soul is supposed to work in *cooperation* with (instead of in *conflict* with) the spirit.

I promised that this book would analyze what part *we* play in dealing with our negative thoughts and feelings and what part *God* plays. Before we can embark on this analysis, we must first briefly explore the difference between our spirit and our soul.

That the soul and the spirit are in fact different parts of our inner world can be seen in verses such as Hebrews 4:12a: "For the word of God is alive and powerful. It is sharper than the sharpest two-edged sword, cutting between *soul* and *spirit*, between joint and marrow." (NLT)

This is not an academic theological textbook, so I do not intend to get into a deep debate about the exact definition of the words "soul" and "spirit." (Similarly, later on, I will not attempt to strictly define words like "heart" or "mind.") These words all carry many nuances and layers of meaning. Splitting hairs over the fine nuances of these words is not necessary in this book—the main principles can be advanced and understood within a framework of general descriptions.

The Spirit Dimension of Our Being

The "spirit" is that part of us which is capable of connecting with God. Until we make such connection, however, the spirit dimension of our being often feels empty and unsatisfied. Seventeenth century French physicist and philosopher Blaise Pascal once talked about the God-shaped abyss within us that only God can properly fill. This deep empty space within is the part of us that seeks spiritual experience, the compass of truth, and the supernatural realm—that yearns to discover whether there is a God, who He is, and how we can relate to Him.

John 3:3–7 talks about how we must be born again, not of the flesh but of the spirit. This involves a new birth within, inviting the very Spirit of God to indwell the spirit dimension of our being.

In a nutshell, this process of spiritual birth involves believing that: there is a God; He loves us; we are sinners (our greatest sin being our rebellion from God); in that state we are separated from God; we cannot save ourselves; and Jesus, as the Son of God, died for our sins so that we might be reconciled to God. If we confess that we are sinners, ask for God's forgiveness, and thereby personally accept what Jesus did for us, we are spiritually born again.

As a result of all this, we receive the promised indwelling of God's Holy Spirit. We do not have to earn this salvation and this spiritual birth. Salvation is a free gift from a gracious God. Spiritual birth is a miracle waiting to happen in each of our lives. It is even more miraculous than natural birth. By admitting that God is indeed God and that we are part of the fallen human race in need of redemption, we can enter into right standing with God.

If you have not experienced being spiritually "born again," then I invite you to turn to Appendix A to discover how you can enter into a personal relationship with God and how the Holy Spirit can come to indwell the spirit dimension of your being.

Once we are born again, we begin to develop spiritual core strength by disciplines and activities such as prayer, Bible study, and fellowship with other Christians. We cannot properly mature and develop *spiritually*, however, if at *soul* level we remain sick, weak, or stressed.

The Soul Dimension of Our Being

All human beings are born with a "soul." The soul is comprised of three parts: the mind, the emotions, and the will.

Our souls develop from earliest childhood. Observe a typical two-year-old and notice how they have an emerging mind of their own, independent feelings, and a strong will. (Napoleon allegedly once said, "Give me ten toddlers and I can take over the world!")

Our soul dimension is usually very full—in fact, our souls are usually *so* full they overflow. The steady inner stream of our thoughts and feelings eventually spill out as words, attitudes, and actions. For better or worse.

Even after we are born again (in the spirit part of our being), each one of us still retains a soul. We still have free will. We still have a continual inner stream of thoughts and feelings. Many of those thoughts and feelings remain negative, unhealthy, and sometimes even sinful.

In our soul dimension, much work must be done as we begin our journey in the Christian life. As we mature *spiritually*, we must also mature in our *soul management*. To the extent we ignore our soul, we often feel a sense of soul dis-ease—nagging interior emotional discomfort—or perhaps even an inner furnace of raging emotions.

It took me years to really grasp that spiritual development and soul management are two different processes. In my early adult years, even though I had become a committed Christian, I often lived as a hostage to my shifting emotions. If I woke up feeling sad, then I went on to have a blue day. If I woke up feeling worried about something, I would work myself into even greater anxiety as the day wore on. If I woke up feeling angry about something, I usually fed that anger throughout the day, and it was even stronger anger by sundown. I let my emotions run their own course.

On many occasions, it took a good turn in circumstances to get me out of a negative, downward emotional spiral. On other days I would wake up feeling happy or excited about something, but an unpleasant change of circumstances would then trigger negative emotions. I often let those negative feelings guide my thoughts, without making enough deliberate choice regarding my thoughts and feelings. I too often accepted whatever thoughts and emotions sprung up in response to my changing circumstances.

At the start of the Christian journey, our soul is often in a terrible mess—the product of wherever our life has been up to that point. We might be full of hatred, bitterness, anger, jealousy, self-pity, and many other destructive emotions. We may have accumulated a lifetime of memories that continue to trigger these emotions. We may also have *some* measure of love, happiness, hope, and other positive feelings, but these have, up until the start of our Christian journey, been solely the product of human effort.

After our new spiritual life begins, at *soul* level we must learn: how to make right choices with our will; how to renew our mind; and how to consciously rule over our feelings. When we learn to do *our* part in this, the Holy Spirit is able to then pour out His measure of love, joy, peace, and other spiritual fruits that transcend what we could ever achieve by mere human effort.

Our *will* can be used to manage our *thoughts,* which then influence our *feelings.*

Our soul, however, often operates in backward fashion: our lives are too easily dominated by the transient whims of our capricious feelings. Our feelings too often govern our thoughts, which then determine how we steer our will to act and speak. This is where our soul really gets messed up.

Instead of letting our feelings hijack our lives, we must train our wills to consciously manage our thoughts, which can then steer our emotions in healthy directions.

In his poem, "Invictus," W.E. Henley once wrote: "I am the captain of my soul."[9] God does expect us to be the "captain" of the *soul* dimension of our lives. We *can* steer our souls.

The Soul is Intended to Cooperate with the Spirit

Our soul (under our control) is intended to *cooperate* with our spirit (indwelt and controlled by the Holy Spirit). The Spirit wants to help us discover the best direction in which to steer our will, thoughts, and emotions hour by hour.

Does this happen smoothly and surely each moment? Unfortunately, the answer is no. Because of our flawed humanity, our imperfect maturity, and the stubbornly remaining traces of our

---

[9] From W.E. Henley's poem "Invictus" (1875, Public Domain).

old nature, there is often an internal war going on between soul and spirit. In Galatians, Paul described this inner struggle: "For we naturally love to do evil things that are just the opposite from the things that the Holy Spirit tells us to do; and the good things we want to do when the Spirit has his way with us are just the opposite of our natural desires. These two forces within us are constantly fighting each other to win control over us, and our wishes are never free from their pressures."[10]

Can you relate to this kind of inner battle—the battle between base human nature and higher spiritual desire? Part of our Christian growth involves letting our soul be led by the Spirit, as Paul instructed us in Romans 8:14. The soul and the spirit are supposed to exist in harmony, not in friction. While we have the responsibility of captaining our will, our thoughts, and our feelings, the Spirit can be a wonderful navigator if we let Him take that role.

Permit me to share one example of how I have sometimes personally impeded this intended cooperation between spirit and soul. I have a tendency to worry, to fret, and to be anxious. Even though I have now been a committed Christian for more than three decades, this part of my personality still continues to operate from time to time.

Spiritually, I desire inner peace. I pray for God to give me His promised peace. I wait for the Spirit to give me this peace. But I have learned that this is not enough. If I *choose* (with my will) to keep on *thinking* anxious thoughts, then I will continue to *feel* anxious. The Holy Spirit will not override my own will. Though He longs to give me the peace that I desire, He will not take charge of my thoughts or my feelings. Those remain my responsibility. The Spirit will not *give* me peace of mind and heart as long as I *choose* to worry and fret. A self-inflicted internal war will carry on for as long as my soul makes choices inconsistent with what my spirit desires.

---

[10] Galatians 5:17.

If, however, I use my will to make the choice *not* to worry but instead to think thoughts about trusting in God, then I will start to calm myself. I will begin to feel a certain measure of peace. It is only then that the Holy Spirit, by His power, is able to complement what I have done in my soul by giving me the peace "that transcends all understanding."[11] What has been done in the natural realm is then magnified and completed by what is done in the supernatural realm. An amazing synergy between my soul's power and the Spirit's power takes place, and the resulting peace within me surpasses the measure of peace I could ever have attained by mere human effort.

The lesson is, quite simply, that I cannot choose to worry and fret and at the same time expect God to "zap" me with His peace. It is only after I deliberately and mindfully choose to stop worrying that the Holy Spirit can then give me His peace.

Here is another practical example of how the soul and spirit sometimes work against each other. Suppose a person is angry because someone has hurt them. Suppose they nurture that initial anger by choosing to constantly replay the hurtful incident in their mind. They will, no doubt, continue to feel angry. And so, they will likely continue to think negatively about the other person and to maintain angry feelings toward them, setting the soul on a destructive downward spiral. In this example, the mind, will, and emotions have conspired, in the soul realm, to sustain anger.

What do you think will happen if that angry person prays for God to give them peace of heart and mind? Of course they want to get rid of the soul discomfort that they are feeling. Even if they plead for peace, however, God will not grant it. God *wants* to give the person peace—indeed He promised to give it even before the person prayed for it. But God has also commanded us to forgive others when they hurt us and to not let the sun go down on our anger. It is only when the person *chooses* (with their will, whether they feel like it or not) to forgive the offender, and

---

[11] Philippians 4:7 (NIV).

to *think* thoughts consistent with forgiveness, that eventually they will begin to *feel* that forgiveness.

Anger must be deliberately displaced with forgiveness. Only after this work has been done in the soul realm, by human effort, can the Holy Spirit come in with the divine peace of heart and mind that He bestows. The Spirit will also add supernatural empowerment to the forgiveness process. As yet a further bonus, the Holy Spirit will begin to heal the hurt that triggered the anger in the first place.

These examples demonstrate how God wants us to partner with Him—to cooperate and to work with Him. In this partnership, the efforts of the soul need to line up with the desires of the spirit.

This is not just "self-help," which has such limited power to overcome anxiety, anger, or despair, nor is it just sitting around waiting for God to do everything for us. This is a "God-help" book—underline both "God" and "help." God is an essential part of healthy soul management. But God is our "Helper" in this—He does not magically and mystically zap us with positive feelings if *we* are choosing to get stuck in negative thoughts and emotions.

God Wants to Partner with Us in All of Life

The principle of partnering our efforts with God's power is not unique to the realm of soul management. This principle of partnering with God should operate in *every* area of our Christian lives. Let's look at the bigger picture for just a moment.

This same principle of human-divine partnership is applicable to our financial affairs. The Bible promises that God will provide for all of our needs and that He will prosper us. But we must also do our part. We can certainly pray and have faith that God will meet our material needs. But we must also work with our own hands. We must use our gifts and skills. We cannot sit back on the sofa, watching television, expecting checks to miraculously arrive in the mail. (While occasionally this kind of miracle happens in response to faith and prayer, it is not the usual Christian experience, and it does not happen to spiritual couch potatoes!) *If* we do our part in the natural, *then* God blesses in the supernatural. We can partner with God in financial management. We must be willing to take the first steps (with both faith and practical action) to set the partnership in motion.

We can also partner with God in our health management. God promises us health, strength, and energy. But once again, we must do our part. We must do everything we can, on a practical level, to promote our own good health. We cannot smoke, eat poorly, never exercise, stay up late, and drink heavily and then expect good health and long lives just because the Bible promises these things. God will not override our poor choices. *We* must do our part, *then* God can do His. We need to pray, have faith, eat well, exercise, rest, perhaps see a doctor, maybe take some medicine, and then God can add His power to the process.

This pattern of human-divine partnership is evident throughout Scripture. In Deuteronomy 28, God said to the people of Israel that *if* they obeyed God and followed all of His commands, *then* He would give them various blessings. Many times, through the prophets, God told Israel that *if* they would repent, *then* He would restore them. *If* they drew near to Him, *then* He would draw near to them. The "if/then" pattern is a repeated biblical theme. By God's design, natural effort usually precedes the supernatural action.

Successful Soul Management:
If We Do Our Part, Then God Does His

If God wants to partner with us in every other area of our lives, it is no surprise that He wants to partner with us in healthy soul management. The same "if/then" process applies. *If* we choose to enjoy our lives, no matter what comes our way, *then* God will pour out His joy upon us. *If* we pursue peace, *then* God will amplify the sense of serenity and well-being within. *If* we choose to not be jealous, *then* God will enable us to be content with our personal lot in life.

God expects us to do our part first. This sounds so simple—yet I admit that it took me years to really grasp how this principle applied to my ever-changing emotional life.

I have heard synergy defined as $1 + 1 = 3$. Perhaps the synergy in this case should more accurately be defined as $1 + 1 =$ infinite power. Our human efforts to control our thoughts and feelings, augmented by God's incomparable and unlimited help, add up to incredible results! Let's move on to more fully explore this miraculous equation in the realm of soul management. Let's discover how, with God in the picture, we *can* develop unassailable core strength in our innermost beings, enabling us to address our inner pain and discomfort. Whether life circumstances have *bent* us out of shape, or we have allowed ourselves to slip into poor shape emotionally, it's possible to get in better shape.

3
CAPTURING OUR THOUGHTS AND EMOTIONS
Timeless Truths

...the Lord sees every heart
and understands and knows every thought.
1 Chronicles 28:9b

A man without self-control is as defenseless
as a city with broken-down walls.
Proverbs 25:28

Keep a close watch on all you do and think.
1 Timothy 4:16a

W HEN MY CHILDREN were young, I planted a vegetable garden in our backyard. The three of us had a lot of fun growing peas, carrots, chives, lettuce, and corn. I taught my children how to tend the garden with great care—removing weeds before they had the chance to grow, watering the seedlings, turning the soil. We loved to feast on the products of our labor.

Then, for a few consecutive summers, we took leave from our work and spent six weeks on medical mission trips to various countries in Africa. How sad the three of us were to come home to our beloved garden patch, only to see it so overgrown with giant weeds, and crawling with nasty insects—its delicious produce raided by rabbits, squirrels, chipmunks, and birds.

At the end of those summers, I had to hire men to aggressively rototil the forlorn garden patch with a large, noisy machine. This process destroyed the roots of hundreds of unwanted weeds and turned the hardened soil.

The soul dimension of our lives can be compared to my family's beloved vegetable garden. This metaphor is timeless and universally apt. In His parables, Jesus loved to use images of seeds, soil, weeds, gardeners, crops, and harvests.

Just like a garden, the *soul* can be tended or untended—carefully and lovingly watered, fed, and manicured or negligently left to the mental and emotional equivalents of weeds, pests, and diseases. A beautiful garden needs constant planting, pruning, nurturing, fertilizing, mulching, surveillance, and protection. All that is harmful—the prickly thorns and thistles, the slimy slugs, the necrotic rings—must be deliberately expelled as soon as possible.

Ecclesiastes 3:2 talks about there being a time to plant and a time to uproot plants. This book will talk about what is worthy of being planted and nurtured in our souls as well as what must be diligently uprooted.

We cannot control all of the circumstances of our lives or the people that we interact with. But we *can* control our inner selves—our wills, thoughts, and feelings.

If we neglect the deliberate tending of our souls, our interior worlds will become as dead, as dry, as unruly, as tangled, as rotten, as ravaged, as pathetic, and as barren of fruit as that neglected vegetable patch those long ago summers.

I invite you to meditate for a moment on the word picture found in Joel 1:10–12: "The fields are bare of crops. Sorrow and sadness are everywhere. The grain, the grapes, the olive oil are gone. Well may you farmers stand so shocked and stricken; well may you vinedressers weep. Weep for the wheat and the barley too, for they are gone. The grapevines are dead; the fig trees are dying; the pomegranates wither; the apples shrivel on the trees; all joy has withered with them." Do we want our souls to be as desolate as the neglected fields that Joel was describing?

We can learn to be good gardeners of our inner selves. Let's look, in greater detail, at *how* we are to tend our minds and our feelings.

The Human Will

First, let's invest some further time addressing the important issue of our will. Just as we need tools to manage our gardens, we need our will to manage our thoughts and feelings. Although this book is primarily meant to be about our emotional lives, our feelings cannot be properly controlled without understanding how they relate to our will and our thoughts.

Because we are born with a free will, we can think whatever we choose to think and feel whatever we choose to feel.

We can even choose to not exercise our will. For example, during our busy days, how often do we pause to think about our streams of thought? Too often, we just passively accept almost every thought that travels through our minds without much deliberate filtering. Similarly, we too often passively feel whatever feelings develop as a result of our unmanaged thoughts. No wonder we too often suffer from that vague sense of soul dis-ease.

The Bible teaches us that we are to put great effort into managing our thoughts and feelings, using our will to do so. We are to develop a high level of self-control. Our thoughts and feelings are not meant to run wild, however poetic that kind of impulse may seem.

Paul challenged his fellow Christians: "...let us be alert and self-controlled."[12] In Galatians 5:23, Paul listed self-control as one of the fruits of the Spirit-filled life.

Peter also urged his fellow Christians to exercise self-control. Over and over, he encouraged others to be alert, clear-minded, and self-controlled.[13]

I have heard many sermons comparing the mind to a television or a computer. Just as we can click a remote control to change

---

[12] 1 Thessalonians 5:6 (NIV).
[13] See, for example, 1 Peter 1:13, 4:7, and 5:8.

the channel on the TV or click a mouse to exit an undesirable page on the Internet, we can use our wills to change the channel or the screen that is playing in our minds.

These analogies are cliché, but they are effective—I suppose that is why they are repeated so often! We cannot be reminded often enough that we *can* and *should* change the channels in our minds as freely as we change the channels on our television sets or the websites on our computer screens. Most of us are highly deliberate about what we choose to rent from the video store. Are we just as diligent in closely monitoring what plays in our heads all through the day?

Just as a movie or a website can affect our emotions, what plays in our mind throughout the day also has great impact on our feelings. Let's consciously remember that we have an inner remote control that we can use to change what we are thinking and feeling when such change is warranted.

As we explore a number of undesirable emotions in this book, we will see that these emotions cannot be brought under control unless we exercise our will. We will see how we can use our will to choose to get rid of unhelpful thoughts before they lead to debilitating emotions. We cannot simply wish them away or pray them away. Like it or not, we have to be self-controlled. We have to willfully decide not to entertain that resentful thought, that propensity to worry, or that attitude of ingratitude. I'm as lazy as the next person, so I don't like all this self-control business any more than you do. But I've come to accept the fact that it's necessary if I want to enjoy my life at soul level.

Hannah Whitall Smith wrote about negative thoughts and emotions knocking at the door of our mind. She stated the obvious—that we do not have to let these kinds of thoughts and feelings walk in the door. We can slam the door in their faces! Yet how often do we so unwisely let harmful thoughts and emotions in the doors of our minds as if they were welcome guests we want to spend time with.

Hannah Whitall Smith said, quite simply, that we must choose to put our will over on the Lord's side. It is only then that God will help us with our mental and emotional battles.[14]

Throughout this book, I will encourage you to use your will to say to yourself: I choose not to be angry; I choose to forgive; I choose not to worry; I choose to have faith and trust; I choose not to be discouraged; I choose hope—and so on. These kinds of choices have to be made first, before we can effectively receive God's help and empowerment.

Canadian psychiatrist Dr. Stephen Stokl said this about the power of the will: "We all have heard of professionals who say that people never really change. They back this up with the metaphor, 'A leopard never loses its spots.' Human beings, unlike animals, have will power and they have the power to malign, hate and destroy, or to build, imagine, laugh, love, and pray. It is this power to choose and the free will to carve out their own attitude and destiny in any given set of circumstances, that gives mankind the ability to 'lose and gain' its spots."[15] In treating his patients, Dr. Stokl understands the incredible significance of the human will.

Although human willpower is not enough *on its own* to effect truly deep and lasting change (we do desperately need God's help and empowerment!), exercising the will is the first step on the road to healthy soul management. No one else can change our thoughts and feelings—not the most gifted psychiatrist, psychologist, doctor, author, pastor, parent, or friend. Each one of us needs to take personal responsibility for what goes on inside our mind and heart.

We cannot blame anyone else for the anger or the hatred or the fear or the despair that lurks within. No matter what terrible circumstances or hurtful relationships we have experienced in the past, we must take authority over—and responsibility for—what happens within our inner world. We are not helpless. We are not

---

[14] Hannah Whitall Smith, *The Christian's Secret of a Happy Life.*

[15] Dr. Stephen Stokl, *Mentally Speaking,* pg. 398.

victims. No matter what tragedies, abuse, or pain we have suffered, we *can* choose to be happy, hopeful, loving, forgiving, peace-filled, grateful, and content people. We can choose to get rid of our bitterness, hatred, and anxiety.

The human will *can* be independent of circumstances and it *can* be independent of those around us.

So let's get the main focus off of the past. The past cannot be changed. In the present, we cannot control the behavior of others. We cannot totally control our environment.

Let's instead focus on what we *can* control—and we can, in fact, control our interior worlds. Let us also get our focus on the God who is able and willing to help us. Let's stop being so *reactive* to our circumstances and *codependent* on how other people behave. Let's choose to be *pro-active*. Click that inner mouse, thumb that inner remote control. Mental and emotional well-being is often just a click away; it is achieved, as a normal state of being, one inner click at a time.

Our Thoughts

The Bible has much to say about our minds and how we are to manage them. One cannot expect to grow spiritually or to be emotionally at ease without doing mental house-keeping on a *daily* basis. I will spend time later talking about what we should do about our memories. At this point, let's consider in more detail how we are meant to handle our moment-by-moment thought processes.

The Bible clearly teaches that our human mind is prone to wrong and sinful thoughts. In Genesis 8:21, the Bible says that "man's bent is toward evil from his earliest youth." Jesus quite bluntly stated: "Your souls aren't harmed by what you eat, but by what you think and say!...*It is the thought-life that pollutes...*"[16]

When we think wrong thoughts, we develop certain mental habits, which eventually become strongholds. For example, if we

---

[16] Mark 7:15–16, 20.

nurse angry thoughts day after day, we will develop a stronghold of anger. Mental strongholds are habitual patterns of thinking. Strongholds are so easy to build—it is much more difficult to tear them down.

Our minds are constantly thinking, sometimes on more than one track. We think every moment, but how often do we stop to think about what we are thinking about? It is as if we carry around an inner I-pod and often lose track of what is playing in our mind. Our thoughts become vague background noise that insidiously impacts our shifting moods.

Paul urged us to be "transformed" by "the renewing" of our mind.[17] Notice the action verb. This verse does not say that God will renew our mind without any effort on our part. Instead, the verse commands: "*Be* transformed..." Once we make the decision to embrace Christian faith, *we* are to change the way we think and what we think about.

In Hebrews 10:16, Paul asserted that God promised to place His laws in our heart and to write them on our mind. But He does not do this unless we purpose to fill our minds with the truths and principles of God. Bible study is so important. It is foundational to the renewal of our minds. That is why this book is full of scriptural references.

Some might ask: Isn't this just a form of brain-washing? I love to quote what a wise old African missionary once said in response: "Yes, it's brainwashing. But boy did my brain need a good washing!" We wash our bodies every day. Why not wash our minds with as much diligence?

Paul said to "fix" our thoughts on Jesus.[18] Paul also instructed us to "take captive every thought to make it obedient to Christ".[19] We are to quite literally capture our thoughts and ensure that they are consistent with our relationship with Jesus. We cannot let our

---

[17] Romans 12:2 (NIV).
[18] Hebrews 3:1 (NIV).
[19] 2 Corinthians 10:5 (NIV).

thoughts randomly drift and go where they please. We cannot accept, let alone pursue, every thought that pops into our head.

Speaking to the Ephesians, Paul said: "You were taught...to be made new in the attitude of your minds."[20] The end goal is to have a mind that thinks like Jesus Himself. In 1 Corinthians 2:16c, Paul made the amazing statement that "...strange as it seems, we Christians actually do have within us a portion of the very thoughts and mind of Christ."

In Philippians 4:8, Paul taught that we must therefore think only about those things that are pure, lovely, noble, and of good report.

This book will provide example after example of how the Holy Spirit has helped many Christians, past and present, to develop the mind of Christ...to put off angry, resentful, hate-filled thoughts and instead to think loving and forgiving thoughts...to stop fretting and worrying and instead to think thoughts of peace, faith, and trust...to stop struggling in discouragement and despair by thinking hopeful thoughts...to quit grumbling, complaining, and envying by choosing to mentally focus on whatever fosters gratitude, contentment, and joy.

A quick test to see if we are *thinking* the way that we should at any point in our busy days is to be aware of how we are *feeling*. If we are feeling down, upset, in turmoil, agitated, or stressed, then we are not bringing all of our thoughts captive to Christ. We are allowing negative streams of thought to ruin the moments that we are presently living in. When we find ourselves feeling unpleasant emotions, we need to stop and think about what we are thinking about.

The more we do this, the more we can identify the kinds of negative thoughts and feelings that are most dominant in us. If we find ourselves feeling down a lot, we are probably habitually entertaining depressing thoughts. If we find ourselves feeling agitated and stressed, we are probably worrying about something or remaining angry at someone.

---

[20] Ephesians 4:22–24 (NIV).

Let's stop living at the mercy of our minds, as if they have the right to control us instead of *us* having the right to control *them*. We are meant to be the masters of our minds, not our minds the masters of us.

We do not tolerate spam in our e-mail stream or viruses in our computers. We instantly get rid of pop-ups on our computer screens. We go to great lengths to set up firewalls and to update our computer's virus protection software. We guard against cyber-contamination. We regularly clean out our computer files, delete what we do not want, and defragment our systems.

Let's just as deliberately reject mental spam when it tries to enter our thought stream. Let's label more of our thoughts as energy-wasting inner junk mail. Let's quickly delete unwanted mental pop-ups. When our minds get stuck on any unhealthy thought stream, let's reboot. Surely we can be as diligent about the state of our minds as we are about the state of our computers.

Of course there are times when we *do* need to think about unpleasant matters for brief periods of time to process them—to decide what we are going to do, for example, about an unpleasant person or an unpleasant circumstance that has presented itself. I am not advocating sweeping all of our negative thoughts and emotions "under the rug," thereby denying or repressing them. *Some* (but not all) negative thoughts, and the consequent emotions, need to be processed to a degree before they can be disposed of. This must be done mindfully and carefully, however, with the clear goal being to ultimately get rid of the negative thoughts and emotions.

It is time to stop letting our minds roam randomly all over the place. The challenge is to become more mentally disciplined and self-controlled. To rein in unhelpful stray thoughts. To get a grip on our careless and lazy mental habits. To focus. To be alert. To pre-empt the formation of negative feelings by nipping our negative thoughts in the bud.

Renewing our minds is a life-long process. But day by day, we can make progress—one thought at a time.

Our Feelings

Our feelings form the third part of our soul. Every soul is usually a mixture of positive and negative feelings that are constantly changing.

We all start with certain personality predispositions. Even as young children, some of us are quiet, shy, and socially anxious. Other children are naturally more cheerful, carefree, and exuberant. Some children have numerous fears and are more prone to worrying and fretting. Others are more intrepid. Some will gravitate more towards anger, others toward despair, still others toward discontentment. As you read through this book, try to discover what your "signature" emotions are. (A shortcut is to ask your mother, room-mate, spouse, or children—they can tell you in a flash! But please do not do this unless you are strong enough and courageous enough to hear their honest answer.)

As a person's personality becomes more defined, these dominant feelings (whether positive or negative) become more and more entrenched in their heart. Unfortunately, the human default is to tend towards what is negative and harmful. Jeremiah recorded: "The human heart is the most deceitful of all things, and desperately wicked. Who really knows how bad it is? But I, the Lord, search all hearts and examine secret motives."[21]

Along life's road, we all eventually experience the full range of human emotions. In Ecclesiastes 3:4, King Solomon talked about there being: "A time to cry; A time to laugh; A time to grieve; A time to dance."

We are meant to control our emotions just as we are meant to control our thoughts—to use our will to exercise self-control, authority, and dominion over all of our feelings. The sad truth is that we are too often just as lazy and careless about our feelings as we are about our thoughts. No wonder we so easily feel down or so quickly work up a sweat about an issue. God did not intend

---

[21] Jeremiah 17:9–10 (NLT).

for our feelings to dominate and tyrannize us. Emotional control must replace controlling emotions.

We can never be reminded enough of this key principle: our feelings are meant to follow our thoughts, which should follow our will. Our feelings are supposed to be *followers*, not leaders or masters in our lives.

We have to become as aware of our feelings hour by hour as we are cognizant of our thoughts. Some people don't like to analyze their feelings, especially unpleasant ones. But we must all learn to name our emotions before we can tame them. One of the goals of this book is to help us all learn to better name and tame each specific emotion.

God wants to help us understand our own hearts so that we can transform them into something much better. God can show us the truth if we let Him—and we know that truth is necessary to being set free.

We must bring our feelings out into the light. We must validate their reality, whether we think they are "good" or "bad." We must learn to process them and then to discard the feelings that are harmful. We cannot properly choose faith until we acknowledge that fear exists. We cannot deeply forgive someone until we acknowledge our hurt, our anger, and our resentment towards them. We cannot even truly embrace God's forgiveness towards us until we first acknowledge our feelings of guilt and shame. We have to deliberately *let go* of all that is negative before we can *move on* to all that is positive. This book will hopefully provide practical strategies (and encouraging examples) so that each one of us can constructively master this kind of effective emotional management.

If we ignore our emotions, there is a danger of becoming numb to them. In Matthew 11:16–17, Jesus talked about children playing wedding, but this did not make them happy; so they played funeral, but this did not make them sad. People can become numb in their emotional lives, going through the motions of all kinds of activities but shutting off their emotions so that they feel very little or nothing at all.

In the meantime, emotions do not disappear just because they are unacknowledged. It takes enormous energy to keep emotions buried deep within. Negative emotions can cause a lot of *diffuse* internal pain. They surface in many of the unhealthy behaviors we discussed in the very beginning—in everything from over-eating to substance abuse or excessive spending. We will not successfully lose weight (and keep it off) or stop our impulse buying until we courageously acknowledge, name, and tame the emotions driving the unwanted behavior.

So let's take authority over our thoughts and feelings—to control them instead of them controlling us—with the end goal being that we *enjoy* our emotional lives. Our emotions are meant to energize, empower, and enliven us, not exhaust us. God does not want us to be stuck in anger, worry, or despair. Instead, He wants us to gratefully live in love, joy, peace, contentment—with faith and hope to encourage us onward.

Search me, O God, and know my heart; test my thoughts.
Psalm 139:23

...Plow up the hardness of your hearts;
....Cleanse your minds and hearts...
Jeremiah 4:3–4a

Above all else, guard your heart, for it is the wellspring of life.
Proverbs 4:23 (NIV)

4
WHY BOTHER?
Six Incentives

MODERN ACADEMIC RESEARCH continues to explore the fascinating interconnectedness of the body, spirit, mind, and emotions. Experts who study these various facets of human existence are paying increasing attention to how each part affects the rest—and how this knowledge can be harnessed to help us. Canadian psychiatrist Dr. Stephen Stokl has written: "It is a known fact that medicine, psychiatry, psychology and religion are mutually compatible and influence each other to promote emotional and spiritual healing."[22]

Academics often make a distinction between the concepts of "feelings" and "emotions"—*feelings* are what we subjectively experience and *emotions* are the measurable physical responses to stimuli. For example, we can experience a sensation of fear as a *feeling*; the *emotion* of fear manifests itself as a racing heartbeat or increased perspiration. In this book, I will use the words "feelings" and "emotions" somewhat interchangeably (because in everyday life that is what we do), but the academic distinction is interesting. It demonstrates that feelings have a very real *physical* component.

Some psychologists analyze emotions/feelings using the ABC model: "A" being arousal on the physiological level, (e.g. heart palpitations, faster breathing, tensed muscles); "B" being the behavioral expression (e.g. smiling or frowning); and "C" being the conscious inner experience (the subjective feeling within

---

[22] Dr. Stokl, pg. 351.

oneself). This model shows that our inner feelings affect our bodies and our social behavior.

Because the body, spirit, mind, and emotions are so interconnected, working to improve our soul management skills can have beneficial impact on *every* part of our lives.

Consider the following six reasons why developing better management of our thoughts and feelings is very worthwhile.

1. Impact on Our Bodies and Our Physical Health

The Bible teaches us about the link between body and soul. In Psalm 31:9b-10a, for example, King David lamented: "...my health is broken from sorrow...my years are shortened, drained away because of sadness." I invite you to notice the biblical link between body and soul as you consider many such verses throughout this book.

More than three-quarters of visits to primary care physicians take place because of stress-related problems. This affirms the common saying: many people suffer health problems not from what they eat, but from what is eating them.

According to my husband, Sam, there is a considerable volume of medical research linking the mind and the emotions with the onset and clinical course of a wide range of human diseases, including cancer and heart disease.[23] Emotions can affect the immune system, the central nervous system, the endocrine system, the gastrointestinal system, and the cardiovascular system. Medical studies especially link anger, anxiety, and depression with disease.[24]

Other studies have linked *positive* emotions with desirable health outcomes, including increased longevity, reduced susceptibility to the common cold, and reduced likelihood of developing

---

[23] See, for example, articles by: Herrald and Tomaka; Kiecolt-Glaser et al; Fredrickson and Levenson.

[24] Ibid.

diabetes or hypertension.[25] Experts are now exploring how positive emotions undo the adverse effects of negative emotions on, for example, the cardiovascular system.[26]

We will further explore the link between emotions, disease, and physical health in the upcoming chapters on specific emotions.

Biochemical Changes

According to Dr. Sam, medical science has shown how negative emotions have the power to adversely affect our physical bio-chemistry. Feelings of anger and fear, for example, have been associated with increased adrenaline and cortisol levels in the bloodstream. These higher than normal levels can really damage the body if the anger or the fear is chronically sustained.

Thankfully, positive emotional states also impact our bio-chemistry. Laughter, for example, increases endorphins, which promote a sense of well-being in both body and soul. Happiness is linked with serotonin, a brain neurotransmitter commonly known as the "good mood" body chemical.

We are not born with biochemistry that is fixed and unchangeable. We *can* change our biochemistry—by physical means such as exercise and medication—but *also* by the way we choose to think and feel.

Changes in the Brain

Even our brain circuitry is affected by our emotional choices. One exciting, cutting edge frontier of neuroscience is called neu-roplasticity. Some neuroscientists are exploring the connection between our thoughts/feelings and identifiable changes in brain circuitry caused by them. Their research results suggest that the

---

[25] See, for example, articles by: Rozanski and Kubzansky; Kiecolt-Glaser et al; Danner et al.

[26] Kiecolt-Glaser et al; Herrald and Tomaka; Fredrickson and Levenson.

brain is not permanently hard-wired. On the contrary, the brain apparently has amazing power to change its own structure in response to a person's unfolding life experiences. The brain remolds and re-organizes itself. Our thoughts and our feelings actually impact the brain's functional anatomy, for better or worse.[27]

Our thoughts and feelings leave detectible traces, footprints, and even pathways in the brain. Some researchers are now finding, for example, that repeated emotional experiences (such as multiple fear-filled encounters with dogs, the dentist's drill, needles, or lightning) actually sculpt the shape, size, and number of neurons in the brain and affect the synaptic connections between neurons. There are about 100 billion cells in the brain, connected by synapses that can form, disappear, weaken, or strengthen, depending on how we choose to respond to our life experiences.[28]

Repeated thoughts and emotions create neural pathways. Psychiatrist Dr. Doidge has compared the formation of these pathways to a sled going down a hill of soft snow. The first time the sled goes down, it leaves a light path. The second and third times, the sled might take the same path or a similar path or a different path. By the end of the day, the sled will likely traverse some paths so many times that those highly-trafficked paths will leave tracks (presumably deeply rutted, packed down, ridged). Once the sled is on one of those well-established paths, it is tough to deviate from the set course. The sledder will want to use the well-established paths because they have become the fastest routes down the hill. It still remains *possible*, however, to create *fresh* paths for *future* trips down the hill.[29]

---

[27] Dr. Norman Doidge, *The Brain that Changes Itself* and Dr. Mario Beauregard et al, *The Spiritual Brain.*

[28] Dr. Beauregard, pg. 102.

[29] Dr. Doidge, pgs. 209–210, 242; Dr. Doidge's analogy is credited to Dr. Pascal-Leone.

When we experience fear, anxiety, depression, or other chronic thought and emotional patterns, neural pathways are established that future thoughts and emotional responses gravitate towards. Some pathways become much more heavily trafficked than others, just like the sled tracks in the snow. The most deeply rutted pathways are made up of our most habitual thoughts and emotions. The pathways that are seldom traveled shrink and sometimes even disappear.[30] We must pay attention to what we are thinking and feeling!

The Bible warns us about choosing right paths instead of wrong ones, wise paths instead of foolish ones. We tend to think of these paths as our *exterior* paths in life, but the advice is just as applicable to our *interior* paths.

Anecdotal Evidence of the Link Between Body and Soul

While there are purely physical reasons for some medical problems, emotions play a huge part in the physical health issues of most people. On a daily basis, Dr. Sam observes the link between body and soul. The majority of the patients he sees each day who have physical complaints will also have underlying emotional/relational/stress issues. Many do not readily see the connection between their emotions and their ulcers, their insomnia, or their headaches. Dr. Sam has frequently observed that, once a patient learns how to deal with the emotions underlying their medical problem, their physical health often improves.

Getting positive control of our minds and our emotions can benefit our physical health both in the short term and over the long haul.

2. Better Mental Health and Performance

Our emotions also affect the performance of our mental faculties and the overall state of our mental health. Our emotions and the effects they have on our brains impact our sense of being up or

---

[30] Dr. Beauregard, pg. 33.

down, agitated or calm, enthused or fatigued, focused or scattered, sharp or dull.

Negative emotions can lead to psychological disorders, narrowed scope of attention, increased stress load, and low self-esteem. In contrast, positive emotions have been linked to psychological good health, higher morale, improved creativity, enhanced learning capacity, and increased self-esteem.[31]

Learning how to better manage our emotions can improve our mental health and performance.

3. Sustained Sense of Well-Being

We all desire to have an ongoing sense of inner well-being and inner rest. Everyone learns, sooner or later, that it is never enough to seek mere physical rest and relaxation. A good night's sleep does not always result in feeling rested and refreshed.

A person can even go on a luxury holiday to a top resort and, after spending a week there, *not* feel rested once they come home. Despite days of sleeping in, indulging in spa treatments, basking in warm sunshine, lounging on beach chairs, and sipping on cool drinks, a person will never feel *truly* rested *if* they have not come to terms with any anger, unforgiveness, worry, disappointment, envy, or ingratitude that is lurking in their soul. The most delightful pleasures of a tropical paradise cannot bring true and lasting rest if the soul is not at rest. I have met some incredibly unhappy people in some incredibly beautiful places. I have, on occasion, personally experienced feeling miserable in five-star surroundings.

Emotional fatigue is much harder to deal with than physical fatigue. A vacation may refresh the body—but it does not have the power, on its own, to *deeply* restore the troubled soul. Furthermore, emotional refreshment and inner rest surpass physical rest—they linger after the glorious sunset fades, long after the massage is over, even when storm clouds cover the sun.

---

[31] Articles by: Barsky et al.; Rowan et al.; Herrald and Tomaka; Fredrickson.

Learning to manage our emotions day by day is the only way to truly achieve a *sustained* sense of feeling rested, relaxed, and refreshed.

4. Improved Relationships

Our soul management also affects our relationships with family, friends, neighbors, and work colleagues. Negative emotions can be highly destructive in human relationships.

It took about eight years to build the World Trade Center in New York City, but only one morning to bring the twin towers crashing to the ground. Similarly, it can take years to build a relationship—and a few hours of destructive emotional outburst to wreak a terrible toll on that relationship. Mismanaged emotions can lead to divorce, estrangement from family, broken friendships, and shattered careers.

Lasting, healthy relationships require deliberate, ongoing emotional management. The more we learn to control our own emotions, the better all of our relationships will be.

5. The Value of Emotional Intelligence in the Workplace

The career world has come to recognize that emotional intelligence (EQ) is often just as important as mental intelligence (IQ). EQ involves the ability to accurately recognize and to appropriately manage emotions.

In my twenty-year association with a big city law firm, I observed that the lawyers who had graduated with high academic grades from law school were not necessarily the ones who lasted at the firm the longest or became its best performers. Some of the B and C students eventually fared better than some of the A graduates.

Why did some average graduates thrive better than some of the top scholars? Quite simply, they had great EQ. Clients enjoyed golfing with them. Other lawyers wanted to lunch with them. They also generally got along well with lawyers from other firms when it came to negotiating agreements, collaborating on business deals, or settling tough cases. They were team players. They had more highly developed abilities to control their tempers, cope with anxiety, or get over setbacks. It seemed to me that, in the long run, their EQ mattered just as much as their IQ.

Sound emotional management will positively impact long-term career success.

6. Spiritual Maturity, Stability, and Fruitfulness

As we have already discussed, simply becoming a Christian does not immediately produce a constant inner state of love, joy, and peace. We all carry old baggage and it needs to be dealt with. If new Christians *persist* in nursing bitterness, sheltering unforgiveness, dreaming of revenge, fretting over everything, complaining that their glass is half-empty, or dragging around any other negative mental/emotional habits, they will not become spiritually healthy or optimally fruitful.

We have all known Christians who have given their lives to God but who continue to harbor all kinds of garbage within. They have their feet barely inside the door of Christian faith, thereby limiting their opportunity to freely enjoy all that is within. They miss out on a large part of the riches, blessings, privileges, fellowship, and fruitfulness that should be theirs.

Some Christians have trouble connecting with God, no matter how faithfully they attend church, read their Bible, or listen to worship music. We will see, in later chapters, examples of people who have held on to anger against God—or who feel so hopeless or ashamed that they believe they are beyond God's love, forgiveness, grace, and provision. These kinds of thoughts and emotions, if not dealt with, can impede a healthy and intimate relationship with God.

Some Christians feel emotionally crippled, stuck on the sidelines, or chronically fatigued because of powerful emotions such as anger, fear, depression, and discontentment. They wonder why they do not *enjoy* their Christian journeys. If you are one of those who try to attend church, read your Bible, pray, and socialize with other Christians, but *still* primarily feel crushed, wounded, weary—maybe even empty, numb, or spiritually dead—hopefully this book will set you on a different emotional path.

All of us will be frustrated in our relationship with God and held back in our spiritual growth and effectiveness if we do not pay heed to our thoughts and feelings on a daily basis. To relate to God and to fulfill God's highest purposes for our lives, we need to get a grip on our thoughts and emotions, so that we can become all that God intended us to be.

This is also an issue of obedience. We will see in the coming chapters how we are *commanded* to forgive, to love, to put off anger and bitterness, to rid ourselves of jealousy, to stop grumbling and complaining, and to manage our thoughts and emotions in many other specific ways. Obedience and discipleship demand growth in this area of healthy self-control.

We cannot mature spiritually if we mismanage our souls—reason number six for reading on—the most important reason of all!

Be Encouraged

Do you want to be spiritually, physically, mentally, emotionally, and socially strong and healthy; to enjoy all of your relationships, especially your relationship with God; and to be highly effective in your work roles and ministries? All of us can become stronger and healthier *across the board* if we learn how to appropriately deal with our thoughts and feelings.

Let's move on to study what God says about many of our most common emotions. As we embark on this study, be assured of this—the effort that will be required of us will be well worth it in *every* dimension of our lives.

5
CLUSTERS OF EMOTIONS
Feelings Find Friends

E MOTIONS TEND TO operate together in clusters. Earlier, we posited that if a person has a problem with anger, they will also likely have problems with resentment, bitterness, hatred, and unforgiveness. If a person is prone to fear, they will also likely struggle with worry and anxiety. If a person often finds themselves in despair, they will also probably battle discouragement and depression. If a person is discontent, they are also usually weak in the areas of grumbling, complaining, and jealousy.

This book will deal with these four clusters of distressing emotions: the Anger Cluster, the Fear Cluster, the Despair Cluster, and the Discontentment Cluster.

There is no scientific or academic basis for the way I have grouped or named these four clusters. It has simply been my experience and observation that these are the most prevalent negative emotions that Christians struggle with, and that certain emotions with similar traits *do* tend to show up alongside one another. These particular clusters of feelings showed up over and over as I researched dozens of biographies of well-known Christians.

For each of those clusters, there are alternative choices of healthy emotions that we can embrace: Forgiveness and Love; Faith, Trust, and Peace; Hope; Gratitude, Contentment, and Joy. Some of these feelings also tend to cluster together. The loving are usually forgiving. The grateful are likely to be joyful.

This idea of grouping emotions together is not original. Mental health researchers and clinicians have been compiling their own lists and groupings of emotions for years. This sort of conceptual framework has been very helpful in dealing with my own feelings.

Before reading further, it would be useful for you to spend some time thinking through what your dominant negative emotions are. What feelings weigh you down? What emotions drain your energy? What steals your happiness? What do you feel when you have trouble sleeping in the middle of the night, or when you first get out of bed in the morning, or when you have time to kill sitting in traffic? What prompted you to pick up this book in the first place? What chapter title caught your attention?

It is easy to pretend that all is well. I have often heard the analogy of the emotional life being just like a full glass of water. A glass of water can look so clean, serene, and inviting when it is sitting on the table. But bump that glass and what is inside spills out and makes a mess. Bump any of our lives with some tumult or tempest and what spills out is often quite messy. The apparent serene perfection of our neat surface image can become an unpleasant emotional mess to be tended to when tough circumstances knock our world.

Let's face our hurt and our pain. Let's inwardly admit our weaknesses and our human frailty. Let's acknowledge, at least to our own selves, what is sinful and selfish in our interior worlds. This will require courage within. Let's decide to bravely confront, with God's help, whatever dark, discomforting, or disturbing emotions live within our souls. There is no point trying to hide our flawed inner selves. God already sees deep within us. Others will eventually see our real selves.

Remember that God is with each one of us every step of the way as we deal with our emotional issues. His love, His forgiveness, His mercy, His grace, His compassion, His power, His strength, and His victory will travel with each one of us as we undertake our journey into inner space.

6

ANGER

The Toxic Soul

A wise man controls his temper.
He knows that anger causes mistakes.
Proverbs 14:29

Y EARS AGO, I waitressed to pay for some of my university expenses. One slow July afternoon, as I served a table by a window, I suddenly heard tires squealing outside. My eyes riveted on a car careening through the parking lot. Then I heard a loud bang, just as a young man fell to the pavement, blood pooling around his body.

An ambulance and police car soon came wailing into the parking lot. Sickened, but fascinated, I watched the scene below me off and on all afternoon. Using yellow tape and pylons, police detectives blocked off what was clearly a crime scene. One of them drew a chalk outline around the fallen body.

Later that day, I heard on the news that the driver of the careening car had gunned down the other man. The two young men had known one another. Anger had built up in their relationship, ultimately growing into out-of-control rage.

The man who had been shot died from his wounds. The other man was charged with murder. Feeling somewhat shell-shocked over the following days, I watched the remains of the chalk outline fade in the summer rains. This had been my first brush with anger of that magnitude. As a courtroom lawyer in later years, I was to encounter lives full of enormous anger on many occasions.

Out-of-control anger is on the rise in Western society. Violent crime abounds. So does domestic abuse, road rage, air rage, rink rage, cyber-rage, school yard bullying, and urban gang warfare. There is even something called lawn rage. I recently read about a man who shot and killed a teenager for taking a shortcut across his immaculately groomed green lawn.

Anger is showing up in the workplace in unprecedented ways. I once knew a lawyer who became so angry after a meeting with his law partners that he smashed his fist right through the drywall in his office. After scribbling obscenities beside the jagged hole in the wall, he stormed out of his office, never to return. Another lawyer in my city achieved notoriety after rudely catapulting the coffee from his cup at a lawyer he disagreed with across the table.

I recently read the story of Soviet dissident Alexander Litvinenko who was allegedly poisoned in London in 2006. Litvinenko's autopsy determined that he had ingested only about one microgram of Polonium. This amount would have weighed less than a grain of salt and been smaller than the period ending this sentence. Yet even this tiny amount made his hair fall out, his muscles shrivel, his bone marrow fail, and his whole body eventually shut down. In the end, this miniscule amount of poison killed him.[32] Just like a trace of poison can destroy a body, even a seemingly small amount of anger can become toxic to the soul.

Common to All

If you have been raised to believe that "good Christians" never get angry, you have been misled. Everyone gets angry from time to time. Truth be told, most of us experience some degree of anger, however minor or fleeting, on an almost daily basis.

Many well-known Christians have had battles with anger. Martin Luther, father of the Protestant Reformation, apparently had a quick temper. The classical composer Johann Sebastian Bach also had an ongoing problem with anger. Once Bach got so

---

[32]From TIME magazine, (Canadian edition), December 18, 2006 issue, pg. 19.

angry at a fellow musician that he slashed the other man's clothing with a sword. Former American President Ronald Reagan struggled to overcome intense anger toward his alcoholic father.

Simply becoming a Christian does not make anger disappear. No matter how long we have been Christians, we all sometimes feel angry.

Is Anger a Sin?

Anger is not necessarily sinful. After all, the Bible tells us that God Himself is sometimes angry.

Feeling that first rush of anger is not wrong or unspiritual; it is human. It is what we choose *to do* with our anger that determines whether we commit sin or not. Psalm 4:4a instructs us: "In your anger, do not sin."[33] This verse implies that we can be angry, yet choose not to sin. In other words, anger can exist without sin.

Processing Our Anger

Acute anger is actually a biochemical reaction to some trigger. Anger has often been compared to fever in our physical bodies — it is a sign to us that something is wrong. Just as a doctor tries to figure out why his patient has a high fever, we can try to understand the underlying reason for our anger.

We can start to *process* our anger by asking ourselves some questions. What triggered the anger? Have we been hurt? Rejected? Taken for granted? Felt frustrated because someone or something has become an obstacle to our goal? Has someone or something failed to meet our expectations? Have we been denied something we feel we have a right to? Has someone else dumped their anger on us? Are we over-reacting because we are tired, stressed, sick, hungry, or experiencing hormonal shifts? These are some of the most common sources of anger.

---

[33] NIV translation.

Making a Choice

Admitting anger, then seeking to understand what triggered it, are very constructive steps. Up to this point, an angry person has done nothing wrong. At this stage, an angry person has a *choice* to make. How will the anger be handled?

There are appropriate, healthy, and sinless ways to handle anger. Unfortunately, there are just as many *in*appropriate, *un*healthy, and sin*ful* ways to respond to anger.

Paul stated in Ephesians 4:26, referring to Psalm 4:4, that in our anger we are not to sin. Christian psychologist and author Dr. James C. Dobson once astutely observed that it is our *will* which separates the first part of the verse (about being angry) from the last part ("do not sin").[34] The will must decide how to respond to the biochemical surge of energy rushing through the body.

The first recorded instance of anger in the Bible occurs in Genesis 4. Cain was very angry because God accepted his brother Abel's sacrifice but not Cain's. "'Why are you angry?' the Lord asked him. 'Why is your face so dark with rage? It can be bright with joy if you will do what you should! But if you refuse to obey, watch out. Sin is waiting to attack you, longing to destroy you. But you can conquer it!'"[35]

After God rejected his sacrifice, Cain stood at a crossroads. He had a *choice* to make. Even after Cain was "dark with rage," he could still have avoided sin by doing what was right. He could have presented a second sacrifice that pleased God. If he had made that choice, his anger would *not* have been sinful.

Cain chose, however, to vent his anger in violent fashion by murdering his brother. He failed to conquer the sinful impulse that God warned him was waiting to attack and destroy him within. Cain will forever be infamous as the first murderer in biblical history and an example of what *not* to do in response to anger.

---

[34]Dr. James C. Dobson, *Emotions: Can You Trust Them?* pg. 87.
[35] Genesis 4:6–7.

It does not help to try to blame someone else for our anger or its consequences. No one else has the power to *make* us angry or to *keep* us angry. We choose to be angry and we choose to handle that anger in some fashion. We must accept responsibility for our anger and the choices that flow from it.

Inappropriate Anger Management

Here are some of the common ways of managing anger that are harmful, unhealthy, and possibly sinful. Later, we will discuss healthy and appropriate alternatives.

Denial

I used to think that just because I did not yell, throw things, or get red in the face I was not actually angry. It took me years to realize that anger can be as icy cold as it is fiery hot. Those prone to denying their anger are usually not hot-headed personalities. Instead, they likely think of themselves as calm, cool, and collected.

Anger can cause some of us to coldly withdraw and to put up defensive walls. We become more distant from the person who triggered our anger, drumming up reasons to avoid them. Smiles disappear, conversation dries up, fellowship ceases.

It is neither helpful nor healthy to deny our anger. Denial is not acting in truth. It is really a way of lying to ourselves. We cannot deal with our anger until we accept the reality of its existence. We risk getting stuck in our anger unless we learn to be honest with ourselves. Remember, there is no shame in admitting anger—anger does not have to result in sin if we will only admit that it exists and then find a healthy way to deal with it.

If you grew up believing that anger is always bad and always sinful and that a "good Christian" or a "mature Christian" never gets angry, there is a good chance that you have a *lot* of denied anger stored up inside of you.

Suppression (Repression)

Suppression is similar to denial. With suppression, however, there is usually at least an *initial* acknowledgment of anger.

This acknowledgment is very fleeting for some people. They have trained themselves to quickly suppress the emotion of anger as soon as they become aware of it. Instead of *processing* or *expressing* their anger, they choose to *bury* it. They succeed in avoiding open conflict with this strategy and applaud themselves for it. For a time, they are oblivious to the harmful *undercurrent* of anger that remains hidden beneath the surface.

According to the experts, this pattern of dealing with anger often begins in childhood.[36] In some homes, when a child shows anger, their parents respond by getting even angrier than the child. Children brought up this way learn to equate expressing their own anger, for *any* reason, with some kind of immediate negative consequence. They discover that when they hide their own anger they avoid a spanking, a loud lecture, or some other kind of punishing adult response.

At first, these children just hide their anger from their parents. Eventually, they stuff their anger down inside so often that they successfully hide their anger even from themselves. They develop no strategies for dealing with their angry feelings other than putting a lid on the steaming pot.

Think back to your own childhood. Do you remember being able to tell your parents that you were mad about something or at someone? Even if that someone was them—or one of your siblings? Could you ever express that you were mad at God when tough circumstances came your way? What did your parents do or say when you got upset, raised your voice, whined about something, slammed a door, or otherwise showed that you were in a mad mood? Did they try to talk to you about your feelings or did they just snap at you to stop it, grow up, or go to your room? Was your expression of anger immediately greeted

---

[36] See, for example, Dr. Dobbins, pgs. 86–87.

with punishment, a lecture, or a sermon on every occasion? Were you told it was always bad to be mad?

The answers to these kinds of questions will help you to get insight into whether you have likely suppressed a lot of anger over the years. If you say you are the kind of person who *never* gets angry, you have most likely either denied or suppressed your anger for so long that you do not recognize how it manifests in your life. We will later examine how suppressed anger manifests itself in many ways that don't look like anger.

Am I suggesting that parents should allow their children to have unbridled temper tantrums, break their toys in a rage, or hit other children? Of course not! Children should, however, be allowed to *say* that they are mad, that something bothers them, or that someone has upset them. They should be given a compassionate hearing—even if they are crying, pouting, or whining. Children need to learn that it is okay to be angry *up to a point*.

Teenagers, every once in a while, should be allowed to say "That sucks!" They should have some freedom to stomp their feet, to load the dishwasher more noisily than usual, or to occasionally slam their bedroom door (just so long as they don't break the dishes or the door!). Wise parents try to engage their angry teenagers in conversation to allow the teens to figure out (and to then express) what's wrong with their world. As parents, we can help them find healthy ways to express their anger. I know, however, this is easier said than done!

Extended Silent Treatment

When some people get angry, they clam up and give the "the silent treatment" to the person who offended them. These silent sulkers are well aware of their anger—they are not denying it or suppressing it. But neither are they properly processing it or openly expressing it. I've been both the perpetrator and the recipient of this unhealthy means of coping with anger.

There is nothing wrong with having an agreed upon time-out to cool down. That kind of brief time-out is being silent in a spirit of love. But *extended* silent treatment—intended to convey some kind of disapproving message to the recipient—is hurtful, rejecting, and unproductive. Such punishing silent treatment can be as wounding as hurtful words. The recipient can feel unloved, devalued, not worth talking to.

People who dish out "the silent treatment" often feel more righteous than those who lose their tempers (been there, felt that). Giving the cold shoulder to those around us, however, is *not* an expression of love. Just because the anger remains silent does not mean it is free of sin. Jesus spoke often of the sins of the *heart*. Even feelings that stay quietly locked up in the heart *can* be sinful.

Meltdowns and Verbal Outbursts

Anger can explode in an uncontrolled torrent of *words*. Galatians 5:19–20 talks about "fits of rage" as ugly evidence of our sinful nature.

Those who explode in verbal abuse are usually people who have denied or suppressed their anger or who have consciously clammed up until the pressure inside has become unbearable. Releasing a stream of angry words can ease the pressure, but relationships in the line of fire can be left in tatters.

In James 3:5–6 we are soberly warned: "...the tongue is a small thing, but what enormous damage it can do. A great forest can be set on fire by one tiny spark. And the tongue is a flame of fire. It is full of wickedness, and poisons every part of the body. And the tongue is set on fire by hell itself, and can turn our whole lives into a blazing flame of destruction and disaster."

Prior to marriage, I was one of those people who believed that I rarely got angry. Marriage changed my self-image. In my first year of marriage, I could not believe how angry I could feel! From seemingly out of nowhere, I suddenly had such intense feelings. They sometimes led to arguments. I quickly learned that marriage is vastly different from other relationships.

Early in our marriage, my husband and I suffered the painful consequences of some heated arguments. Unnecessary words were spoken by both of us. We were bright enough to eventually realize that we had to learn the rules of fighting fairly whenever we disagreed or stepped on one another's toes. We learned the hard way the wisdom of Proverbs 29:11: "A fool gives full vent to his anger, but a wise man keeps himself under control."[37] Over the decades, I have talked to enough other married friends to know that this kind of intense anger and immature conflict often occurs early in a marriage (unless both people are deniers and suppressors—in that case it will take time, maybe years, for the pent-up anger to challenge the marriage).

Do Sam and I ever get angry at one another now, after almost twenty five years of marriage? Of course we do. But we have both matured in our abilities to manage our anger in reasonably healthy ways (most of the time).

Some measure of conflict is inevitable in most close relationships, not just in marriage. We might as well accept this reality and learn how to take authority over our tongues during the conflict so that our anger does not become destructive. In Proverbs 29:11, it is not the simple fact of being angry that is foolish—the problem lies in giving full vent to the anger instead of bringing it under reasonable control.

The Bible warns us about being easily provoked. In 1 Corinthians 13 we are told that love is *not* easily provoked. We must develop a long fuse so we can walk away from most quarrels before they even begin.

Over more than five decades of living, I have come to realize that very few issues are actually worth fighting over. Proverbs 20:3 advises: "It is an honor for a man to *stay out* of a fight. Only fools insist on quarreling." Proverbs 26:21 states: "A quarrelsome man starts fights as easily as a man sets fire to

---

[37] NIV translation.

paper." Ecclesiastes 7:9 warns: "Do not be quickly provoked in your spirit, for anger resides in the lap of fools."[38] This is echoed by Paul in Romans 12:18: "Don't quarrel with anyone. Be at peace with everyone, just as much as possible."

On the civil litigation side of my law practice, I observed on a daily basis how prevalent conflict is in our society. While I believe that seeking justice through the court system is merited in many instances—and can be a useful way to process conflict between disagreeing parties—I also believe that too many people engage in brutal legal fights too lightly, with blind hot-headedness, inflicting damage with the weaponry of words.

Many proverbs tell us that our words can bring either "life" or "death" and that we can have either a "wise" or a "foolish" tongue. Let's choose to be wise the next time we're tempted to use our words as weapons.

Aggressive Physical Behavior and Violence

When I first bought a microwave oven, I took a lesson on how to use it. The instructor taught us to *never* cook an egg in its shell in the microwave. The steam building up inside the egg would eventually cause the egg to explode. Supposedly, the explosion would be powerful enough to blow the microwave door right off its hinges.

Just like an egg in a microwave, anger that is not dealt with in a healthy way will build up inner steam and might eventually physically explode, leaving the soul blown off its hinges. Chronically angry people can become physically aggressive, even violent.

As a law student, I worked one summer with my province's legal aid services. While interviewing one pleasant young man, I was surprised to learn that he had been charged with man-slaughter, a type of homicide. He told me his sad story.

---

[38] NIV translation.

He and his common law partner had developed money issues. They had avoided discussing these issues so both of them had just simmered with anger on the inside.

One day, the young man bought (on steep credit) the sports car he had always wanted. When his partner saw him pull into the driveway in his new car, she stormed outside, brandishing a kitchen utensil.

Using the heavy utensil, she began to violently smash the front window of the sports car. The young man struggled with her, trying to get the utensil out of her hands. By that point, he was also feeling explosive rage. He grabbed the heavy utensil, but somehow, in the midst of the struggle, it struck the side of his partner's head. She died from the blow.

He wept as he told me that he could not remember whether he had purposely hit her or whether it was an accident. All he could remember was the violent, out-of-control rage he felt as he saw the smashed front window of his new sports car. He had reached his breaking point.

On the criminal side of my law practice, I saw other examples of fairly normal people snapping under the emotional pressure of pent-up anger, committing acts they never dreamed they were capable of.

The Bible records many episodes of anger exploding into physical aggression and violence. One example is the story we referred to earlier, about Cain murdering his brother Abel. Generations later, Jacob's sons were so angry at the rape of their sister Dinah that they brutally slaughtered the men in the city where the crime had occurred.[39] In story after story, the Bible provides ample warning that mismanaged, unresolved anger can lead to highly destructive violence.

---

[39] Genesis 34.

The Fall-Out from Mismanaged Anger

Physical Health Issues

Mismanaged anger can be destructive to our physical health. According to Dr. Sam, anger triggers the release of adrenaline, norepinephrine, and cortisols into the bloodstream. These chemical changes in the body were intended by our Maker to be a *short-lived* response to anger-inducing stimuli. When left unchecked over a *sustained* period of time, however, these chemical changes can seriously damage our physical health. The body was not designed to handle *chronic* anger.

There are long-term health effects when anger is denied or suppressed. When we keep our anger bottled up inside, the potent force of this biochemical energy turns *against* our own bodies.

According to Dr. Sam, buried anger can cause (or contribute to) numerous physical problems such as: fatigue, high blood pressure, muscle aches, digestive disorders, headaches, chronic pain (with no identifiable cause), and insomnia. Chronic anger has also been linked to health problems such as cardiac disease, cancer, asthma, ulcers, and arthritis.[40]

Suppressed anger will, over time, create what Dr. Sam calls a soul hunger or ache that cries out to be filled or soothed. This, he believes, is often a silent, invisible culprit behind many addictions, such as drug and alcohol abuse, as well as some eating disorders. In many cases, those who struggle with these issues have no insight into their internalized anger.

According to Dr. Sam, anger that is inappropriately vented, through violent actions or verbal outbursts, can cause: elevated blood pressure, increased muscle tension, headaches, and actual physical injuries.

---

[40] Articles by: Kiecolt-Glaser et al; Raikonen et al; Fredrickson; Herrald and Tomaka; Everson et al; Ahmed; Kneip et al.

Mental, Emotional, and Relational Health Issues

If anger is left unresolved, it can progress into resentment, bitterness, hatred, and a hardened mindset of unforgiveness. These escalating thoughts and feelings block out love, joy, peace, and contentment. Eventually, unresolved anger can change a person's personality, character, and reputation.

Dr. Sam agrees with Dr. James Dobson, Dr. Dobbins, and other Christian experts that chronic anger also sometimes surfaces, *in disguise*, as depression or anxiety.[41] In some cases, chronic anger turns into low self-esteem.[42]

Anger ultimately impairs our relationships. Anger creates distance. Anger builds walls. Anger makes a person prickly—easily irritated and easily provoked—and very self-centered. Unresolved, mismanaged anger can lead to estrangement, divorce, and other kinds of relational death. Jesus warned, for example, that a home filled with strife, argument, and division will destroy itself.[43]

Appropriate Anger Management

What are some healthy, appropriate ways to manage anger? Here are a number of approaches, scriptural and practical, advocated by Christian counselors.

Prayer

One of the best ways to handle anger, at the outset, is to pray about it. God is fully aware of our circumstances. He heard the cruel words someone threw at us. He saw the painful rejection. He knows when we have been unjustly and unfairly treated. He

---

[41]Dr. James Dobson, *Emotions: Can You Trust Them?*, especially page 93–94, 105.

[42] Article by Herrald and Tomaka.

[43] Mark 3:24–25; Luke 11:17.

understands why we are frustrated. He knows that our reasonable expectations have not been met.

God feels our pain. Jesus wept while here on earth. We can imagine that He weeps for us now when we suffer. God the Father, Jesus the Son, and the Holy Spirit all experientially understand what hurt and rejection feel like. God also knows what frustration feels like—He has had to compassionately and patiently deal with the fallen human race!

We have an empathetic, sympathetic, loving Ear waiting to hear about our pain. We can pour out our hearts to Him. As we pray, we can use up the biochemical energy that anger generates. We can freely admit our anger to Him. We can *release* the anger in His loving Presence—like the fine steam being released from a dishwasher or vaporizer.

While praying, I have often felt my anger dissipate. I have thereby avoided an unnecessary confrontation with the person who offended me. After praying, my surge of biochemical energy often feels spent and I do not have enough energy left to strike out at someone.

In prayer, we need to be sensitive to what God might be trying to tell *us*. Perhaps we have said or done something that ignited the negative situation. Perhaps we have triggered the other person's anger. Perhaps we have been selfish, proud, impatient, or critical. We should not just focus on what the *other* person has said or done (or neglected to say or do). As we pray, God can speak to our hearts to show us *our* contribution to the unpleasant situation.

Prayer is the key to inviting God's help. In response, He will get involved in the situation—working in our hearts, in the hearts of others involved, and in the surrounding circumstances. God will help us get through to the other side of our negative situation.

I have found that it is best not to pray, in painful detail, over and over about the same matter. If we tell God the *whole* miserable story *each* time we pray, we keep feeding our anger and intensifying our pain. Both the anger and the pain will grow instead of dissipate, imbedding the whole mess ever deeper into our memories. I have learned to pray, in full detail, only one time.

When I pray about the matter again later, I remind myself that God was present when the offence happened *and* He heard me the first time I prayed, so repeating details is not necessary for *His* benefit. I refer briefly to the person who offended me, leaving out all of the nasty details that have the potential to re-ignite my anger. ("Father, you know that I have a problem of anger against so-and-so. Please help me to forgive and forget. Please help me to move on. Please help me to overcome all remaining anger. Please heal my heart…").

The emphasis of all ongoing prayer should *not* be on the original offence. The emphasis should instead be on forgiving, forgetting, overcoming, healing, and *moving on*. We cannot undo the past. We do not have to ruin the present or the future by constantly re-living, in brutal detail, what triggered our anger.

Capturing Our Thoughts

We must get a grip on our thoughts. We should not let them freely go wherever they want, without restraint. Thinking over and over about the offence is just as unhealthy as repetitively praying about the offence in great detail.

While *some* mental processing of our anger is necessary, we need to be wise to recognize when enough is enough. We do not have to change the channel the very first instant we feel anger (otherwise we are just denying or suppressing it). But if we are *still* stuck in our angry thoughts *long after* we should have dealt with them, it is time to take authority over them.

Paul, using strong action verbs, instructed us to do this: "*Stop* being mean, bad-tempered and angry."[44]; "you must *rid your-selves* of all such things as these: anger, rage, malice…"[45] Sooner or later, we must make this choice.

[44] Ephesians 4:31a.
[45] Colossians 3:8 (NIV).

Physical Activity

We talked earlier about how anger, in its acute phase, triggers an immediate surge of biochemicals and hormones in our bodies. According to Dr. Sam, this surge can make our muscles tense, our senses more alert, our hearts pound, and our blood pressure go up—our bodies feel ready for action. A very healthy way of dealing with anger is to *spend* this energy in some immediate, vigorous physical activity.

Christian psychologist Dr. Richard Dobbins once wisely recommended that we should think of anger management as energy management. He suggested that, by finding practical ways to spend all the energy that anger generates, we can turn anger into a friend instead of an enemy. Anger can actually be turned into positive, *useful* energy.[46]

When something or someone has angered me I love to dig in my garden, tackle a household chore, play a game of tennis, or take a brisk walk. Anger can be a stepping stone to fun or fruitful activity!

Talking it Out

Sometimes praying, changing our mental channel, or physical exercise are not enough to dispel our anger. Sometimes, we also need to *talk out* our anger with someone we trust.

It can be counterproductive to talk to too many people about what has made us angry. Just as I used to replay an offence over and over in my prayer life or in my thought life, I also used to talk out the offence with multiple listeners on multiple occasions. This habit also resulted in feeding my anger.

In the immediate moment, each re-telling made me feel good. Telling others about the offence was a way of striking back, indirectly, at the offender. I got some measure of seductive revenge by telling others just how terrible the offender was. But

---

[46]Dr. Dobbins, pgs. 24–25.

this was neither right nor constructive—the memory of the offence just became more deeply entrenched with each retelling.

It is best to pick one friend and tell them the full story *once*. The first telling of the story might be productive, cathartic, and necessary to receive counsel. Each retelling just adds unnecessary fuel to the internal fire. Remember what James said about one spark from the tongue being able to set our whole lives on fire.

There are, of course, exceptions in very serious situations (for example rape, violent assault, extreme abuse). In those situations, the story might have to be retold to police, medical personnel, a pastor, and other counselors. In the majority of situations, however, we do not need to endlessly retell the story.

We are not to *wallow* in our anger, *get stuck* in it, *nourish* it, or *cherish* it. The ultimate goal is to put it off, to stop it, to get rid of it, as the apostle Paul exhorted. If talking it out once helps this process, then it is a viable means of dealing with our anger. If repetitively talking about it moves us further away from being able to put off our anger, then it's time to *move on* and to *stop talking* about the offence.

Who is the best person to talk to about our anger? Dr. Larry Crabb observed that modern Christians often think that help for life's emotional problems has to come from professional counselors. We undervalue the help that "ordinary" people can offer. Of course, Dr. Crabb believes that trained counselors have a legitimate role to play—but he believes that most of us can benefit from time spent on the living room couch of a compassionate relative or friend. Ordinary people can be remarkably full of wisdom, insight, discernment, empathy, encouragement, and helpful advice.

We have the *gift* of Christian brothers and sisters if we are involved in a church community. In Dr. Crabb's opinion, Christian community ought to take on more of a counseling, healing, supportive role as we deal with our troubling emotions.[47]

---

[47] Dr. Larry Crabb and Dr. Dan B. Allender, *Hope When You're Hurting*, especially see pages 58, 142–145, 167–168, 197.

Thankfully, professional Christian counseling *is* available in those situations where the next level is required. Professionals *do* have a valuable role to play, and with deep anger issues they may be necessary. Medical doctors, psychologists, psychiatrists, and pastors are all trained to counsel those needing help with anger issues.

Forgiving

The ultimate goal is to *forgive* the offender—and, if possible, to get back into loving relationship with them. Many minor everyday offences can be dealt with almost immediately with a spirit of forgiveness. Proverbs 19:11a tells us that "A wise man restrains his anger and overlooks insults."

Forgiving more major offences will be covered in a detailed chapter on the critical topic of forgiveness.

Communicating With the Offender

There are times when it may be necessary to communicate our anger to the person who has offended us. This is especially the case when the hurtful language or the damaging behavior keeps on happening. But we need to exercise caution.

I made the repeated mistake, early in my marriage, of trying to talk to my husband every time he did something to annoy me. I had read about a dozen marriage books before my wedding and each one stressed the importance of honestly communicating with your spouse. So I thought I was doing something healthy and constructive by regularly "communicating" my every angry feeling. I soon learned that this caused a lot of unnecessary conflict over minor matters and sabotaged too many precious moments.

I eventually learned, the hard way, not to raise every single habit, word, action, or choice that upset me. At some point, we all need to grow up—to stop *impulsively* flying off the handle with an *immediate* reaction in the heat of every angry moment. Believe me, it took agony of soul to learn what I have been suggesting in this chapter: to pray; to get physically busy; to occasionally seek out a sympathetic ear; and to more often just forgive, forget, let go, and move on. Over the years, as I have practiced these methods, I have found that the majority of matters that once pushed my buttons no longer do. I don't need to discuss most irritations and annoyances with my husband. What inner freedom has come from that realization!

Every so often, however, an issue arises that simply must be talked out. Sometimes, for example, a husband or wife can say things that are hurtful to one another without even knowing it—for example, teasing remarks. As spouses, we all do things out of habit that are thoughtlessly selfish or inconsiderate without realizing how much they hurt or irritate the other person. One person might be less tidy than the other and they do not realize that their messiness upsets their spouse. One person might enjoy a lot of noise (TV, the car radio) without knowing that this disturbs the other person's peace and quiet. So *some* communication along these lines is necessary when habitual conduct by one spouse continually upsets the other. The goal is to speak the truth in love. The goal is to build a marriage where both partners can be comfortable.

There are many excellent marriage books that discuss communication in detail. They give lots of wise counsel about "fighting" fairly and expressing grievances in a healthy, mature manner. While I initially misapplied some of what I had read, I found these kinds of books helpful in the long run.

Communication of what has triggered anger is also sometimes necessary between parents and their children, siblings, friends, fellow Christians, work colleagues, and neighbors. Like it or not, it is a skill we all need to develop.

Seeking the Ongoing Help of the Holy Spirit

God knows that our human strength and willpower are no match for the potential ferocity of anger. After doing *our* part by employing the above constructive strategies and avoiding the destructive ones, we can be encouraged by this: we are never alone in our anger. The Spirit will *help* us to pray, to bring our thoughts under control, to physically spend our energy, to forgive, to seek out a friend or a counselor, and to speak the truth in love when necessary. We can rely upon the help and empowerment of the Holy Spirit.

Pastor David Wilkerson, who worked with teen gang members in New York City, has told the story of Maria. She was a heroin addict. She also developed an anger problem, which was one of the reasons she had turned to the comfort of drugs in the first place. Heroin helped her escape her anger—at least for as many hours as she stayed high.

Once Maria became a Christian, she became progressively aware of the Holy Spirit's remarkable work within her. On her own, she would not likely have overcome her longstanding heroin addiction or her intense anger. With the Spirit's help, however, she was able to eventually deal effectively with both problems.

Soon after becoming a Christian, Maria was robbed and stabbed by two members of her former gang. She was naturally tempted to lash out, but instead the Spirit prompted her to pray. She knew it was the Spirit, because praying was totally contrary to her usual instinctive reaction. Her former tough self would have responded with fierce anger to this cruel assault.

Maria did not fight back—either against her assailants *or* against the inner working of the Spirit. She chose not to relapse back into her old behavior. Because she was willing to rely on Him, the Holy Spirit helped her to win her *inner* battle instead of engaging in a street battle.

After she dressed her wounds later that night, Maria was able to fall asleep in deep peace.[48] There was clearly more than mere human effort involved in this outcome. The welcomed empowerment of the Holy Spirit had made all the difference.

---

[48]Maria's story is told in David Wilkerson's *The Cross and the Switchblade.*

Don't Let the Sun Go Down: Prompt Resolution of Anger

Ephesians 4:26–27 states: "In your anger do not sin: Do not let the sun go down while you are still angry, and do not give the devil a foothold."[49] The *ideal* is to get rid of all anger before the sun goes down each day.

With minor offences this is quite possible. With more major issues, however, it is not realistic to think that every trace of anger can be resolved by sundown. But *each day* we can take some healthy steps to whittle away at our anger. Each day we can pray. Each day we can meditate on and memorize helpful Scripture. Each day we can spend some of our anger-induced energy in constructive ways.

Each new day may bring a fresh battle. Each new day we can fight *that* day's battle.

Consider, for example, the wife of a husband who has left her for another woman. The hurting wife will not be able to deal with all of her anger in one day. Let's get real! But she can take small steps, one day at a time, to overcome her anger. On a certain day, for example, the hurting wife might come across a photograph that stirs up anger. She can decide before she goes to bed what to do with the photograph so that it does not cross her path again the next day. On another day, she might come across a credit card receipt that shows her husband was buying gifts for the other woman. *That* day, before the sun goes down, she can decide how she will deal with the receipt.

The battle can be fought one trigger and one issue at a time. Each fresh trigger, each resurfaced memory, each negative thought, each fresh assault, can be tackled within the ensuing twenty-four hours. The anger can be tamed in progressive twenty-four increments.

---

[49] NIV translation.

Sustained Anger at God

It is normal, at some point in our lives, to feel anger towards God. When a loved one dies or serious illness strikes or a tragic accident occurs, it is only human to angrily question God.

Moses, in the midst of his frustrating encounters with Pharaoh, was "hot with anger."[50] He was angry at Pharaoh's stubbornness, deceit, and hard heart, but he was also upset at God. God had commissioned Moses to set His people free, but in the short-term, the suffering of the Israelites was increased. For a while, Moses felt like a fool. But Moses did not turn away from God, and eventually God helped to bring him through both his trying situation and his anger.

Ethel Waters, a well-known singer and actress of a bygone era, experienced a traumatic childhood. She was conceived when her mother (only twelve years old at the time) was raped. Her biological father was poisoned to death a few years later by another woman. Raised in poverty by various relatives, Ethel was exposed to a sordid world of excessive drinking, drug addiction, and prostitution. After being physically abused, she sometimes chose to sleep out on the street. She learned early in life to steal and fight and curse.

Not surprisingly, young Ethel developed anger at God. At church, she had been told that God was up in heaven watching over her. She would look up at the sky, hoping to see Him. As the tough times continued, she became even angrier at God. From her point of view, He was neglecting to take proper care of her.

Although she was later to find peace with God (eventually becoming a singer for the Billy Graham Crusades), for *years* Ethel struggled with this anger at Him.[51] Only God could help turn such anger and pain into such beautiful song!

---

[50] Exodus 11:8.
[51] Ethel Waters, *His Eye is on the Sparrow.*

Lisa Beamer was also once angry at God. Lisa is the widow of Todd Beamer, one of the American heroes who brought down an airplane hijacked by terrorists on 9/11.

Lisa is an excellent example of Christian principles of emotional management. Like the rest of us, though, she did not reach this emotional maturity overnight. During her teenage years, long before her husband's tragic death on 9/11, she had learned much about battling difficult emotions. Her father died of an aortic aneurysm when she was just fifteen years old and Lisa responded to this painful loss with fear, hurt, and anger. Sometimes she yelled at God, but mostly she endured unspoken rage. Her faith in God was seriously challenged. Eventually, over a period of years, she resolved her anger towards God. She chose instead to trust Him.

As a result of this early life lesson, Lisa was remarkably equipped to emotionally handle her husband's sudden death some years later. She was able to set an almost larger-than-life example for the world in the wake of 9/11, when anger against man and God was rampant.[52]

Those who have gone through difficult childhoods will understand Ethel's and Lisa's feelings. *Everyone* experiences some pain in their childhood, whether at the hands of parents, siblings, peers, teachers, schoolyard bullies, or life circumstances. At one point or another in life, everyone will be upset with God, wondering how He could let them suffer pain. God can help us turn that suffering into song if we're willing to stop shaking our fists at Him.

What is accomplished by sustained anger against God? He has promised that everything that happens to us will work out for our good.[53] (All things are not *in themselves* good, but they will *work out* for our good.) God allows some tough trials to come our way, but He promises to strengthen us, comfort us,

---

[52]Lisa Beamer, *Let's Roll.*
[53] Romans 8.

meet our ongoing needs, deliver us, and guide us—no matter how treacherous the path becomes.

There is no point in seeing God as the enemy. He is, in fact, our loving Father. Jesus is our Brother and our Friend. The Holy Spirit is our Comforter and Companion. Sustained anger at God only alienates us from the greatest Power in the universe, who has infinite capacity to help us get through whatever circumstances we find ourselves in. Remaining in sustained anger against God is one of the poorest emotional choices any of us can make. If you are stuck in that place, I compassionately encourage you to make your peace with God—and seek His help as you work through your pain.

In Conclusion

In the famous Sermon on the Mount, Jesus gave special attention to anger.[54] Jesus made this dramatic statement: "You have heard that it was said to the people long ago, 'Do not murder, and anyone who murders will be subject to judgment.' But I tell you that anyone who is angry with his brother will be subject to judgment." Jesus wanted to emphasize the seriousness of this common emotion. If He takes it so seriously, then we must too!

Most of us will not drive a careening car through a parking lot and shoot down, in cold blood, those who trigger our anger. But there are chalk outlines and yellow tape at many "crime scenes" in each of our lives. Thankfully, we can turn to God for help in learning how to constructively manage our anger in healthy, appropriate ways.

It is hard to stop a quarrel once it starts, so don't let it begin.
Proverbs 17:14

...wise men turn away anger.
Proverbs 29:8 (NIV)

----

[54] Matthew 5:21–22a (NIV).

Dear friends, never avenge yourselves.
Leave that to God, for he has said that
he will repay those who deserve it.
Romans 12:19ab

7
RESENTMENT
AND
BITTERNESS
Twisted and Tangled

Each heart knows its own bitterness…
Proverbs 14:10 (NIV)

Watch out that no bitterness takes root among you,
for as it springs up it causes deep trouble,
hurting many in their spiritual lives.
Hebrews 12:15b

Get rid of all bitterness…
Ephesians 4:31 (NIV)

I N MY MID-TEENS, I worked at the Canadian National Institute for the Blind, teaching a variety of adaptive life skills to new adult residents. Most of the residents that I worked with had developed a fairly rapid onset of blindness and were still adjusting to their loss of sight.

Eleanor, despite her complete blindness, was one of the cheeriest souls I have ever met. She often walked with me in the CNIB rose gardens. She could identify each type of rosebush by its fragrance and was so aware of birdsong. Curious about everything, she found great joy in conversation. Our half-a-century age difference was irrelevant to our delightful relationship. She was endlessly interested in my hopes and dreams, but also loved talking about herself and her family. Her life was clearly very rich. Most of the time, I forgot that she could not see. Her blindness had not blunted her ability to passionately enjoy life.

I also grew fond of an older gentleman who liked to travel on the bus with me to various shopping destinations. He knew, by memory, how many steps it was from the CNIB to the bus stop. He had also memorized the number of footsteps between favorite shops in every mall. He intensely experienced the smells of a bakery, the cold refreshment of an ice cream cone, and the laughter of passing children. Like Eleanor, he was very alert to the presence of even the smallest of blessings in his life.

There were other residents of the CNIB, however, who were very bitter about the loss of their sight. I vividly remember one man in particular. On various afternoons, I tried to teach him how to safely iron his clothes. He would not cooperate at all. He just wanted to vent his deep bitterness—not just about his blindness, but about everything and everyone. He hated his life. Even my efforts to help him seemed to irritate him. I do not mean to sound critical of this man; it must be extremely difficult to cope with such a painful blow in life. But the contrast between this man and the other two cheerier residents left a life-changing impression on my young mind.

Working with the CNIB residents, I learned the practical truth of the folksy advice I have heard from various pastors over the years: life either makes you bitter or better—it all depends on the "I." When the storms of life come, we all face the choice as to whether or not we will respond with bitterness.

Blind hymn writer Fanny Crosby faced the same choice as the CNIB residents that I have just described—only she had to face her blindness as a child. Even at a tender age, she chose to reject bitterness.

At age eight, she wrote these amazing lyrics: "Oh, what a happy child I am, although I cannot see! I am resolved that in this world, contented I will be. How many blessings I enjoy that other people don't! So weep or sigh because I'm blind, I cannot nor I won't!"[55] The set of her will was to live her life to the fullest despite her blindness. Fanny eventually wrote eight *thousand*

---

[55]From the hymn collection of Fanny Crosby (Public Domain).

hymns, including the much-loved "To God Be the Glory" and "Blessed Assurance."

The Roots of Resentment and Bitterness

Hebrews 12:15 warns us about permitting bitter roots to grow in us—they will later cause much trouble to many.

I am an avid gardener and am well acquainted with the growth of roots. One summer, I planted some annuals in the stone urns on my front porch. The flowers grew for only a few months before the autumn frosts came and it was time to remove the plants. I could not believe what a thick and tough mass of roots had formed in those two urns. It took a few hours and a lot of muscle power to dislodge that tangled mess of tenacious roots! It takes even more work to deal with the tough roots of bitterness.

What causes roots of bitterness to grow in our inner soil to begin with? Here are four common causes that I noted as I researched Bible stories and Christian biographies.

Unresolved Anger

If seeds of anger are allowed to grow, it is only a matter of time before roots of bitterness and resentment begin to form. If not uprooted and cast away, they *will* grow, becoming an increasingly thick, twisted, tangled mess in our souls. The noxious plants they produce will eventually bear fruit such as malice, unforgiveness, hatred, and revenge.

In Genesis, we are told that Esau became bitter towards his brother Jacob when he realized that Jacob had tricked him out of his father's blessing. Esau "burst out with a loud and bitter cry" and thereafter "held a grudge" against Jacob.[56] Esau was so angry he wanted to kill Jacob. After Jacob fled, the brothers were estranged for a long time. To his credit, Esau was eventually able to forgive Jacob when they reunited decades later.

---

[56] Genesis 27:34, 41 (NIV).

I learned much about bitterness during my first year of marriage. Earlier, I mentioned how amazed I was at the intense feelings of anger that I sometimes experienced as a newlywed. I was baffled and confused as to how I could feel such anger towards the person I also so deeply loved! I was immature and inexperienced in dealing with anger of this intensity. As a result, my anger was not always resolved as it ought to have been. Sure enough, roots of bitterness and resentment began to grow.

I was not initially aware of my bitterness. Roots, of course, grow *beneath the surface—in the darkness*. We find out they exist when shoots break through the surface, eventually bringing forth visible, tangible, poisonous fruit.

Soon after we were married, my husband and I took a year off from our careers. We spent that year traveling together across Europe, the Middle East, and the continent of Africa. Traveling for a whole year as newlyweds (being together almost constantly) was wonderful most of the time, but challenging some of the time. We talked about almost every imaginable subject and issue. Occasionally, our conversations led to conflict or caused old wounds to surface. We exchanged hurtful words, as most newlyweds eventually do. However, I was oblivious, for some months, to the degree of bitterness that was building up deep inside.

As we journeyed from country to country, we visited Christian friends, churches, and missionaries. A common element began emerging in various conversations, sermons, books, and devotional readings I encountered—the theme of resentment and bitterness. The Spirit began to shine His loving light on the depth of the bitter roots that were growing in the darkest corners of my interior life.

I still remember one particular church service in Jerusalem. Derek Prince, a well-known Christian author, spoke that Sunday evening about uprooting bitterness. The Spirit really got through to me that night. I saw clearly that I was not properly resolving my anger towards my husband.

That night, I promised myself that I would make a determined effort to *recognize* bitterness and *uproot* it as soon as I became aware of it—to get a better grip on my thoughts and to understand how all of this connected with forgiveness and real Christian love. I earnestly sought the Spirit's help and empowerment, knowing that I could not do this on my own. My eyes had been opened wide to the ugly potential of bitterness in my soul.

All marriages are perfect breeding grounds for bitterness. Hurt is inevitable. The sins, weaknesses, imperfections, and failures of one another sometimes inflict pain, which can lead to anger and then bitterness.

In fact, *any* relationship can be fertile soil for the poisonous roots of bitterness. Years ago, I found myself being unjustly treated in a relationship. My hurt, and the consequent anger, began to turn into bitterness against the other person. Bitterness has a tendency to *creep stealthily* into our souls. In some ways, this unwanted invader is less obvious in relationships outside of marriage because we can more conveniently choose to avoid those individuals. I tried to avoid the person who had offended me, but could not avoid them entirely.

One Saturday morning, not long after some particularly harsh conduct on the part of this person, my husband kindly offered to watch our young son for a while. Sam told me to *relax*, to take a much-needed break. Thankful for his gesture, I retreated into a steaming shower.

I soon began to realize that I was *not* relaxing. Instead, I was becoming tenser with each moment. I caught myself bitterly thinking about the person who had hurt me and replaying some recent conversations. Instead of the shower being soothing, I realized I was seething. I felt agitated by the inner turmoil and deepening discomfort.

It dawned on me that my thoughts (and the intense feelings they were generating) were becoming *more* destructive than the words and actions of this person. I had allowed these thoughts and feelings into my soul—into my morning, into my time to relax. This intrusion into my morning was *my* fault, not the other person's.

It hit me that morning, in a powerful way, that I had a *choice* as to how I was going to respond to the ongoing behavior of this person. I could choose to forgive, forget, let go, turn it over to God, and move on with my life each time they said or did something to bother me. Or I could choose to simmer and seethe and let these roots of bitterness grow. It was an epiphany similar to what I had experienced in Jerusalem a few years before.

That morning, I made a quality decision to reject bitterness. This choice was made as much out of loving self-preservation as it was out of any level of spiritual maturity or nobility of heart. I felt a sense of freedom as soon as I consciously made that choice. I got a grip on my thoughts, changed the channel of my soul, and finally began to relax in the shower. Intuitively, I asked the Spirit to help me with this whole process.

The emotional power that this person had exerted over me was broken that morning—in fact, I realize now, they never really had any power over me at all.

I had to keep on making this same choice, over and over, whenever I had further hurtful encounters with this person. Sometimes I failed to make the right choice and I found myself seething again.

I used to think I was getting some measure of revenge by thinking nasty thoughts about this person—fantasizing about what I would say or do in retort to their words and actions. I realized, however, that this revenge was an illusion. I was not hurting this other person one little bit by savoring these scenarios. I was just hurting myself.

So every time I was faced with a fresh temptation to think nasty thoughts, I instead tried to think of these words: "I choose to forgive, forget, let go, trust God, and move on." On many occasions, this nipped fresh anger in the bud and prevented it from turning into bitterness. This is a very helpful little phrase to memorize. These few words succinctly demonstrate the partnership our soul is to have with the Spirit in battling an emotion such as bitterness.

. Profound Disappointment

Disappointment is another potential root of bitterness. We all face disappointments in life. Sometimes these are related to *unmet expectations* in our relationships. Other times, they are related to *shattered dreams* or a *tough turn* in our life circumstances.

When Joseph was second in command to Pharaoh, he was able to arrange for his extended family to come and live in Egypt. At first, this was a blessed turn in their circumstances. They were fed and cared for in the time of famine. They initially prospered in their new Egyptian home.

But as years passed, the circumstances of this family and their descendants took a tough turn. Later generations of Egyptians enslaved the Israelites. The oppressed Israelites became bitter. Exodus 2:23 tells us that they groaned beneath their burdens and *wept bitterly*.

Because they wisely turned to God in the midst of their bitterness (at least for a while), God heard their cries and helped them. God sent Moses to bring His people out of Egypt.

The Israelites, however, did not thoroughly destroy their roots of bitterness. Even after God miraculously delivered them out of Pharaoh's hand and was leading them to their Promised Land, they grumbled and complained and allowed all of their disappointments to turn into bitterness. Exodus 16:2 records that, in the difficulties of the wilderness they had to pass through, "the people spoke *bitterly* against Moses and Aaron." The Israelites kept finding new reasons for disappointment. They cultivated their bitter spirits instead of fully uprooting their bitterness. Most of that generation did not make it to the Promised Land.

Hannah is a more positive biblical example of a person who was bitterly disappointed. She desperately wanted to have a child, but as the years passed she began to believe that she was barren. In 1 Samuel 1:10 we are told: "She was in deep anguish and was *crying bitterly* as she prayed to the Lord."

We can learn from Hannah. Although greatly disappointed to the point of bitterness, she came to the Temple and poured out her heart to God in prayer. She threw herself into His arms. She chose a constructive way to deal with her bitter agony. God answered her prayers and soon provided her with a son, Samuel.

God is compassionate towards the disappointments we feel. Like Hannah, we can uproot our bitterness by turning it over to Him, trusting in His love and care. We can pray the bitterness out of our system. God will eventually take this bitterness from us, *if* we are willing to give it up to Him. He will also eventually bring us out of our disappointing circumstances into a better place.

Naomi is another biblical example of a woman who initially battled bitterness when life took a difficult, deeply disappointing turn. Her husband and her two adult sons died. In her terrible pain, Naomi said: "Don't call me Naomi….call me Mara, because the Almighty has made my life very bitter. I went away full, but the Lord has brought me back empty…The Lord has afflicted me; the Almighty has brought misfortune on me."[57] In contrast with the name Naomi, which connotes "Joy," the name Mara means "Bitter." Notice how Naomi initially blamed God for her painful circumstances.

Dealing with her bitterness over time, Naomi did not wallow in it or get stuck in it. She moved on with her life. Choosing to treat her daughter-in-law Ruth with kindness, love, and concern, she focused on finding a new husband for Ruth.

God ultimately brought Naomi out of her tough circumstances when Ruth married Boaz. Naomi became an integral part of that new family, helping to care for Ruth's son Obed (who became the grandfather of David and an ancestor of the family line that Jesus was born into). Naomi left her painful past behind

---

[57] Ruth 1:20–21 (NIV).

and was able to enjoy the relationships that unfolded in her new circumstances.

Job is yet another well-known biblical example of how bitterness can arise from the profound disappointment and excruciating pain of very difficult circumstances. Job lost his children, his wealth, and his health. At one point, Job cried out: "I will speak out in the anguish of my spirit, I will complain in the *bitterness* of my soul."[58] Who can blame him?

God had compassion on Job and helped him to get a proper perspective on his life. Job, for example, was able to recognize that God was aware of every detail of what was happening to him; that even though God appeared to be slaying him, Job should still trust Him; and that no matter what was coming against him, he could resolve to come forth out of the fire as purified gold.[59] Job refused to get entangled in his bitterness and instead *chose* to have these better attitudes even while his horrible circumstances continued. In the end, God gave Job twice as much as he had before.

In the New Testament, Peter reacted bitterly to a crushing disappointment. Remember this scene? Jesus had just been arrested. He was about to be crucified. Afraid for his own life, Peter denied that he knew Jesus three separate times. Recognizing how he had betrayed Jesus, Peter "went away, *crying bitterly*."[60] Peter was deeply disappointed in the evolving circumstances and then in himself.

Note how compassionate Jesus was towards Peter's inner bitterness and his difficult circumstances. Jesus appeared to Peter after His resurrection and assured Peter of His love, notwithstanding Peter's cowardly denial of Him. God soon granted Peter a generous outpouring of the Holy Spirit and Peter became one of the greatest leaders of the early Christian church.

---

[58] Job 7:11 (NIV).
[59] See Job 23:2; 13:15; 23:10.
[60] Matthew 26:75b.

The above examples show bitterness in response to profound, painful disappointment arising from *tough life circumstances*. In Peter's situation, there was also bitter disappointment *in his own self*.

We can also become bitter in response to disappointment in our *relationships*. So often in life, we encounter unmet expectations in our relationships. We all carry around an idea of what perfect parents, a perfect mate, perfect children, and perfect friends should be like. We imagine what Christmas should be like. We have idealistic expectations of birthdays, anniversaries, Valentine's Day, romantic getaways, and family reunions. Real life and real relationships do not always match our hopes and dreams.

We will discuss in a later chapter how human love has the potential of being disappointing—sometimes profoundly disappointing. All of us must guard against developing roots of bitterness in response to the disappointment we feel in certain close relationships. Just as we must let go of hurt, we have to let go of our expectations. We have to follow that same path of forgiving, forgetting, letting go, and letting God help—and then *move on* with a fresh outlook.

Bad Parenting

Roots of bitterness can start growing in childhood. Some children grow up in dysfunctional homes where emotional illness, substance abuse, or domestic violence scars their souls before they have the maturity to manage their troubled thoughts and feelings. Other homes suffer from being too strict, too punitive, or too deficient in warmth and love.

Paul warned parents about this potential root of bitterness: "Fathers, do not *embitter* your children, or they will become discouraged."[61]

---

[61] Colossians 3:21 (NIV).

It is not a child's fault that roots of bitterness begin to develop in them at a tender age—but it *is* the responsibility of an older teenager/young adult to begin making right emotional choices. As God reveals the bitterness in their hearts, they must make a deliberate decision to uproot the bitterness. The *maintaining* or *nurturing* of a bitter spirit by an adult person *is* their fault.

There is no point in thinking of oneself as an "innocent victim." While it may be true that some people *were* innocent victims as *children*, there is no upside to spending the rest of one's life wallowing in a victim mentality. This only toughens the bitter roots and fertilizes the eventual bitter fruit.

Unconfessed Sin

Unconfessed sin can cause roots of bitterness to grow deep within. The sin and the bitterness get all tangled up together. When Moses warned the Israelites about the specific sin of worshipping idols, he instructed them: "make sure there is no *root* among you that *produces such bitter poison.*"[62] Sin of any kind that is not dealt with ultimately produces bitter poison. Mismanaged, unresolved anger is clearly not the only sin that leads to the growth of bitter roots.

Proverbs warns over and over about sexual immorality. Proverbs 5, for example, talks about engaging in sexual sin with a prostitute. King Solomon warns in Proverbs 5:4 that "afterwards only a *bitter conscience* is left to you." Sin can taste sweet at first, but the consequences eventually taste bitter.

Jeremiah warned the Jewish people about the consequences of their ongoing sin and rebellion against God. In Jeremiah 2:19b, the prophet asserted: "You will see what an evil, *bitter* thing it is to rebel against the Lord…" In Jeremiah 9:15b, the prophet brought the wayward Israelites this message from God: "I will feed them with *bitterness* and give them *poison* to drink."[63]

---

[62] Deuteronomy 29:18b (NIV).

[63] NLT translation.

Though warned about this, God's people continued to sin and rebel.

In the Book of Lamentations, Jeremiah later had much to say about the bitter fruit of that ongoing sin. Describing Jerusalem, he wrote: "How deserted lies the city, once so full of people! How like a widow is she, who once was great among the nations!... *Bitterly she weeps at night,* tears are upon her cheeks....she is in *bitter anguish*...Jerusalem has sinned greatly..."[64]

Yet, for those willing to turn back to God in repentance, Jeremiah offered hope. After describing the affliction, groaning, grieving, distress, destruction, desolation, and death that God's people suffered as a result of their sin and rebellion, Jeremiah stated: "Yet this I call to mind and therefore I have hope: Because of the Lord's great love we are not consumed, for his compassions never fail. They are new every morning....The Lord is good to those whose hope is in him, to the one who seeks him....Let us examine our ways and test them, and let us return to the Lord. Let us lift up our hearts and our hands to God in heaven and say: 'We have sinned and rebelled...'"[65]

Even though the people did repent, God did not *immediately* remove His people from the bitter situation their sin had brought upon them, nor did He immediately help them uproot their deep inner bitterness. But He did have compassion over time. Jeremiah was able to accurately prophesy: "O Daughter of Zion, your punishment will end; he will not prolong your exile."[66] God's people were in exile in Babylon for seventy years. But God eventually brought them back to Jerusalem. The Temple was rebuilt. Singing and laughter returned one day. Most importantly, most of the people repented of their sinful rebellion and chose to return to serving and worshipping God.

Repenting from sin prevents *new* bitter roots and bitter fruit from growing. It does not necessarily spare us from eating some

---

[64] Lamentations 1:1ab–2a, 4b, 8a (NIV).

[65] Lamentations 3:21–25, 40–42 (NIV).

[66] Lamentations 4:22a (NIV).

of the old bitter fruit. Sometimes, in His mercy, God destroys the old bitter fruit. But not always. Take Esau for example. In Hebrews 12:16–17, Paul warned: "Watch out that no one... becomes careless about God as Esau did: he traded his rights as the oldest son for a single meal. And afterwards, when he wanted those rights back again, it was too late, *even though he wept bitter tears of repentance.* So remember, and be careful."

God *forgave* Esau. But He did not *undo* all of the consequences of Esau's flippant disregard of his birthright and the special paternal blessing that ought to have attended it. We saw earlier how Esau had to overcome his bitterness towards his brother Jacob, who "stole" both his birthright and his father's blessing. Esau also had to overcome the bitter fruit of his *own* wrongdoing.

Getting Stuck in Bitterness

Bitterness, bearing a grudge, having fantasies of revenge—these thoughts and feelings can seem deceptively delicious for a while. Hannah Whitall Smith wrote: "Have you ever tasted the luxury of indulging in hard thoughts against those who have...injured you? Have you never known what a...fascination it is to brood over their unkindnesses and to pry into their malice and to imagine all sorts of wrong and uncomfortable things about them? It has made you wretched, of course; *but it has been a fascinating source of wretchedness that you could not give up.*"[67]

It is like eating a food that you know is unhealthy for you—it is hard to stop indulging in it because it is so tasty. Bitterness may seem like a pleasurable enough indulgence for a while, but it takes a terrible toll on our physical, emotional, relational, and spiritual health.

We have all known people who have become stuck in their bitterness and resentment. These people protect their bitterness as if it were of some value. They have decided that they are

---

[67]Hannah Whitall Smith, *The Christian's Secret of a Happy Life,* author's italics.

entitled to harbor their resentment. Not surprisingly, Dr. Sam has observed that many of these people develop a host of physical aches and pains, often compounded by cycles of insomnia and fatigue. All of this puts them at risk for chronic depression. Some of them become invalids.

Their interior worlds are full of hardened unforgiveness. Eventually, they alienate most of their family and friends. Who wants to be around someone with a long list of grudges, offences, and complaints?

Many bitter people continue to grow older, unable to enjoy most days—increasingly lonely and estranged from others, still professing Christian faith but unable to bear much meaningful fruit.

John and Molly Wesley

John Wesley (an 18th century preacher, evangelist, and hymn writer) and his wife Molly both battled bitterness and resentment. They married when they were already in their forties. Almost from the outset, the marriage fared poorly and deteriorated further over the subsequent twenty years.

Molly was not happy when John frequently left her to preach all over the country. The couple did not get along any better when she accompanied him on his trips. Molly was known for her fierce temper and poisonous tongue. It's tough to judge her though. John apparently held the philosophy that his life and ministry as a married man should be no different than it had been as a single man. He chose to unwisely correspond with and counsel other women who admired him, naturally arousing Molly's jealousy and anger. And so roots of bitterness grew in them as they locked horns over various issues.

John and Molly endured years of unresolved resentment and bitterness before their marriage ended in separation. Wesley rationalized, after Molly's death, that if they had enjoyed a happier marriage, he might not have been as single-mindedly committed to his work as preacher and evangelist. Wesley was unquestionably one of the great spiritual giants of his time. His ministry powerfully impacted Britain, America, and parts of Europe. He preached tens of thousands of sermons to crowds that numbered tens of thousands. Although he blessed countless others, it is sad that his own personal life was so marred and diminished by longstanding marital bitterness.[68]

Mary Livingstone

Mary Livingstone, wife of African medical missionary and explorer David Livingstone, also battled resentment and bitterness over many years.

David and Mary first fell in love when she was just twenty-three. She had nursed him after he had been badly mauled by a lion. Early in their marriage, they were able to travel around Africa together. During these years of togetherness (some of the happiest in Mary's life), their marriage was relatively healthy. In those days, David considered his wife a blessing—a kind and hardworking woman who knew how to comfort him and how to be an enjoyable companion.

David's dream was to open up the African continent. As the years passed, due to bouts of ill health and the demands of motherhood, Mary could not always accompany David on his travels. Sometimes she was left to take care of their many children as a single parent—surely not easy in the African bush. Other times, she had to return to England with the children while David remained in Africa. For a while, she had to live with her British in-laws (with whom she did not enjoy a good relationship).

David was sometimes away on his explorations for a few years at a time. During these long marital separations, Mary's physical illnesses were eventually compounded by failing emotional health. Deep bitterness developed as the years rolled by, and Mary increasingly resented her lot in life. During one

---

[68]William J. Petersen, *25 Surprising Marriages,* chapter 13.

four year period of separation from her husband, she started to speak negatively about the mission organization which sponsored her husband. She also began to drink. As she bitterly watched her husband rise to be an adored national hero, her life steadily unraveled.

The growing bitterness temporarily abated during a six-month period of togetherness when David came home to England. Mary was briefly able to share in the honor being bestowed on him. Furthermore, she hoped that she would be able to go with her husband on his next African trip. She actually started out on that next journey, only to discover she was pregnant, resulting in her return to England without David.

Her bitterness crept back. It showed up in heavier drinking, significant weight gain, negative moods, strained social relationships, and a spiritually dark outlook. Bitterness was to remain her chosen companion until her death at age forty-one. Her final brief reunion with her husband in Africa, where she died of malarial fever, was not able to alleviate the deeply-rooted bitterness that had grown over too many years.[69] She is a sad example of a woman who became stuck in bitterness that accompanied her to the grave.

I do not intend to judge or criticize the Wesleys or Mary Livingstone. I have not had to deal with their unique and particularly challenging circumstances. My point is to make all of us more wary of the insidious potential of bitterness. Even Christians highly esteemed for certain aspects of their public life of faith have failed to deal with bitter roots in their souls. It could happen to any of us if we are not careful.

Uprooting and Resisting Resentment and Bitterness

I am deeply touched by the stories of those who have refused to get ensnared in resentment and bitterness, even after going through some very difficult relationships and circumstances.

---

[69]Petersen, chapter 17.

Corrie ten Boom

Many older Christians have read about the inspiring life of a Dutch woman named Corrie ten Boom. Her life story provides some of the finest examples of how Christians are meant to manage their toughest emotions.

Corrie spent part of World War II in a Nazi concentration camp after she was arrested for hiding Jewish refugees in her home. In that Nazi camp, she suffered near-starvation, crowded barracks infested with fleas, standing at early morning roll call (sometimes naked, no matter how terrible the weather conditions), the vicious brutality of Nazi guards, and the unjust deaths of loved ones.

After the war, Corrie traveled to Germany and many other nations, speaking about the need to forgive. One aspect of her postwar ministry involved establishing a home in Holland for Dutch victims of Nazi brutality. After working with these traumatized individuals, Corrie observed that those who chose to forgive their former enemies were better able to build new lives. In contrast, the people who nurtured their bitterness wasted the rest of their lives.[70]

Corrie had her *own* personal struggles with bitterness. It took her time, for example, to get over the bitterness she felt towards a fellow Dutch man—supposedly a friend—who had betrayed her whole family during the war. He was the person who had told the Nazi occupiers in Holland about Corrie and her family hiding Jewish refugees in their home. Most of Corrie's family was thereafter arrested by the Nazis and several of her family members ultimately died during their unjust imprisonment, including her dearly loved father and sister.

Corrie learned that forgiveness was the only way to overcome bitterness. She had to *give up* her bitterness and *choose* forgiveness. She had to seek the help of the Holy Spirit. Only then did God wash away the bitterness and hatred that had

---

[70]Corrie ten Boom, *Tramp for the Lord*, pgs. 56–57.

seized her heart, allowing her to actually begin to love her enemies.

After the war, Corrie encountered the same Dutch man who had betrayed her and her family. Tough as it was, she chose to expressly forgive him. In fact, Corrie was able to lead this Dutch man to Christ. [71]

Dr. Helen Roseveare

Dr. Helen Roseveare, a medical missionary in the Congo for many years, encountered her share of reasons for feeling resentful and bitter. She also learned to get rid of bitterness before it became deeply rooted.

An example of this occurred the day after the first Congolese nurses she had trained passed their state nursing exams. She had worked so hard to prepare these nurses for their qualifying exams. Instead of being congratulated by her fellow missionaries on the success of her students, she was abruptly told the following day that she was going to have to move her medical work seven miles from the central mission center. In her moment of shining achievement, she felt that she was being treated as a rejected outcast.

Dr. Roseveare was initially full of bitterness and resentment. For a time, she was understandably consumed with these emotions. She was so full of fury that she even resisted praying. She did, however, wisely allow someone else to pray for her. Dr. Roseveare was thereafter able to get a grip on her thoughts, her emotions, and her tongue. God gave her the grace she needed to agree to the decision to move away from the central mission. She ultimately chose to discard her bitter, resentful feelings and to *get on* with her medical missionary work.[72]

Dr. Roseveare had to put these emotional skills into further serious practice in later years. The Congo achieved independence from Belgium in 1960. Most white people were either

---

[71]Ibid, pgs. 50–52.
[72]Helen Roseveare, *Give Me This Mountain.*

captured or killed soon after, or they quickly fled the country. Dr. Roseveare chose to stay, because doctors were desperately needed.

She was aware of the acute danger she was in. In that tumultuous era, other missionaries who chose to stay were being assaulted or robbed by roaming bands of rebels. It was not long before she herself was burglarized and almost poisoned to death. The worst was yet to come. In 1964, Dr. Roseveare was held captive by rebels for *five months*, beaten up, and brutally raped. Understandably, Dr. Roseveare battled serious negative emotions after this trauma, including bitterness.

Over the months after her captivity and rape, Dr. Roseveare had to process a deep level of forgiveness towards the rebels who had so savagely imprisoned and violated her. In response to her cries for His help, God eventually gave her an even greater love for the people of the Congo. She was able to resume her medical work in the country in 1966, and went on to serve there for seven more years.[73]

Barbara Johnson and her son Larry

Best-selling author Barbara Johnson and her son Larry have been candid about the bitterness to which they both once succumbed. Barbara and her son were essentially estranged for about eleven years, while Larry pursued a gay lifestyle.

Admirably, they ultimately chose to put off their bitterness and to work at ending the pain of estrangement, even after so much time had passed. Eventually, there was healing and restoration of the relationship between mother and son. The Johnsons have been publicly open about their emotional struggles so that others can be warned about the powerful grip that bitterness can have on a family.[74]

---

[73] Dr. Helen Roseveare, *Give Me This Mountain*; Dr. Helen Roseveare, *The Spirit's Enablement* (a talk given by her at the 1981 Urbana Conference in Illinois).

[74] Barbara Johnson, *Splashes of Joy.*

I am thankful for honest Christians like Barbara and Larry, who are willing to share their pain, their struggles, and their ultimate victory. It helps the rest of us to admit (to ourselves and others) our own struggles with difficult emotions. Their story also gives others hope that deeply rooted negative feelings like resentment and bitterness can, with personal determination and with God's help, be overcome.

Lisa Beamer

Lisa Beamer, widow of 9/11 hero Todd Beamer, has also been candid in sharing her battles with bitterness and resentment. We talked earlier about how she battled anger after the sudden death of her father when she was fifteen. Because that anger remained unresolved for some years, she also struggled with the consequent bitterness and resentment that developed.

She learned that bitterness and resentment do indeed grow over time. They cannot be quarantined in a small, dark corner of the soul; they begin to insidiously permeate the rest of life. Watching how hard her mother had to work after her father's death triggered her bitterness. So did pondering why God let her father die. Life felt unfair. As time passed, she became increasingly aware of how ugly the emotions of anger, bitterness, and resentment were, but did not know what to do with them.[75]

Lisa eventually learned how to stop asking "why" questions, to stop focusing on life being unfair, to start trusting God again, to seek His help, and to dwell on what was still right and good in her life. Once she stopped feeding the bitterness regarding her father's death, it dissipated.

Later, when her husband Todd lost his life on 9/11 at the hands of terrorists, she chose from the outset not to get stuck in resentment and bitterness. She *refused* to start new roots of bitterness in her life. She *rejected* the temptation to give in to these negative emotions. No one would have blamed her for

---

[75]Lisa Beamer, especially pgs. 81–82.

being angry and bitter. She had learned, however, that harboring and nurturing these ugly emotions wastes precious time and energy—and in the end they achieve absolutely nothing.[76]

Further Comments on the Spirit's Empowerment

We can seek the empowering help of the Spirit in our struggle with the potent emotions of resentment and bitterness. Hannah was right, in her profound disappointment regarding her barren womb, to weep in the Temple, in the presence of God. The Israelites, weary of their slavery to the Egyptians, were right to cry out to God. Job was wise to engage in a long dialogue with God, not just his friends. Corrie ten Boom was wise to seek the help of the Spirit to uproot her bitterness towards her Dutch betrayer and her Nazi captors. Dr. Roseveare was willing to let someone pray on her behalf, asking for God to give her grace. Lisa Beamer learned that the only way to get rid of her anger, resentment, and bitterness was to turn to God—to trust in Him and His help even when she did not understand the "why" of it all.

Whatever the reason for our bitterness and resentment, we can turn to God and ask for His help. We can seek the partnership of and empowerment from the Holy Spirit. They are ours for the asking.

We may have to ask for God's help day after day until the bitterness and resentment are fully uprooted. This may not happen overnight, especially if the roots are deep. Corrie has shared about how her bitterness kept trying to come back, attempting to re-establish its tenacious roots. She realized that, on a daily basis, she had to *stand her ground* against the temptation to become bitter and resentful. Eventually, her bitter and resentful thoughts fell away.[77]

God, through his Spirit indwelling within us, will help us stand our ground. He will help us face the recurring temptations to get stuck in bitterness and resentment. He will help us bring

---

[76]Lisa Beamer, especially pgs. 308–309.
[77]Corrie ten Boom, *Tramp for the Lord*, pg. 53.

our thoughts captive. He will help us forget the memories that give rise to the thoughts we struggle with. He will help us dig out *all* bitter roots—until they are *completely* removed.

The Challenge

God sees bitterness in a very serious light. In Romans 1:29, Paul wrote about those whose "lives became full of every kind of wickedness and sin..." In a list that includes murder and lying, Paul mentions bitterness. We do not know much about whether Paul personally struggled with bitterness. We know he was beaten, imprisoned, insulted, and ultimately beheaded. What-ever the nature of his personal battle with bitterness, he spent years preaching against its destructive power and sinful grip.

We must do whatever it takes to destroy these roots before they bear poisonous fruit. We will not be ready to choose forgiveness or love until we do so. Joy, peace, and contentment will also elude us.

When our years advance and life throws us a curve ball such as blindness, let each one of us be numbered with those who can still enjoy the fragrance of the roses. What we cultivate in our souls *now*, for better or worse, will profoundly impact the choices we will make in our lives *then*.

...you husbands must be loving and kind to your wives
and not bitter against them...
Colossians 3:19

So I want men everywhere to pray
... free from sin and anger and resentment.
1 Timothy 2:8

Don't bear a grudge...
Leviticus 19:18b

...love...does not hold grudges...
1 Corinthians 13:5bd

Get rid of all bitterness, rage and anger
...along with every form of malice.
Ephesians 4:31 (NIV)

8
HATRED
Unhinged

So let us feast upon him and grow strong in the Christian life,
leaving entirely behind us the cancerous old life
with all its hatreds and wickedness.
1 Corinthians 5:8a

I N MY TRAVELS, I have come into chilling contact with the horrific hatred that has marred so many periods of history in so many places. In Carthage, Tunisia, I stood on the ground where Christians were cruelly martyred centuries ago. In Kabul, Afghanistan, I saw the soccer stadium where the Taliban executed men for crimes such as listening to Western music and women for accidentally showing an ankle beneath their burkas. Speechless, I walked through the rooms in Dachau, Germany, where young and old were gassed to death during the years that the Nazis systemically murdered six million Jews. In Monrovia, Liberia, I drove down streets where men, women, and children had been butchered with machetes, their severed limbs left to litter the sidewalks. Appalled, I viewed hideous instruments of torture in the Tower of London museum. Like countless others, I felt numb as I stared at the gaping hole of Ground Zero in New York City.

Our world is full of hatred, some of it so brutal it is beyond comprehension. I am not a sadistic person in search of the gruesome or the macabre—without even looking for it, evidence of hatred has assaulted me all over the place.

Hatred is on the rise in our world. In the past decade, for example, hate crimes have increased more than 90% in Toronto, the Canadian city I live near. Gun violence in Toronto has been exploding, especially in recent years. Hatred on a titanic scale is not just *back then* or *over there*. It is openly expressed in *our* communities, classrooms, and courtrooms. It lives inside the walls of too many homes on *our* streets. We do not have to travel to Kabul, Dachau, or Ground Zero to observe its impact. Nor does it just live in the hearts of ruthless dictators or foreign terrorists. Its ugly potential lurks in *every* human heart.

Proverbs 10:12 tells us: "Hatred stirs old quarrels..." Hatred continually fertilizes all the old unresolved hurt, anger, resentment, bitterness, and unforgiveness deep within. Hatred does not let these other emotions heal or wither or die. On the contrary, hatred sustains the vitality of this ugly cluster and attracts other unwanted emotions. Psychiatrist Dr. Stephen Stokl warns: "By chronically sustaining anger, hatred, and an unforgiving attitude, a person can only end up in depression, anxiety, and misery."[78]

Tragically, the original anger might have been triggered by hurt. Hurt and hatred go hand and hand in this fallen world. Those who hate the most have, in many cases, been hurt the most.

Hatred Destroys Ordinary Lives

While still a law student years ago, I assisted a well-known criminal lawyer with a murder trial. Our client had been married to his wife for many years, but she unexpectedly left the marriage and had retained a family lawyer to advance her interests in court. The Judge granted her custody of their children and possession of the marital home and our client was ordered to pay for the support of his former family. Coming from a culture where women were expected to meekly obey their husbands, my client could not accept that his wife and her lawyer were able to assert such control over his children, his home, and his paycheck. As these acrimonious divorce proceedings had unfolded, his anger

---

[78] Dr. Stokl, pg. 396.

and bitterness had escalated into intense rage and unbridled hatred—and ultimately into a sudden violent outburst in the corridor outside the courtroom. He shot and killed his wife's lawyer.

One of my assignments, in preparing for the murder trial, was to find as much evidence as I could of how nice, decent— even loving—this man had been prior to the passionate courthouse shooting of his wife's lawyer. The goal was to obtain the most appropriate prison sentence for this level of homicide and these particular circumstances. For days, I looked through old family photographs, letters, and diaries. I was struck by two surprising discoveries as I worked on this case.

The first unexpected discovery was how pleasant, polite, and even charming the accused was. How could an accused murderer be so ordinary and so human? I enjoyed being in the company of this man. I learned, as I worked on that case, that murderers are not necessarily psychotic, mentally deranged, sub-human monsters.

The second unexpected discovery was the amount of love that could be observed in the family photographs of happier times— and the degree of tender affection that could be detected in the warm words once written. *This family had once been so happy and so loving.* Where had the intense hatred come from? How could it have escalated into the nightmare that had transpired? I realized, at that early stage of my law career, that hatred does indeed potentially lurk in the hearts of very ordinary humans.

In my later work with a Christian prison ministry, I noted how many times hatred, festering in a marriage or family, had ultimately led to murder. The convicted murderers that I met (both men and women) were not what one would expect. Some had a delightful sense of humor and a warm smile. Others had intelligent minds, engaging personalities, and interesting talents. A number of these convicted criminals seemed to be too *nice* to be serving time in maximum security prisons for the heinous crime of murder.

So many of them had started out as ordinary people in ordinary families, with hopes and dreams similar to the rest of us. They, too, had photo albums full of wedding kisses, smiling babies, Christmas celebrations, birthday parties, happy holidays, and anniversary toasts. In the midst of seemingly normal lives, the cycle of hurt, anger, bitterness, unforgiveness, and hatred had been triggered. In some cases, alcoholism, drug abuse, infidelity, and strife had arisen from, and then fueled, the emotional turmoil. In the end, it was not knives or bullets that tore apart these marriages and families—hatred was the real deadly weapon.

Hatred Is Not an Option

The Bible teaches us that hatred is *never* acceptable. It is not justifiable or excusable. It is clearly sinful. In Galatians 5:19–20 and in Romans 1:29, Paul wrote about lives that were full of every kind of wickedness and sin, including hatred.

The teaching of Jesus in this regard has always been radical. He told His followers plainly: "You have heard that it was said, 'Love your neighbor and hate your enemy; But I tell you: Love your enemies...'"[79] We are not allowed to hate even our worst enemies. Moses taught that we are not to hate our brother.[80] Jesus extended this to *not hating anyone*.

The apostle John wrote: "whoever hates his brother is in the darkness and walks around in the darkness; he does not know where he is going, because the darkness has blinded him."[81] Whenever we try to justify our hatred, we are in the very realm of darkness and self-deception that John warned about. John went so far as to equate hating our brother with the seriousness of murder.[82] When we hate our brother, we are no better in God's eyes than the convicted murderers I have just described.

---

[79] Matthew 5:43–44 (NIV).
[80] Leviticus 19:17.
[81] 1 John 2:11 (NIV).
[82] 1 John 3:15.

God knows better than we do the horrible potential of
unchecked hatred. If we allow hatred to grow in our hearts, can
any of us guarantee that we will be able to adequately control its
escalating force?

Biblical Examples of Hatred

The Bible is a very graphic exposé of the human heart. It frankly
(sometimes shockingly) reveals what lies within the souls of
ordinary men and women. We have already seen how Cain *hated*
his brother Abel and how Esau *hated* his brother Jacob for many
years.[83] Cain eventually murdered his brother and Esau certainly
thought of doing the same. Who knows what Esau would have
done if Jacob had not fled for his life and lived in a distant land
for a few decades?

Although Jacob later became one of the great patriarchs of
Jewish history, he and his own family were far from perfect.
Genesis 37 records how Jacob favored one of his sons, Joseph,
more than the other eleven. This became especially evident when
Jacob gave Joseph a special coat. When Joseph's brothers "saw
that their father loved him more than any of them, they *hated*
him."[84] When Joseph began to have dreams of his brothers one
day bowing down to him, they hated Joseph even more. Their
hatred grew to the point that they plotted to kill Joseph. Fortunately, Reuben was able to talk his other brothers into sparing
Joseph's life. Instead, they sold Joseph to a passing caravan.

Acts 8, 9, 22, and 26 record some other striking examples of
hatred. The apostle Paul was known as Saul prior to his dramatic
conversion on the road to Damascus. Saul was once very familiar
with raw, brutal hatred—it controlled *his* heart.

Saul approved the fatal stoning of Stephen, one of the first
Christian martyrs. Saul viciously hated all Christians. Becoming
one of their most feared persecutors, Saul tried to destroy the
early church. He went from house to house, hunting down and

---

[83] Genesis 4; Genesis 27:41.
[84] Genesis 37:4 (NIV).

then dragging off Christians, delivering them to prison and sometimes death.

Just before his encounter with Jesus, "Saul was still breathing out murderous threats against the Lord's disciples. He went to the high priest and asked him for letters to the synagogues in Damascus, so that if he found any there who belonged to the Way, whether men or women, he might take them as prisoners to Jerusalem."[85]

When Saul became Paul, and later wrote so much about the sin of hatred, he knew only too well what he was writing about. Sometimes we forget this dark side of Paul. Although he would eventually write the great 1 Corinthians 13 passage about *love*, (arguably the greatest treatise ever written about love), Paul was once a man whose heart had been full of intense hatred.

Choosing to Overcome Hatred

We can choose whether or not we will hate someone. We do not have to give in to hatred, no matter how grievously we have been hurt.

If we already have hatred in our hearts, we can choose to dig it out and destroy it, rather than letting it destroy *us* and others. Paul was able to do that. Once mired in hatred, Paul became a shining example of profound love and forgiveness. He taught that, with the help of the Holy Spirit, we *can* overcome hatred, no matter how tight its grip on our lives.

Chuck Swindoll

Most Christians, if they are willing to be emotionally transparent, will admit to having hated someone at some point in their lives. Chuck Swindoll, well-known author and speaker, has made this kind of frank admission. In one of his books (quite appropriately a study of the life of Paul), he confessed to having once hated another person. In fact, Swindoll hated that man so

---

[85] Acts 9:1–2 (NIV).

immensely that his hatred began to consume him. At some point, he recognized that the hatred was only hurting himself, not the object of his hatred.[86] Being the wise and mature Christian man that he is, he chose to get rid of his hatred.

Another Lesson from Corrie

Earlier, we introduced Corrie ten Boom, survivor of a World War II Nazi concentration camp, and discussed her battles with bitterness. In some cases, Corrie allowed her bitterness to escalate into hatred.

Corrie chose to hate one of the German nurses who worked in the Nazi camp—a nurse who was being particularly cruel to Corrie's dying sister, Betsie. The hatred intensified when Corrie stumbled across the lifeless body of Betsie, slumped against a washroom wall in the camp, amidst a pile of other corpses. Who can blame Corrie for hating the German nurse who had mistreated her sister in her final days?

One decade later, after the war, Corrie met that same nurse in a mutual friend's house. As soon as Corrie recognized the woman, she realized how much she *still* hated her. Corrie also realized that her hatred was contrary to the message of love and forgiveness that she was busily preaching to the post-war world.

Corrie prayed and fervently asked for God's help. In her own human strength, she struggled to obey God's command to love her enemy.[87] With the empowerment of the Spirit, however, Corrie was ultimately able to overcome her deeply imbedded hatred. In fact, Corrie was eventually able to lead this former Nazi nurse to Christ. I invite you to notice the pattern of how this remarkable woman was able to lovingly lead even her former enemies to Christian faith.

Like Corrie, we all need the empowerment of the Holy Spirit to truly get rid of hatred. It is up to us to make the initial choice to do whatever *we* can to rid our lives of any hatred growing within.

---

[86]Charles R. Swindoll, *Paul*, pg. 105.
[87] Carole Carlson, *Corrie ten Boom: Her Life, Her Faith*, pg. 141.

We must set our wills in that direction. We must take authority over our thoughts. We must then prayerfully partner with the Holy Spirit in the painstaking process of getting rid of our hatred.

The Gangs of New York City

In his years of working with teen gang members in New York City, David Wilkerson often encountered hatred. There was a long history of violent clashes between the warring gangs that Wilkerson was reaching out to. Over the years, most of the teens had been both the victims and the perpetrators of the violence. As Wilkerson preached on the streets of Brooklyn to these wayward teens, he knew that he had to specifically address their hatred.

He told these hate-filled youths that God loved them just as they were. God knew everything about them. God knew all about their anger, bitterness, and hatred. But God loved them anyways and already knew the potential of what they could become *in Him*.[88]

After hearing Wilkerson speak on the street, tough teen gang members would sometimes kneel on the sidewalk and choose to become Christians. Wilkerson understood the importance of praying, then and there, for God to help these young teens overcome their hatred. Many had experienced *years* of soul-crushing gang warfare, the brutal murders of their peers, and the breakdowns of their own families. Drugs, alcohol, and promiscuous sex had not been able to soothe their pain.

Only God's power was strong enough to break down the strongholds of hatred in these hardened young hearts. Only God's love could wash away the underlying pain. It was not unusual for these young men and women to sob as they prayed with Wilkerson for the first time—releasing a flood of pent-up anger, bitterness, and hatred.[89]

Wilkerson knew that human beings cannot do very much to truly change themselves, to heal their own pain, and to replace

---

[88] Wilkerson, pg. 58.
[89] Wilkerson, see for example pg. 74.

hatred with love and forgiveness. The hardened human soul
must be brought to God. Only He can deeply transform the
hurting heart and hating mind.[90]

Bishara

On a similar note, Brother Andrew has told the poignant story of
a Palestinian Christian named Bishara. For years, Bishara battled
hatred in his heart towards the Jews in Israel.[91] Bishara's father
had been gunned down in Jerusalem in 1948, by an Israeli para-
military force, when Bishara was just nine years old. That same
night, he and his family had to abandon their home, never to see
that home again.

His widowed mother could not make enough money to
support all her children. So Bishara grew up in an orphanage,
where he often went to bed lonely and hungry.

Years later, after the Six Day War of 1967, Bishara became the
principal of a high school for Palestinian boys in a town adjacent
to Jerusalem. Bishara wanted to help the boys in his high school,
recognizing how deeply scarred they were from the prolonged
conflict between Israelis and Palestinians. Many of the boys had
lost one or both parents or had been separated from them. Not
surprisingly, these boys were angry, filled with hate, and sometimes violent. Bishara could relate to their feelings.

Bishara tried to teach them to love God, love one another, and
even to love their enemies. None of these boys were initially
interested in Bishara's Christian faith. On the playground, the boys
continued to play-act, pretending they were getting revenge
against the Israeli soldiers who had harassed and humiliated them.

Bishara had a personal emotional breakthrough in the spring
of 1974. He came face to face with his own un-Christ-like feelings,
which included his unresolved hatred towards the Jewish people.
He realized that he could not help the boys overcome *their* hatred
if he did not deal with his *own* deeply buried hatred.

---

[90] Wilkerson, pg. 78.

[91] Brother Andrew, *Light Force,* chapter 13.

He still blamed the Israelis for the death of his father and the loss of his family home years before. He further blamed the Israelis for the twelve tough years he had lived in an orphanage, away from his mother. The cumulative hatred had been percolating beneath the surface of his life for years. He had been so quick to observe the ugly hatred in the lives of his students, but the time had come to admit the hatred in his own soul. He had been a Christian for a dozen years. It was time to finally deal with his longstanding hatred.

He prayed out loud one night, in tears, for God to forgive his feelings towards the Israelis. He wanted to be finally free of the hatred. He *knew* that he needed God's help. As he cried out to God, he could sense God already beginning to release him.[92] Over time, God helped him to deal decisively with his hatred.

Bishara went on to develop a Christian college, training many Palestinian Christians to minister the love of God. He has also accompanied Brother Andrew in face-to-face meetings with some of the most militant leaders of Hamas, sharing with them the Christian message of love and forgiveness. These important seeds are being planted in hostile ground.

Bishara has continued to live for three decades amidst the conflict, violence, and tension between the Israelis and Palestinians. He is a powerful example of one man who has personally overcome his hatred. If one man can conquer his hatred, there is hope that others will too. Forgiveness and reconciliation are unattainable goals in the Middle East as long as deep hatred breeds in human hearts. *Hatred is the real enemy*. Men like Bishara understand that.

Martin Luther King, Jr.

In a previous generation, black civil rights leader Martin Luther King Jr. learned the same lesson as Bishara. Early in life, King hated white people and saw them as the enemy. Later, he realized

---

[92] Brother Andrew, *Light* Force, pgs. 106–107.

that it was the wrong policy and practice of racial segregation that was the real problem. So he stopped hating, learning to love his previous enemies. With that attitude, he became one of the greatest civil rights leaders in American history.[93]

Self-Hatred

Self-hatred, arguably the most prevalent form of hatred, needs to be addressed. Self-hatred is the natural end result of unresolved guilt, inner shame, and self-condemnation. One of the heaviest burdens known to humankind, self-hatred corrodes the soul with self-torment. The afflicted person wrongly believes that they have no right to *ever* be happy, to be free, to enjoy their lives, or to be worthy of love.

Guilt and Shame

There are two types of guilt: (1) healthy guilt produced by our God-given conscience, under conviction by the Holy Spirit, after we have sinned; and (2) false guilt, imposed upon us by parents or other persons in authority who try to make us feel shame for behavior that is not sinful or for past sins that have been confessed.

Appropriate Guilt

The first kind of guilt—appropriate guilt—arises from truly wrong behavior. We *should* feel guilty *if* we have hurt someone because of our wrongdoing. We should feel guilty if we are indulging in secret sins. This kind of appropriate guilt is what brought us to Christ in the first place.

In Romans 9:1, Paul described our conscience as a valuable tool of the Holy Spirit. Paul later wrote, in 1 Timothy 3:9, that we are to have a *pure* conscience. In Titus 1:15 we are warned about having a *defiled* conscience. If we ignore our conscience too often,

---

[93] Bordon Books, *Mothers of Influence*, pgs. 41–43.

we are further warned in 1 Timothy 4:2 that it will become a *seared* conscience. A *healthy* conscience should lead us to appropriate confession and repentance whenever we sin, so that we can receive the forgiveness of God. Properly managed guilt leads to emotional freedom.

We can seek God's gracious forgiveness for every one of our sins and shortcomings. He can wash away our guilt and shame. He can remove all condemnation, no matter what we have done. In Isaiah 1:18 God tells us: "Come, let's talk this over! says the Lord; no matter how deep the stain of your sins, I can take it out and make you as clean as freshly fallen snow. Even if you are stained as red as crimson, I can make you white as wool!"

We are then in a position to love and forgive ourselves. We can feel clean and pure and free. Because Romans 8:1 tells us the wonderful news that there is *no condemnation* to those in Christ Jesus, we can stop hating ourselves.

False Guilt

False guilt is often more difficult to recognize and deal with than appropriate guilt. Inappropriate self-condemnation sometimes occurs after we have made an innocent mistake or let somebody else down. Simply *feeling* guilty does not mean that we have proper reason to feel guilty.

How can we tell the difference between appropriate guilt and false guilt? Let us look at what God Himself has to say about the matter. God has set forth his standards in the Bible. If we have violated the standards of the Bible, then we are experiencing true guilt that can only be dealt with by confession and repentance.

If, however, the Bible does not condemn what we have done, then we need not feel guilty and should not condemn ourselves. There is no need for confession or repentance. In other words, we should not feel guilty unless we are in deliberate, disobedient, rebellious, and unrepentant sin as defined by the Bible.

A person should *not* feel guilty if they have accidentally hurt (or even killed) someone. Try to tell that to the driver of the vehicle whose brakes would not grip an icy road—and whose wife or children died in the resulting accident. Try and tell that to the parent whose child has choked or fatally fallen. Lawyers, pastors, doctors, and other counselors face this kind of false guilt regularly when they deal with the hurting survivors of human tragedies.

Let me touch on some other common examples of false guilt.

Some Christians grow up in homes where they are taught (incorrectly) that all sex (including marital sex) is dirty and carnal. When they begin to develop normal sexual desires, they feel guilty and ashamed. When they later marry and try to enjoy a normal sexual relationship, they continue to feel guilty. This is not guilt arising from a defiled conscience. This is false guilt arising from improper teaching—guilt arising from incorrect *parental* standards, not *biblical* standards.

Other well-meaning but misguided parents teach that it is wrong for Christians to *ever* feel anger or anxiety, depression or discouragement—and so their children grow up feeling guilty for having these normal human feelings. These children learn to hide their troublesome emotions instead of properly processing them. They suffer from false guilt imposed on them by unhealthy emotional expectations in the home.

Some children grow up thinking that they will never be "good enough." They are not smart enough. They don't always tuck in their shirts. They should have more friends. They are too shy. They do not compete well in sports. They feel that they have not met their parents' expectations in areas that have nothing to do with *sin* or *moral choices* or *biblical standards*. They live in an environment of conditional love, with parental approval based on performance and achievement. Unhealthy perfectionism sets in. If these children "fail," they feel guilt and shame. Once again, this is false guilt: guilt imposed by parents, not by a healthy, Spirit-controlled conscience.

All parents probably set too high standards *some* of the time. Most parents love their children and want them to do well, desiring that they seek excellence and not settle for mediocrity.

Yet, as parents, we need to be so careful that we are not sending the wrong message—making our children feel guilt, shame, self-condemnation, and even self-hatred when they perceive that they are not "good enough."

I believe that this is one of the most difficult challenges of parenthood! How do we help our children reach their highest potential without undermining their self-esteem on those occasions when they don't get a good grade, don't score a goal, don't remember to do their homework, or don't want to get out of bed for that early morning game? There is such a fine line between encouragement and implied criticism, between correction and disapproval, between excellence and perfectionism. Needless to say, almost everyone grows up with at least some little pockets of self-condemnation arising out of a sense that their parents disapprove of *certain aspects* of who they are.

Marriage is another incubator of false guilt. Many spouses feel that they will never be "good enough." Women typically think that their marriage would be better *if* they could only lose some weight, dress a little better, look a little sexier, and still have time to cook a gourmet meal. (Of course, they also need to be professional superwomen and exemplary mothers!) Husbands may feel that they can never work hard enough, make enough money, buy enough gifts, give enough compliments, do enough domestic chores, or spend enough time with family.

Many husbands and wives feel guilty when they do not meet these impossible standards—standards which might have been imposed by their spouse, their own perfectionist selves, societal expectations—or by some lethal combination of the three. As one who has battled perfectionism, I know what it feels like to try to meet unrealistic inner expectations and self-dictated performance levels.

Here is the most tragic example of false guilt. Some people believe that they will never be "good enough" for God. This is the result of distorted theology and perhaps a shame-based childhood. For those who relate to that kind of thinking, there is good news. *None of us are good enough for God. All have sinned and fall short of the glory of God.* That is the precisely the reason that Jesus had to die for our sins.

The further good news is this: we don't *ever* have to be "good enough" for God on our *own* merits and by our *own* efforts. We only need to accept, in faith, that Jesus died for our sins. On that basis, and that basis alone, we find right standing with God. We do not earn this right standing. We do not achieve it. We do not work for it by trying to be nicer, kinder do-gooders. Thank God for this!

Those who have been programmed to believe in a "theology of works" will spend their lives feeling a floating sense of chronic, ill-defined guilt and condemnation. It is not the kind of healthy guilt inspired by a Spirit-controlled conscience. It is not guilt based on a specific wrong word or deed. It is hazy, cloudy, murky—yet ever present—an endlessly exhausting burden, a depressing weight.

True guilt can always be correlated to something very clear, defined, specific, and real—to a concrete statement, act, omission, thought, or attitude. False guilt is always nebulous, unclear, and general—not tied to some act or omission that we can put our fingers on or wrap our heads around.

Christian psychologist Dr. Dobbins made an astute observation about false guilt. He has said that we can know when guilt is unhealthy when it does not yield to forgiveness, no matter how often one has prayed for it.[94] When a person remains burdened with guilt after genuine confession and repentance, they must recognize that the residual guilt has been imposed on them by their own standards or the standards of someone other than God.

If you are one of those people who pray over and over for forgiveness but find no relief, then your task is to figure out *whose voice* is condemning you. It is not the voice of God. It is not the voice of Jesus. It is not the voice of the Holy Spirit. You must discern the owner of the voice that keeps condemning you. Satan

---

[94] Dr. Dobbins, pg. 113.

is the "accuser" of the brethren, but he often uses the voices of human beings to falsely accuse those repentant souls who ought to have no condemnation in Christ Jesus.

Self-hatred and self-condemnation are so destructive. Dr. Sam has observed that perfectionism, false guilt, and self-hatred often make up the hidden forces behind overeating, substance abuse, shopping addictions, sexual obsessions, and many other unhealthy means of trying to relieve and placate that incessant inner pain.

There is great hope for those wearied by such burdens. Just as the Holy Spirit can help us overcome hatred towards others if we ask Him, He can help us overcome all false guilt, self-hatred, and self-condemnation.

We are not meant to go through our lives bearing heavy burdens of false guilt and self-loathing. We do not have to walk in the shadows, wearing a cloak of shame. If we regularly confess our sins, then we *can* regularly receive God's loving forgiveness. Then we *do* have the capacity to be happy, to be free, to enjoy our lives, and to know that we are worthy of love. From this day forward, let's hear God's voice in this regard and choose to silence any voices playing in our minds which try to tell us otherwise.

...get rid of your feelings of hatred.
1 Peter 2:1a

I demand that you love each other,
for you get enough hate from the world!
John 15:17–18a

You have heard that it was said 'Love your neighbor
and hate your enemy!
But I tell you: Love your enemies...
Matthew 5:43–44 (NIV)

9
FORGIVENESS
Nobility of Spirit

...you are a God of forgiveness, always ready to pardon,
gracious and merciful, slow to become angry,
and full of love and mercy...
Nehemiah 9:17b

The Girl in the Photograph

K IM PHUC WAS a nine-year-old child on the June day in 1972 that military planes targeted her South Vietnamese village. The low-flying planes, on a mission that had been authorized by the American and South Vietnamese joint command, released napalm—jellied acids that caused horrific burns and other physical harm to those in the path of its falling rain. The napalm was intended for Viet Cong soldiers entrenched near the village, but some of it fell on innocent targets.

In the chaos, villagers ran in every direction. As she fled, Kim was sprayed with a heavy shower of napalm, sustaining serious burns to half of her body. Her skin immediately radiated intense heat and large chunks of flesh were instantly charred. She frantically ripped her burning clothes off of her tortured skin.

Moments later, a cameraman took a photograph of a very terrified Kim, as the young girl ran naked and screaming along the village road. The shocking photograph was printed around the world, winning every major international photographic award that year, including the Pulitzer Prize. It became a powerful symbol of the madness, carnage, and tragedy of the war in Vietnam. To this day, it remains a symbol of senseless wartime suffering.

Kim sustained significant and permanent scarring, although mercifully her face and hands were spared. She was in critical condition for about a month. More than a year of excruciating treatment and rehabilitation had to be endured, including multiple surgeries. Headaches, recurring nightmares, emotional pain, and sensitivity to climate changes continued over the decades.

Kim had ample reason to develop into an angry, bitter adult with a huge chip on her shoulder. Instead, a decade after the napalm strike, Kim chose to embrace the Christian faith and its core principles of love and forgiveness. After becoming a Christian, Kim began to experience peace, inner joy, and emotional healing. Over time, she has been able to forgive all those involved in the napalm strike.

This process of forgiveness was neither instant nor easy. Kim read, in Luke 6:27–28, that Jesus said we should love our enemies. She had trouble doing that at first because of the scale of the pain and suffering she had gone through and the limits of her own humanity. She prayed that God would help her to learn how to forgive and to love her enemies. It has taken much work, reliance on God's help, and daily prayer over the years, but Kim is now able to testify that she truly feels *free* from anger, bitterness, and hatred.[95]

In 1996, a few decades after the brutal assault on her village, Kim Phuc visited Washington, D.C. She had been asked to speak to a few thousand people who had gathered at the Memorial Wall for a Veterans' Day Ceremony. After the service, she met face to face with one of the American military men involved in the dispatch of the napalm-bearing planes on that horrible day in 1972. Kim had strong human reason to hate this man. But instead she made the hard choice to listen to what he had to say to her.

He told her that, after the war in Vietnam, he had gone through a divorce and a drinking problem. Those dark years ended after he became a Christian. In fact, he later became a

---

[95] Meg Johnstone, *The "girl in the picture" is flying.*

pastor. This man had already sought and received God's forgiveness for the war atrocities that had troubled him, but on that day in Washington, he sought the gift of Kim's forgiveness. Kim was able to tell him that she genuinely forgave him and to hold him in warm embrace.

Kim Phuc is no longer an emotional prisoner of the terrifying moment that the famous photograph was taken. She is no longer just a symbol of the brutality of war. She has become a world-renowned symbol of the ability of Christian love and forgiveness to *transcend* war, tragedy, pain, anger, bitterness, and hatred. I have had the privilege of hearing her speak and have seen for myself the unique radiance and beauty that light up the face of a person who can bestow that measure of love and forgiveness.

I am proud to call Kim a fellow Canadian. She is now a married mother, a gifted speaker, and a UNESCO goodwill ambassador. She started the Kim Foundation, which reaches out to child victims of war around the world. The power of Christian love and forgiveness continues to pour out of her life.[96]

Massacre in the Jungle

The week that I am writing this marks the fiftieth anniversary of the slaughter of five American men by Auca tribesmen in a remote jungle in Ecuador. In the 1950's, these five courageous young men purposed to introduce this isolated tribe to the message of God's love, mercy, and forgiveness. Although the tribe was known to be violent and especially hostile to any foreign intruders, these American men slowly and patiently attempted contact by offering friendship gifts lowered in a basket from a small airplane. When the tribesmen responded by placing their own reciprocal gifts in the basket, the American men believed that it was safe to attempt a face-to-face meeting. As a result, the Americans set up camp on a riverbank near the Auca village.

---

[96] Details of Kim's story taken from Denise Chong, *The Girl in the Picture,* and from a talk presented by Kim Phuc at Yorkview Community Church in Newmarket, Canada on June 4, 2000.

The Aucas were initially friendly—but soon after first contact, a raiding party returned to murder all five young men. The wives of the Americans were widowed as a result of this brutal massacre, left to raise fatherless young children. The normal human reaction of these widows would have been to develop anger, bitterness, and hatred. After all, their five husbands had come to the tribe in peace and demonstrated nothing but friendly goodwill to the men who had killed them. The murders were senseless and unwarranted.

Yet, within a short time of these murders, the widows instead chose to pray for this tribe. One of them, Elisabeth Elliot (widow of Jim Elliot), met some of the Auca women who had left the tribe. These Auca women were touched by Elisabeth's love and kindness. At the invitation of these tribeswomen, Elisabeth and her four-year-old daughter went to live in the Auca village, among the very men who had not long before murdered their beloved husband and father.

The Elliot widow and child were accompanied by Rachel Saint, (the sister of Nate Saint, one of the other martyred young men). Remarkably, Rachel continued to live amongst the Aucas for almost *forty years* and was joined from time to time by Steve Saint, the son of Nate. Steve had been only five years old when his father was murdered.

These family survivors of the massacre have been able to powerfully demonstrate Christian love and forgiveness to a tribe that committed the worst possible human offense against them. Half a century after the massacre, about a quarter of the Auca tribe are now committed Christians. They have changed the name of their tribe to the Waodani. Once a tribe with a very high homicide rate, the Waodani are now known as a peace-loving people.

Three of the tribesmen who participated in the murder of the five young American men are now elders of the Christian church. Two of them baptized Steve Saint in the very place where the massacre of his father had occurred. One of them, Mincaye, has traveled in America with Steve Saint, speaking about how God's love and forgiveness has transformed his life and many other lives in his tribe. It is incredibly moving to see Steve and Mincaye embrace as they share a speaking platform together.[97]

Everyone Needs to Forgive

Most of us have not had to face such horrific circumstances as the men and women previously described. Yet *all of us* will encounter some measure of pain, violation, and offense in our lives. We will all be hurt, often by the people who supposedly love us: our parents, husbands or wives, siblings, children, or friends. We, in turn, will hurt many others, including those *we* try to love. We are all imperfect. We all have our moments of selfishness, thoughtlessness, fatigue, anger, impatience, pride, careless slips of the tongue, and other human weaknesses. The Bible so accurately states that we are *all* sinners *and* victims of the sins of others.

I vividly recall a church conference dealing with both physical and emotional healing that I attended a few years ago. One morning was committed to the subject of forgiveness. After hearing powerful speakers on this topic, the few thousand people in attendance were invited to come forward for prayer and personal counsel if they needed to forgive someone. The following categories of people were asked to come forward— those who needed to forgive: a father or mother; a brother or sister; a husband or wife; an adult child; a friend; a teacher, pastor, or some other authority figure; a motor vehicle driver; someone who had physically, sexually, or emotionally abused them; a rapist or murderer.

Many moved forward to the front of the church as each category was called. Some moved from one group to another as a fresh category was called forward. While pastors, speakers, and

---

[97] Elisabeth Elliot, *Through Gates of Splendour*; Tom Heinen, *Of Forgiveness and Friendship*; *The End of the Spear* (motion picture released in 2006).

counselors prayed for the various groups and individuals, loud sobbing could be heard. Many people fell to their knees, visibly shaking, doubled over in agony, weeping uncontrollably. Of the few thousand present, not many were left seated in the pews. An almost overwhelming magnitude of pain could be felt in that room.

Heart-felt prayers and whispered counseling continued for some time. The first goal, for each person who had come forward, was to reach the point of *choosing to forgive* one or more offenders. The subsequent goal was to invite God's help and empowerment into the process. Eventually, a wave of peace and calm flooded the room. The sobbing subsided. God's presence could be felt.

Over the following days of the conference, many attendees reported significant breakthroughs in their quests for physical and/or emotional healing. Many testified that, after they made the choice to forgive someone who had hurt them, they began to feel some measure of relief from the intensity of their physical and emotional pain. Enormous burdens lifted. Chronic headaches, neck aches, back aches, and stiffness improved or even disappeared. Many reported sensing a fresh lightness and inner freedom. The testimonies spoke of the healing power that was unleashed in people as they each made the deliberate choice to forgive and then sought God's enabling Spirit to help them with this choice.

In some cases, people had to forgive themselves. At the session on forgiveness, there had been a sizable group who had come forward as drivers of motor vehicles that had crashed, either injuring themselves or killing and/or injuring one or more loved ones who had been passengers. There were, of course, many *other* kinds of tragic accidents, mishaps, and mistakes that people had to forgive themselves for that morning. As a lawyer who had been involved in personal injury and fatal accident litigation for years, I watched this process with awe—I had so often observed the deep emotional pain and guilt that resulted from serious accidents.

I learned afresh at that conference that *everyone* has forgiveness issues, past or present. Each one of us must make our own personal journey of forgiveness—a journey that will continue throughout our lifetime, involving multiple offenders and offences both large and small. Personally speaking, not a day goes by in which I do not need to forgive someone—and to forgive myself—and not a day goes by in which I do not need to seek the forgiveness of God for the ways in which I have hurt others. Such is the weakness and imperfection of my own humanity, no matter how hard I try to live the Christian life.

Sometimes the toughest matters to forgive are the little everyday offences: forgiving our family members when they leave dirty dishes lying around the house; forgiving an office mate for a rude comment; forgiving an aggressive driver who cuts us off in busy traffic; or forgiving our spouse when they are critical. A spirit of forgiveness is fostered and matured—most of all, and first of all—in this realm. If we cannot learn to forgive on this level, we will never reach the spiritual stature of Kim Phuc or Steve Saint.

God's Promise to Forgive Us

We cannot *extend* true mercy and forgiveness to others until we have *received* God's forgiveness and have thereby been able to deeply forgive ourselves.

Have you received God's forgiveness? Do you *feel* that forgiveness in the deepest levels of your soul? Or do you still carry around feelings of guilt, shame, self-condemnation, or self-hatred? Do you struggle with receiving God's forgiveness, forgiving yourself, and forgiving others?

Do you even recognize that you are a sinner and need God's forgiveness? King Solomon wrote: "…there is not a single man in all the earth who is always good and never sins."[98] The apostle

---

[98] Ecclesiastes 7:20.

Paul echoed this in Romans 3: 23: "Yes, *all* have sinned; *all* fall short of God's glorious ideal;..."

From early in childhood until our oldest adult years, we all experience self-centeredness, pride, disobedience, lying, and other wrong conduct. The ultimate sin is rebellion towards God Himself and His authority over our lives. Each one of us needs to recognize that, no matter how "good" we think we are or how "spiritual" or "religious" we have become, we are still sinners, ever in need of God's mercy, forgiveness, and grace.

Thankfully, God *is* a loving and forgiving God. In Isaiah, the prophet recorded God's declaration: "...I alone am he who blots away your sins for my own sake and will never think of them again....I've blotted out your sins; they are gone like morning mist at noon!"[99]

The Basis of God's Forgiveness

In Old Testament times, people received God's forgiveness by offering animal sacrifices to atone for their sins. The New Testament asserts that, at a defining point in history, God provided the incomparable sacrifice of His own Son—a sacrifice that, once and for all, paid the full penalty for all human sin. Luke wrote: "In this man Jesus, there is forgiveness for your sins! Everyone who trusts in him is freed from all guilt and declared righteous..."[100]

The apostle Paul wrote this incredible passage:

"Now God says he will accept and acquit us—declare us "not guilty"–if we trust Jesus Christ to take away our sins. And we all can be saved in this same way, by coming to Christ, no matter who we are or what we have been like. Yes, all have sinned; all fall short of God's glorious ideal; yet now God declares us "not guilty" of offending him if we trust in Jesus Christ, who in his kindness freely takes away our sins....Then

---

[99] Isaiah 43:25; Isaiah 44:22a.
[100] Acts 13:38c–39

what can we boast about doing, to earn our salvation? Nothing at all. Why? Because our acquittal is not based on our good deeds; it is based on what Christ has done and our faith in him. So it is that we are saved by faith in Christ and not by the good things we do.[101]

What do we have to do? We simply have to recognize that we are sinners, confess our sins, and receive for ourselves what Jesus did on the Cross for all of us. Of course, we do not have to catalogue every single sin we have ever committed; if we had to, none of us would ever get up off our knees! We should generally acknowledge that we have sinned and then perhaps confess some of the major sins that are troubling our conscience. In our ongoing daily prayers, we can confess the most significant ways we have sinned in the recent past.

It bears repeating that we do not have to *earn* forgiveness. We do not have to perform enough good works to be saved and forgiven. We just have to be honest enough about our true human condition. John wrote: "If we claim to be without sin, we deceive ourselves and the truth is not in us. If we confess our sins, he is faithful and just and will forgive us our sins and purify us..."[102]

There is room at the Cross for all of us. It does not matter what we have done or who we have been. All of us can receive God's full pardon and forgiveness. We can come to God *just as we are* on the basis of what Jesus did for us. We do not need to be afraid to recognize, acknowledge, admit, uncover, and confess our sins. Jesus has nailed each and every sin to the Cross.[103] God will not punish us for confessed sins—it is *safe* to confess to Him. There is divine amnesty for the repentant heart.

God will wash us white as snow, however dark the stain of our sins; He will remove our sins as far as the east is from the

---

[101] Romans 3:22b–24; 27–28.
[102] 1 John 1:8–9 (NIV).
[103] Colossians 2:14.

west.[104] We can receive God's mercy and His grace. (Grace is defined as God's undeserved favor.) We can exchange our miserable sins, failures, and mistakes for God's love, blessing, and favor. Those who truly experience this incredible exchange have a hard time understanding why anyone else would refuse this great gift of forgiveness that brings priceless right-standing with God.

Problems Receiving God's Forgiveness

For some, the reason they do not receive God's forgiveness is that they do not realize that it is available. For many others, the major road-block to receiving God's forgiveness is the environment that they grew up in.

I was blessed to have forgiving parents. Whenever I did something wrong, I was appropriately reprimanded and suitably punished. But then my wrongdoing was promptly forgiven and forgotten. There were no grudges against me. Old offences were not stored, dusted off, and rehashed at later times. I felt loved even after I had been disobedient, after I had broken the rules, and after I had made foolish mistakes.

My parents sometimes sought forgiveness for *their* wrongdoings. One day, while I was still kindergarten age, my mother lost her temper at me and sent me to my room somewhat unjustly. Within minutes, she came into my room, apologized for getting angry, and asked me to forgive her. Almost half a century later, I still remember that moment. Because my human parents modeled forgiveness, (both by extending it to me and asking for it), it was not difficult for me to believe that my Heavenly Father was willing to forgive me.

Others have not been so fortunate. If you have grown up in a home where you were constantly criticized—where you felt that you could never do anything right, where grudges were held onto and past failures repeatedly resurrected, where you never felt "good enough" and saw no way of becoming "good

---

[104] Isaiah 1:18; Psalm 103:12.

enough"—you might have trouble believing and receiving God's forgiveness.

If you relate to that kind of childhood, settle in your mind *this day* that God the Father is not the same as your earthly mother or father might have been. God's love is perfect and unconditional. God *will* forgive. He will not bear a grudge. He will never again remind you of the failures that you have brought to Him. God will no longer see your confessed sins, because you will have been washed as white as snow. God will thereafter only see the blood of his son Jesus, the blood that was shed for you and for me. You don't have to *beg* for God's forgiveness or *wonder* if you have in fact received it.

Simply ask for God's forgiveness and then receive it. On the basis of what was accomplished on the Cross, you *can* be "good enough" in God's eyes. This day, you can forever silence the voice of an earthly parent, or anyone else, who has told you otherwise.

Forgiving Ourselves

When we truly grasp that God, the Creator of the whole universe, has offered to freely forgive all of our sins, and when we accept that offer, we are then in a position to forgive ourselves. If God has forgiven us, is there any reason whatsoever why we should not forgive ourselves?

We must consciously forgive ourselves. We can then stop beating up on ourselves. We can look in the mirror and love the person we see. We can treat ourselves with kindness and compassion. We can decisively stop giving an ear to those who still want to condemn us.

In some cases, we may still have to ride out the natural consequences of what we have done. For example, a person who has confessed to sexual sin will be forgiven by God, and can therefore forgive themselves, but God will not necessarily step in to undo a pregnancy. A person might still have to tough out the human consequences of their sin, but they no longer have to carry the heavy weight of guilt and condemnation.

Forgiving ourselves is not always easy. I struggle with this whenever I make a mistake or give in to a temptation. I have always been tough on myself. I have had to learn that forgiving myself is important, not just to get rid of my inner sense of guilt and self-condemnation, but to properly prepare my heart to forgive others. There is more at stake than just my inner well-being. All of my earthly relationships hinge on my ability to forgive myself. I cannot extend genuine mercy, grace, and forgiveness to others unless I have extended mercy, grace, and forgiveness to myself.

Forgiving Others

Forgiving those who hurt us is a core element of Christian living. It is, in fact, a requirement and a command. When Jesus taught His followers how to pray, He told them to ask God the Father: "Forgive us our debts, as we also have forgiven our debtors."[105]

Receiving God's forgiveness is not linked to performing good deeds, but it *is* linked to forgiving others. Jesus explained: "...if you forgive men when they sin against you, your heavenly Father will also forgive you. But if you do not forgive men their sins, your Father will not forgive your sins."[106] This ties in with what Jesus told His disciples in Matthew 10:8b: "Freely you have received, freely give. (NIV)"

Peter once asked Jesus: "Lord, how many times shall I forgive my brother when he sins against me? Up to seven times?" Jesus answered: "I tell you, not seven times, but seventy-seven times."[107] Jesus then told the following gripping parable:

> ...a king...decided to bring his accounts up to date. In the process, one of his debtors was brought in who owed him $10,000,000! He couldn't pay, so the king ordered him sold for

---

[105] Matthew 6:12 (NIV).
[106] Matthew 6:14–15 (NIV).
[107] Matthew 18:21–22 (NIV).

the debt, also his wife and children and everything he had. But the man fell down before the king, his face in the dust, and said, "Oh, sir, be patient with me and I will pay it all."

Then the king was filled with pity for him and released him and forgave his debt.

But when the man left the king, he went to a man who owed him $2,000 and grabbed him by the throat and demanded instant payment. The man fell down before him and begged him to give him a little time....But his creditor wouldn't wait. He had the man arrested and jailed until the debt would be paid in full.

Then the man's friends went to the king and told him what had happened. And the king called before him the man he had forgiven and said, "You evil-hearted wretch! Here I forgave you all that tremendous debt, just because you asked me to—shouldn't you have mercy on others, just as I had mercy on you?"

Then the angry king sent the man to the torture chamber until he had paid every last penny due. *So shall my heavenly Father do to you if you refuse to truly forgive your brothers.*[108]

This story seems harsh until we examine its underlying premise. Remember, we are all sinners. While we were in a state of sinful rebellion, we deserved God's judgment. Justice would have demanded that we pay the full penalty for our own sins. Because of what Jesus did on the Cross for us in our place, God's justice has been vicariously satisfied. So instead of God's judgment, we who come to the Cross can receive God's mercy.

It is not right to believe, however, that Jesus died only for *me*. He died for the whole world—for each one of us—even for our enemies. *We cannot accept God's mercy for ourselves and then demand God's judgment for others.* This would not be fair.

The choice is ours—God's judgment *or* His mercy and forgiveness. The only catch is that whatever *we* choose to receive, we must be willing to give to others. If we want mercy and forgiveness, we must extend mercy and forgiveness.

---

[108] Matthew 18:23–34.

As a lawyer, I can appreciate the fairness, the logic, and the inherent justice of God's position that we must extend to others the forgiveness we receive. The bottom line is that, if we want forgiveness and mercy for ourselves, we must be willing to mercifully forgive others.

A Lesson from Joseph

The story of Joseph in Genesis is one of the most amazing stories of forgiveness.[109] After Joseph's eleven brothers cold-heartedly sold him to a passing caravan, Joseph ended up in Egypt, working as a servant in the house of Potiphar.

Although Joseph worked hard for Potiphar, he was once again unjustly treated. When Joseph did not respond to the amorous advances of Potiphar's wife, she lied to her husband, falsely claiming that Joseph had tried to rape her. Joseph was imprisoned for a number of years.

In prison, Joseph interpreted the dreams of two of his fellow inmates, the butler and the baker. In return, the butler promised to tell Pharaoh about Joseph, but forgot to do so until some time later when Pharaoh himself had some troubling dreams he wanted to unravel. When Joseph was able to interpret those dreams, he came into Pharaoh's favor, eventually becoming the second in command of the whole nation of Egypt.

By this time, Joseph could have become an angry, bitter, resentful, revenge-seeking man. He had experienced so much unfairness, mistreatment, and injustice. From his position of power, Joseph could have acted out of hatred toward his brothers, Potiphar's wife, and the butler, who had all wronged him in varying measure. Instead, Joseph ultimately chose to extend forgiveness to them all.

Joseph was not completely a saint, however. Like the rest of us, he had human weakness. He initially gave his brothers a hard time. Not recognizing who Joseph was, the brothers had

---

[109] Genesis chapters 37–50.

come to him (as Pharaoh's second in command), to ask him for grain during the years of terrible famine.

Joseph played some unnecessary tricks on his brothers, such as hiding some silver goblets in their sacks. He then unjustly threw them in jail for a few days, falsely accusing them of being spies. He made them go all the way back to Canaan to bring the youngest brother, Benjamin, back to him. When they attempted to depart again, Joseph repeated the trick of hiding some goblets in Benjamin's sack. He then told his brothers that Benjamin would have to stay in Egypt instead of returning to their father with the others.[110] These acts on Joseph's part display *some* anger, bitterness, and desire for revenge. His ability to forgive did not magically develop overnight. Initially, he succumbed to some of his negative feelings.

Ultimately, however, Joseph chose to fully forgive his brothers. After their father died, the brothers specifically asked Joseph to forgive them. On that occasion, Joseph cried and extended sincere verbal forgiveness. In later years, he graciously fulfilled his promise to take care of them and their children for the rest of their lives.[111]

Esau

Jacob tricked Esau out of his birthright and their father's blessing. You will recall that Esau then became murderously angry and Jacob wisely fled for his life.

After years of living in another country, Jacob finally returned to his home. He was naturally afraid of how Esau would greet him. Esau could have killed Jacob. He could have greeted Jacob with anger, bitterness, hatred, and revenge. Instead, we are told in Genesis 33:4, that "...Esau ran to meet him and embraced him affectionately and kissed him; and both of them were in tears!" The brothers went on to live near to each other in harmony. If only all bitter family estrangement could end this way.

---

[110] See Genesis 42–44.
[111] See Genesis 50:15–21.

Imitating Christ

After the death of Jesus, the early Christians began to experience persecution. One of them, Stephen, was dragged out of Jerusalem by an angry, shouting mob. The crowd proceeded to cruelly stone him to death. Stephen prayed, in the midst of his pain: "Lord, do not hold this sin against them."[112] In his dying moments, Stephen was able to forgive his murderers. This nobility of spirit never fails to take my breath away.

Stephen died in imitation of Christ. Jesus also died a brutal, violent death. He was crucified on the Cross after being whipped and beaten. Jesus also, at His own point of death, cried out to God: "Father, forgive them, for they do not know what they are doing."[113]

Jesus forgave those who tortured and murdered him. He forgave those who personally wronged Him during His life on earth. He also extended His forgiveness to all men and women for all of their sins for all of time. Jesus reigns throughout history as the supreme example of forgiveness.

The Story of Ruby

Like Stephen, we are called to be imitators of Christ. As I struggle to do this, I am challenged when I hear about others who have managed to forgive offences far worse than those I have had to deal with. I was, for example, deeply touched by the story of a young girl named Ruby.

Ruby's story has been told by Dr. Robert Coles, a professor at Harvard and a psychiatrist, who encountered Ruby in 1960.[114] That year, a federal judge in the U.S. had ordered a white school in New Orleans to register four black girls, including six-year-old Ruby. In response, many white parents angrily boycotted the school. Ruby was the only black student brave enough to go to

---

[112] Acts 7:60a (NIV).
[113] Luke 23:34a (NIV).
[114] Kelly Monroe (Ed.), *Finding God at Harvard*, pgs. 34–40.

school each day, having to pass through yelling, swearing mobs of adults who opposed the racial integration. Some of them even threatened to kill her. Yet every morning Ruby came back to school, escorted by federal marshals.

Dr. Coles expected young Ruby to be very stressed by this frightening situation. Yet, although this went on for some months, Dr. Coles observed that Ruby was eating and sleeping well. She appeared to be happy and was successfully learning how to read. As a psychiatrist, Dr. Coles did not know what to make of Ruby's ability to withstand the angry and profane crowds.

Mystified, Dr. Coles questioned Ruby and learned that little Ruby was *praying* for the vicious crowds. Dr. Coles asked Ruby why she prayed for the people who were hurting her day after day. With profound maturity, Ruby explained that the minister at her church had told her about Jesus. She knew that some people had caused Him a lot of trouble. She knew that Jesus had asked His Father to forgive the very people who were hurting him. This six-year-old girl, in extremely stressful circumstances, was able to understand and then imitate the forgiving grace of Jesus.

What is *my* excuse for not imitating the forgiveness of Christ?

Forgiveness is Not Based on Our Feelings

Forgiving others has *nothing* to do with how we feel. If we wait until we *feel* like forgiving, we might wait a very long time. True forgiveness is an exercise of the will. It can be made while we are still trying to sort out our raw feelings of hurt, anger, bitterness, even hatred. The choice to forgive will later help us to deal properly with those other feelings.

Corrie, the Nazi concentration camp survivor, traveled the world for three decades after World War II, speaking about Christian principles of love and forgiveness. She learned over and over that her forgiveness could not just be in the abstract. Earlier, we mentioned how she forgave the man who had betrayed her family, leading to their arrest by the Nazis, and the cruel nurse who had mistreated her dying sister in the camp. She also had to forgive several Nazi guards who had inflicted much pain on her and her family. After the war, Corrie met many of these guards face to face.

After a speaking engagement in Berlin in 1947, one of the most brutal Nazi guards approached Corrie. She instantly recognized him—and just as instantly, a mess of noxious emotions were dredged up from her past.

He dared to ask for her forgiveness. He told her that he had become a Christian after the war. He knew that God had forgiven him, but he also wanted her forgiveness. Then he extended his hand towards her. Corrie, still overwhelmed with her memories, did not *want* to forgive him. She knew that, in her own strength, she was incapable of forgiving him.

She also knew that her response to this man could not be based on her *feeling* a desire to forgive him. It had to be based on sheer obedience to God's command to forgive and on the inner strength that only God could provide. She silently prayed, asking for God's help. She knew *her* part was to reach out to respond to the handshake being offered.

As she stiffly and mechanically extended her hand, an astonishing thing happened. Corrie could feel a sense of warmth within. Corrie was then able to not just shake the Nazi guard's hand, but to also verbally forgive him.

Corrie frankly said that her choice to forgive the guard on that day was a "cold-blooded" decision, independent of the initial temperature of her heart. The naked decision to forgive was made *despite* negative feelings that still needed to be fully processed and dealt with. She had to wait a further period of time until she was able to feel the joy and peace that come from fully letting go of old grievances and hurts.

Sustaining Forgiveness Over Time

With minor offences, forgiveness can often take place at one point in time and be done with. If a friend is late for a get-together, a co-worker makes some snide remark, a teenager forgets to clean up a mess, or a spouse reacts irritably to a comment, we can choose to forgive right then and there and never have to revisit the issue. We can simply choose to forgive, forget, and move on. The normal relationship can continue undisturbed. For more serious offences, however, true forgiveness may not be achieved so quickly or simply—it may need to be nurtured for a while until it has formed deep and strong roots in the soul.

Best-selling author Stormie Omartian experienced working at forgiveness over a sustained period of time. Stormie was physically and emotionally abused by her mother during her childhood. After becoming a Christian, in her adult years, Stormie realized that she had to forgive her mother. This was not simple for her. Forgiveness did not, and could not, occur for her on one single occasion. The abuse had been too painful, too traumatic, and spread over too many years.

The gradual process of forgiving her mother had to be worked on daily for a long period of time. She had to choose and affirm forgiveness *over* and *over*. Every time she saw her mother, old feelings such as anger, bitterness, and hatred would wash over her. Each and every day, she had to persevere with the process of forgiving her mother, whether she felt like it or not. She had to continually chip away at the old feelings, one day at a time, one moment of resolve at a time. This was the path to eventual freedom from her old negative feelings. Stormie has described forgiveness as an art that needs to be practiced again and again.[115] We slowly become better at it.

Stormie also had to forgive her father for not coming to her rescue on the occasions when her mother abused her. Typically, her unforgiveness towards her father was more repressed because her father had not been the abuser. She nonetheless had to forgive him too, for just standing by. Stormie knew that she would never be emotionally and spiritually whole until she dealt with *all* the unforgiveness and anger she felt towards both parents.[116]

---

[115] Omartian, pg. 122.
[116] Omartian, especially pgs. 122 and 163.

Help from the Holy Spirit

In situations of serious hurt and abuse, it may be extremely difficult, or even impossible, to realistically sustain full and true forgiveness in our own strength. Our hurt is sometimes too deep. The offence might have been repeated over and over again or the consequences of the hurtful conduct might still be affecting us. The human will can only take us so far on this journey of forgiveness.

As Christians, we have the wonderful privilege of the Spirit's partnership in the ongoing process. As usual, we are expected to do what *we* can. We can pray. We can try our best to uproot all of the old anger, bitterness, and hatred. We can keep choosing to forgive, one hour at a time. We can guard our thoughts and try to think, speak, and act in a manner consistent with forgiveness (even if it sometimes feels wooden or unreal). Then we must trust that *God* will get involved—that He will help us, strengthen us, and empower us from within. We must leave it all in God's hands, believing that He will bring His supernatural power to bear on the situation.

Corrie modeled this when she prayed, telling God that she could go through the mechanical motion of sticking her hand out to meet the extended hand of the Nazi guard who sought her forgiveness. She then told God that He was going to have to supply the *feeling* and the *power* to carry the process through. God was faithful to Corrie. We can trust that He will be faithful to us too.

Forgiveness Does Not Mean Condoning the Hurtful Act or Inviting Further Abuse

The choice to forgive does not mean that we *accept* or *condone* what the offender has done to us. It does not indicate that they were right or justified in what they did. The very act of forgiveness is necessary precisely because the other person has *sinned* against us, *hurt* us, *offended* us, or in some way *violated* us. The choice to forgive them does not change the gravity of the wrong, sinful, hurtful, offensive, immoral acts against us.

Nor does the choice to forgive mean that we are inviting further abuse. A wife can forgive a husband who has physically abused her. If the abuse is ongoing, she does not necessarily have to continue living under the same roof with him. An adult child can forgive a parent who has deeply hurt them, but the choice to forgive does not necessarily mean that they have to resume a normal relationship with that parent. Until it is emotionally safe to do so, that adult child might need to keep some physical distance from the parent and express their forgiving spirit in the context of a redefined relationship, perhaps by making phone calls or sending cards on special occasions instead of visiting in person. Just because we have forgiven someone does not mean that we have to put our head back on the chopping block. We never have to put ourselves in a position of being subjected to further abuse.

Although forgiveness often means returning to the *normal* relationship, as if the offence had never occurred, and getting on with the business of everyday living, this is only possible when it is emotionally safe to do so. Where violence, alcoholism, drug use, serious verbal abuse, or any kind of physical abuse are involved, forgiveness usually has to be *from a distance* until sufficient positive change has occurred in the abuser's behavior. Some people are dangerous. Forgiveness does not necessarily require close relational *connection* with the offender. If the abuse continues, it is an indication that the abuser does not want (or cannot be part of) an emotionally healthy relationship with us. In those situations, we need to stay away. Even at a distance, however, we can continue to cultivate a forgiving spirit within our own heart.

Forgiveness Does Not Have to Wait

In the spring of 1999, twelve American students and one teacher were shot in a Columbine, Colorado high school. One week later, seventeen-year-old Jason Lang was fatally shot by a fellow student at his Canadian high school.

Jason's father, Reverend Dale Lang, and his mother, Diane, stunned the Canadian public when only *days later* they publicly expressed their forgiveness toward the student who had killed their son. The fourteen-year-old gunman was acknowledged by the Langs to have been a victim himself of schoolyard bullying and teasing (though not by Jason). The Lang family's forgiveness of the teen killer was expressed in press interviews and at a school memorial service held in the immediate aftermath of Jason's death. At the memorial service, Reverend Lang also prayed for the young killer.

The Langs, after insisting that they are as human as anyone else, explained that their ability to so quickly forgive was a result of their personal relationship with God and His enabling power.

When school resumed in the fall of 1999, just months after Jason's tragic death, Diane Lang was at the school, hugging and praying in person for the killer's mother. What an incredible scene that must have been.

Reverend Dale Lang has spoken all over Canada since Jason's death. Like Kim Phuc, Steve Saint, and Corrie ten Boom, he talks about the power of Christian love and forgiveness.[117] He challenges people to forgive sooner rather than later. Forgiveness does not have to wait.

The ability to forgive has brought peace to the Langs. Reverend Lang has said that, although he initially felt anger when he found out his son had died, he was able to overcome that anger relatively quickly. He focused on processing sorrow and grief instead. He saw no point in holding on to his anger.[118]

It is not always possible to choose to forgive immediately after an offence has been committed against us. Sometimes it can take all of our strength and emotional resources just to keep from striking back at the offender. But it seems best not to wait

---

[117] Debra Fieguth article and Kathy Blair article.
[118] Kathy Blair article.

too long to forgive. The earlier the process of forgiveness begins, the less complicated it will be.

I am very challenged by the example of the Lang family. There is no offence more grave than the murder of a fine teenage son who had done nothing to provoke the violence. If the Lang family could respond with almost immediate forgiveness, what excuse do we have to *hold on* to our anger or bitterness?

If you have been harboring unforgiveness, I encourage you to decide *today* that you will begin the process of forgiveness. Make a list of those you feel you need to forgive. Then make the choice *now* to forgive. Do not let another hour pass, cultivating the destructive (and reproductive) fruit of anger, bitterness, resentment, and hatred. It is not always true that time heals wounds. In fact, many wounds just get more infected with the passage of time. The process of true inner healing requires forgiveness.

Forgiveness Does Not Always Require Words

Some people avoid forgiving others because they think they have to *express* forgiveness to the person who has offended them. They do not want to have to face that other person or talk about the hurtful conduct. Perhaps they are afraid of the other person.

In fact, the Bible does not *necessarily* require us to express our forgiveness to anyone other than God. Although Kim Phuc and Corrie were confronted with their offenders face to face, this does not always happen. We must, however, at a minimum, be prepared to forgive others *in our hearts*. We can exercise our will to make that base-line choice. We can thereafter try to think, speak, and act toward that other person, to the extent we interact with them, in a manner consistent with forgiveness. But we do not necessarily have to approach them, of our own accord, and expressly tell them that we have forgiven them.

In many cases, such verbal expressions of forgiveness might not even be well-received. C. S. Lewis once made a delightful observation about the ordinary everyday business of forgiveness.

He noted that some Christians make an unnecessary spectacle of the act of forgiveness, often embarrassing others. They dwell on trifling matters and are especially insufferable in making too much drama of granting forgiveness to their offenders for every minor offence. C. S. Lewis dryly commented that he much preferred ordinary people who let renewed shared activities, a good night's sleep, or some humor mend the relationship.[119] Penitence and forgiveness can be expressed by our *actions*—by our willingness to humbly resume normal interaction with the other person involved in the offence. In the everyday business of life, words are not always necessary.

I have found this to be true in my family. The number of times any of us have asked for forgiveness, or expressly granted forgiveness, is quite small. It is not because we are proud, grudge-bearing, or unforgiving. On the contrary, we are all simply more comfortable forgiving one another within our own hearts and then getting on with the business of living. We know when we have forgiven one another when everything is back to "normal." This is indirectly expressed by tone of voice, body language, and level of interaction. News articles commented on over morning coffee, a meal shared together with unstrained conversation, a favorite television program watched together, little tidbits of routine conversation as we pass in the hall—these are the ordinary ways we let one another know that all is well, all is forgiven. Most "everyday" forgiveness does not require verbal expression.

Forgiveness needs to be expressly granted only when it is essential for the inner well-being of one of the parties or necessary for the relationship to go forward. We have already seen examples of this: the American military veteran who asked Kim Phuc to forgive him; the Nazi guard who similarly sought Corrie's verbal forgiveness and handshake; the brothers of Joseph, who needed assurance that all would be well between them and Joseph after their father Jacob died.

---

[119] C. S. Lewis, *The Four Loves*, pg. 123.

Don't be held back by thinking that you have to *verbally* express your decision to forgive. Simply begin the process in the privacy of your heart. Talk to God about it. Perhaps the time will come to talk about it with the person who hurt you. Perhaps the time will never come. Perhaps the person who hurt you is no longer alive. Lisa Beamer, for example, will never be able to talk to the men who hijacked her husband's plane on 9/11.

Forgive in the quietness of your soul. The Spirit within will let you know if, one day, words have to be exchanged with the other party. If that day comes, God will empower you to verbally forgive if you ask Him to.

Seeking Forgiveness from Others

There are times when we must be the *seeker* of forgiveness. We will know when this is necessary. How? We will not have *inner peace* until we seek the forgiveness of the person we have hurt.

I love Corrie ten Boom's frank admission. She thought that, after having been a Christian for almost eighty years, she would be mature enough to no longer commit acts against others that required forgiveness. Even in her old age, however, she found herself committing acts and causing hurts that required her to seek the forgiveness of others.[120] She never considered herself so mature or so spiritual that she no longer had to seek forgiveness from others.

As mentioned above, in the everyday business of living, we do not have to run around seeking forgiveness for every small offence. In loving relationships, forgiveness is often graciously conferred on us without words being exchanged.

The Fruit of Forgiveness

Forgiveness bears tremendous fruit. As we exercise forgiveness towards others, we are better able to overcome our anger, resentment, bitterness, and hatred. The bondage of these negative

---

[120] Corrie ten Boom, *Tramp for the Lord*, pg. 169.

emotions is broken. By forgiving others, we find freedom. A huge load is lifted. There is fresh lightness in our souls. Room is made within our hearts and minds for peace, restored joy, and increased ability to love God, ourselves, and others.[121]

Our mental and physical health are both affected by our ability to forgive. According to an article by Dr. Puchalski, published in the *Yale Journal for Humanities in Medicine*, unforgiving people have increased anxiety symptoms, paranoia, frequency of psycho-somatic complaints, and incidence of heart disease. In contrast, decisions to forgive can result in decreased anxiety and depression, better health outcomes, improved ability to cope with stress, and better relationships.[122] The ability to forgive one's own self will lead to higher self-esteem and lower levels of anxiety and depression.[123]

As of 1997, in the field of psychiatry, there were only fifty-eight published studies on forgiveness. As of 2005, there were about 1200 published studies.[124] The fields of medicine, psychology, and psychiatry are becoming exponentially interested in the tremendous benefits of applying Christian principles of forgiveness. Experts are studying the link between forgiveness and everything from cancer to cardiovascular health.[125] The John Templeton Foundation has funded such exciting initiatives as the Stanford Forgiveness Project.[126]

Canadian psychiatrist Dr. Stephen Stokl affirms that forgiveness is a "liberating force" which "enables the injured person to move forward." Forgiving people are "relieved of their hurt, anger, depression, agitation and loss."[127]

---

[121] Dr. Puchalski article.

[122] Dr. Puchalski article.

[123] Ibid.

[124] Arterburn, pg. 123.

[125] See, for example, article by Lawler et al and further articles cited therein.

[126] Dr. Luskin and Dr. Puchalski articles.

[127] Dr. Stokl, pgs. 245, 248.

I saw this liberation play out in the lives of legal clients who were able to forgive those who had caused them injury or loss. My husband, Sam, has also seen this liberating force in the lives of many patients who have chosen to forgive. He agrees that forgiveness brings inner freedom and breaks the grip of many other harmful emotions.

Paul understood the importance of forgiveness. He wrote in 2 Corinthians 2:11: "A further reason for forgiveness is to keep from being outsmarted by Satan; for we know what he is trying to do." Satan wants to sow continual destruction in our lives—in our physical health, mental and emotional well-being, and in our relationships with God and other people. Forgiveness outwits and outplays the Enemy of our souls.

God blesses those who choose to forgive. A few years ago, I had the privilege of hearing one of our Canadian politicians speak. Stockwell Day, a Member of Parliament for several years and a prominent Cabinet Minister, talked about a journalist who had sometimes unfairly and untruthfully reported on his political career. Day told the story of how he was driving to work one day, his hands gripping the steering wheel so tightly that he was white-knuckled. He was full of anger about something the journalist had just written.

As he fumed about the matter, the thought crossed his mind that, as a Christian, he had to love his enemies and pray for them. Day was in no mood to do this. But the inner awareness that he must *forgive* this journalist and *pray for him* would not go away. Gritting his teeth, Day obeyed his conscience. He did not feel like doing this, but he did it anyways. As he prayed for the journalist, he felt his hands relax on the steering wheel. The white-knuckled tension was gone.

The very next day, Day was amazed to read another article by this journalist. For the first time, it was a *positive* article. The journalist had no way of knowing what Day had been thinking and praying less than twenty-four hours before. Literally over-night, the relationship between the politician and the journalist improved. God responded to Day's inner choices by allowing Day's external circumstances to change for the better.[128]

Author, radio host, and counselor Stephen Arterburn has reported similar fruit in his own life. He went through some tough times after his wife of many years initiated a divorce. He battled all the predictable feelings but was finally able to come out the other end of the divorce with a spirit of forgiveness towards his former wife. His negative emotions had not changed overnight. But one day he woke up and noticed that the quality of his life had changed. He realized that he was no longer a victim of his past. What had once dominated his life and permeated his thoughts was no longer a part of his present life. Forgiveness had released him from all of the old pain.[129]

A Challenge

Let's be challenged by the powerful examples of men and women like Kim Phuc, Steve Saint, Stormie Omartian, Corrie ten Boom, the Lang family, and others. If they can forgive the violence of war, the crime of murder, cruel and unjust imprisonment, and the pain of abuse, is it not possible for us to forgive our offenders?

The Christian life is all about new beginnings. God gives each one of us a new beginning when we become Christians. In fact, He promises us a new beginning *each morning*. As we faithfully confess, each day, how *we* have sinned, failed, and fallen short of what we can be, God gives us a fresh start. God keeps giving us this precious gift.

We can give this gift to others. We can give them the chance of a new beginning too. God has set us free. All He asks is that we be willing to set others free. We ourselves will never have complete freedom inside until we set others free. We did not deserve God's forgiveness. We must not wait until others

---

[128] From a talk given by Stockwell Day at the National Conference of the Christian Legal Fellowship in Toronto, Canada, in September 2005.

[129] Stephen Arterburn, *Healing Is A Choice*, pg. 122.

deserve ours. God grants to us the sacred trust of being bearers of His grace and mercy in this pain-wracked world.

Bear with each other and forgive whatever grievances you may have against one another. Forgive as the Lord forgave you.
Colossians 3:13 (NIV)

10
LOVE
The Radiant Soul

...God is love.
1 John 4:8 (NLT)

May the Lord bring you into an ever deeper
understanding of the love of God...
2 Thessalonians 3:5

...enjoy other people... and finally you will grow
to love them deeply.
2 Peter 1:7

Y HUSBAND, SAM, and I have known each other for more than twenty-five years. In that time, he has given me roses, surprise parties, gifts, cards, and kisses. He tells me that he loves me. Most mornings, he gets up first, makes the coffee, and brings in the newspaper. He calls me from work, no matter how busy a day he is having. He often plays tennis with me as his doubles partner, even though I drag down the level of play. These are all special gestures that make me feel loved.

He might be surprised to know that I have felt *most* loved on some unusual occasions. Once, for example, we were in the middle of a heated argument. The conflict was in escalating mode. All of a sudden, quite unexpectedly, Sam reached out and hugged me. His anger was replaced with a quiet tenderness. He said that we should stop arguing, that if we calmed down we would be able to work out whatever the issue was. I looked into his eyes and saw a warm love there. I was so surprised (and so relieved) at the sudden change in atmosphere. We stopped arguing, hugged some more, and went out for a wonderful lunch at a French bakery.

I have never felt more loved than I did that morning. I had encountered love in its most divine expression. This was true *agape* love—a love that transcended mere human emotion. My husband had loved me even while I was saying words that hurt him. I knew that I had encountered Christ in him that day.

An Alphabet of Dysfunctional "Love"

Not all love is so divine. Let's be real. Let's look, for just a moment, at the kind of "love" we might experience, at some point or another, in this fallen world. Here are some words describing what "love," without God and without Christian principle, sometimes feels like. We have all likely been, to some degree large or small, both the *victim* and the *villain* in some form of distorted, dysfunctional "love."

A: "Love" can be abusive.

B: "Love" can bruise and batter, emotionally or physically. It can blind us and it can betray us.

C: "Love" can be crushing, cruel, consuming, controlling, or confusing. Sometimes it can feel like a cyclone in the heart. "Love" can be like clouds without rain—a promise never fulfilled. We can be left feeling cheapened or cheated.

D: "Love" can be disillusioning and disappointing. It can leave us feeling deceived, discouraged, degraded, discarded, or dangling.

E: "Love" can be ego-intoxicating for a season, but it can leave us feeling empty, exhausted, embittered, or exploited.

F: "Love" can be frustrating, faltering, fickle. It can end as a failed fantasy—leaving us feeling like forgotten fools in the game of "love."

G: "Love" can be gut-wrenching, greedy, or groping. In its ashes, we can feel guilty.

H: "Love" can be hurtful, leaving us feeling hopeless, helpless, or heavy-hearted.

I: "Love" can be irrational and ill-advised. It can be infatuation in disguise.

J: "Love" can be judgmental, jarring, jilting. We can become jaded.

K: "Love" can be about kisses that never come or kisses that bring regret.

L: "Love" can be purely lustful. It can leave us feeling lost, lonely, or let down.

M: "Love" can be mocking, moody, or melancholy. It can be a mirage. Who hasn't felt mistreated or misunderstood?

N: "Love" can leave us feeling numb, neglected, or naïve.

O: "Love" can be an addictive opiate. It can be overwhelming or obsessive.

P: "Love" can be painful, power-clashing, or punishing. It can leave us feeling played or put down.

R: "Love" can be reckless, restless, or ruthless. It can end in rejection.

S: "Love" can be suffocating, selfish, standard-lowering, and soul-shattering. We can be left feeling sad, scarred, or stood up.

T: "Love" can be torture. Have you ever felt trampled, torn up, or thrown away?

U: "Love" can be undermining, unhealthy, unrequited, or unfaithful. We can feel uncertain, unappreciated, unfulfilled, and undone.

V: "Love" can be vain, vulgar, volatile, or vengeful.

W: "Love" can be wounding. It can leave us feeling wistful, weary, wondering, wronged, worn down, or worn out.

Y: "Love" can be yearning—or yielding too quickly to the selfish will of another.

Z: "Love" can be purely zoological—raw animal instinct. We can feel zapped and zonked and not understand what has hit us!

Maybe you can relate to *some* of these words. Maybe not. Maybe some words capture what you have felt in a family relationship, a friendship, a dating relationship, a marriage, or a divorce. I invite you to pause to consider which words resonate with some of your hurtful life experiences.

Almost one out of every two marriages ends in divorce, and the demise is usually not pretty. Of the marriages that "survive," many are unhappy. We have already mentioned the difficult marriages of David and Mary Livingstone and John and Molly Wesley. Many people don't find a relationship worth pursuing to the altar in the first place. Even men and women in relatively healthy, happy Christian marriages occasionally feel sad, hurt, rejected, ignored, or confused.

Yet men and women continue to search for love—sometimes recklessly and desperately. The search is particularly reckless and desperate for those who have grown up in homes where they never really felt loved.

God Is Love

The search for true, satisfying love will not end until we discover God and *His* love. God is a God of love. In fact, He *is* love. The Bible tells us that God loves us far more than we can ever fathom! He is a God of *extravagant* love—especially towards those who choose to enter into personal relationship with Him.

In Exodus 20:6, God tells us: "...I *lavish* my love upon...those who love me and obey my commandments." In Isaiah 30:18a, the prophet wrote: "...the Lord still waits for you to come to him, so he can show you his love..." In Jeremiah, God declares: "I have loved you, my people, with an *everlasting* love."[130] John wrote: "How great is the love the Father has *lavished* on us, that we should be called children of God!"[131]

God loves us with a perfect love. It does not matter to Him if we are intelligent or good-looking, witty or charming, popular or talented. It does not matter if we are rich or poor, black or white, young or old, male or female. He will love us even if we lose our money, our job, or our reputation. God's love is not connected to these temporal matters.

God loves us just as we are. He loves us when we are tired, cranky, frustrated, having a bad hair day, eating too much ice cream, or barking at the dog. He loves us even when we are looking, thinking, feeling, or acting our worst. No matter what, He loves us with perfect, extravagant love.

Perhaps you cannot see God as a loving Being. Perhaps you have always thought of Him as angry—ready to pronounce judgment—harsh, severe, and punitive. The people who have trouble seeing God as a *forgiving* God usually have trouble seeing God as a *loving* God. This might be because of exposure to fire-and-brimstone Christianity or to a pastor, church, or individuals who were hurtful, judgmental, critical, and condemning. Or perhaps you grew up in a home where one or both parents were cold, uncaring, distant—not very loving or affectionate. If our *human* parents neglect, reject, or abuse any of us, it is difficult to imagine a loving Heavenly Father.

I recall a church service I attended one Father's Day. At the end of the sermon, the pastor asked people to come forward if they were having trouble perceiving God as a loving Father, especially if this was connected to their relationship with their human father. As I watched from my pew, I was astonished at the number of people who streamed forward, some of them

---

[130] Jeremiah 31:3a (NLT).
[131] 1 John 3:1a (NIV).

weeping. The problem was far more prevalent than I had thought.

Each one of us must settle in our soul that God is indeed a God of love. We cannot have a healthy relationship with God unless we recognize that He is a loving Being. We will never properly love our own selves, or be able to properly love others, if we cannot *perceive, believe,* and *receive* the love of God. This is absolutely foundational to a mature ability to love without selfish motives or strings attached.

Many people have been through a lot of pain and suffering in life. This can also prevent them from believing that God loves them. I cannot address this topic in great detail in this book—it is a topic unto itself!—but suffice it to say that many of life's problems come to us because we live in a fallen world. We all sin and then reap the harvest of that sin. The sins, weaknesses, faults, and mistakes of others also affect us, often quite unfairly, even in our relationships with our brothers and sisters in Christ. And let us not forget that there is an Enemy who is determined to steal, kill, and destroy.[132] We must not too quickly ascribe our woes in life to God. Instead, we should come to Him, seeking His loving help in overcoming our problems, healing our pain, and meeting our emotional needs.

Jesus: God's Love Made Manifest to Us

John 3:16–17 expresses this wonderful news: "For God loved the world so much that he gave his only Son so that anyone who believes in him shall not perish but have eternal life. God did not send his Son into the world to condemn it, but to save it." In Romans 5:8, Paul wrote: "...God showed his great love for us by sending Christ to die for us while we were still sinners."

My first real awareness of God's love came at a Sunday morning service at my grandfather's church when I was just six years old. The pastor talked about how much God loves us. He

---

[132] John 10:10.

told us that God was waiting to receive us—His loving arms stretched out towards us—if we were willing to believe that His Son Jesus died for our sins. I did not really understand what all of this meant. *I just wanted to run into the loving arms of my Heavenly Father.* So, when the pastor invited people to come forward, I ran down the aisle. The word "love" was such a powerful magnet to my soul. Decades later, I still have a very vivid memory of running down that aisle towards the love of Father God and His Son Jesus.

I did not become a committed Christian until my late teens, at a point when I fully understood what it meant to accept Jesus as both Savior and Lord. But I *do* know that something wonderful happened that Sunday morning in my childhood. I felt embraced by my Heavenly Father and His Son. I continued to sometimes feel that warm, protective, loving embrace over the next years as I awakened spiritually. That feeling of being loved by God increased significantly once I began a committed Christian life in my late teens.

Over the years, God has demonstrated His love for me in a thousand ways: by guiding me, protecting me, rescuing me, healing my body and my heart, meeting my needs, sustaining me, comforting me, encouraging me, strengthening me, disciplining me, equipping me, and blessing me far beyond my wildest hopes and dreams.

Although I have felt these myriad expressions of God's exquisite and extravagant love for so much of my life, I realized in recent years that I had never truly appreciated what it meant for God to *give* His only Son to us—to *allow* His Son to suffer and to die for our sins. One April afternoon, almost a decade ago, I entered into a much more conscious level of appreciation.

Prior to that afternoon, my twelve-year-old son had been in the hospital for several days, suffering from excruciating hip pain. A team of medical experts had not been able to diagnose the problem. They decided to aspirate the fluid around the hip joint so that they could perform further diagnostic tests. A thick needle had to penetrate deep into the hip joint.

Although my son had received some morphine and some measure of local anesthesia, the aspiration procedure was still incredibly painful. I could hear his heart-wrenching screams for some time as I waited in the adjacent room. As his mother, I felt my own intense pain. Helpless to stop his pain (and knowing that by agreeing to the medical procedure I had actually authorized the pain), I was an emotional wreck. I went to the ladies washroom, with tears streaming down my face. Even there, I could hear the prolonged screams of my son's agony. The specialist was having trouble aspirating enough fluid and the procedure dragged on.

After my son was settled back into his room and had fallen into exhausted sleep, I went outside for a walk in the fresh air. I needed to pound the pavement to deal with my stress. I cried out to God. I told him about the deep hurt I was still experiencing, part of which was my confusion as to why God would allow my son to go through all of this seemingly senseless pain.

As I prayed, pouring out to God my deep anguish and frustration, a gentle voice within me quieted my soul and let me know that God was aware of all that had happened. My inner response was a cry to God that my son's pain not be wasted. The same gentle voice within assured me that God the Father empathized with me as a parent agonizing over my son's suffering. He reminded me that He had endured the excruciating and heart-wrenching pain of watching His *own* Son go through something far worse. Father God had not just authorized a medical procedure—He had authorized his Son's death warrant. And God told me that it was the cry of His *own* heart that *His* Son's pain not be wasted.

My own crushing pain subsided as I spent some time thinking about what Jesus had endured just before the Cross and then on the Cross—the cruel mockery, the crown of thorns, the whippings, the struggle to carry the heavy Cross, the pounding of huge nails into His hands and feet, the slow death, the unquenchable thirst, the public humiliation, the scathing rejection, the approach of death—added to the incomprehensible pain of bearing all the sins and sorrows of the human race. Jesus had submitted to this pain because His Father had said that it was necessary. Jesus trusted His Father.

As the *parent* of Jesus, Father God must have felt far greater agony than I had felt earlier that afternoon. Father God had to watch the crucifixion unfold. Reflecting on my own pain as a parent on that afternoon, I realized that I had experienced but *a glimpse* into the pain of God the Father and Jesus the Son. What is our human pain compared to theirs that long ago day?

A deeper appreciation of God's love for me and the love of His Son Jesus pierced through me that April afternoon. As I walked along the road near the hospital, I initially felt like weeping. But instead, I began to feel a wave of God's love washing over me. God reminded me that my son was now peacefully sleeping and on a morphine drip. For those precious moments alone, I could fully release my soul to soak in God's love. I became aware of the warmth of the spring sunshine. I noticed the loud and cheerful chirping of dozens of birds and how green the grass was. I saw the beauty of daffodils, tulips, and hyacinths emerging through the fragrant earth. I spent an hour caught up in exquisite awareness of God's love and intimate presence—God as Father, Son, and Holy Spirit.

God's love was bigger than my pain and confusion. When we measure our human pain against the pain that Jesus bore for us on the Cross (and the pain of Father God watching what His Son was enduring), we can no longer question God's incomparable love for us. We may not understand our toughest circumstances, but we can learn to trust that a loving God has a purpose for our every moment of pain—just as He had such enormous purpose for His own Son's pain. One day we will see through the glass less darkly.

I began to more acutely notice God's love over the following days of my son's hospitalization. God's love came in so many ways. Most significantly, my son made a steady recovery—how wonderful it was to see him laugh at Mr. Bean videos! I noticed the warmth of my husband's hugs, the smiles of strangers passing me in the hospital corridors, soothing hot cups of tea, the good cheer of visitors, compassionate nurses, and the comfort of many Bible verses. God's love tangibly surrounded me and my family.

Since that experience, whenever I have heard the words of John 3:16, I have let them dwell *very deeply* in my soul. I have stopped to consciously appreciate the measure of the Father's love in letting His Son go through the terrible pain of the Cross and the measure of Jesus' love for us, that He would willingly submit to that painful death. I have paused to recall the heart-wrenching cries of my twelve-year-old son. In those meditative moments, John 3:16 is over and over again achingly real to me.

How sad that so many reject such great love. Blessed are those who choose to fully embrace it. My prayer for each reader echoes the words of Paul:

> And I pray that you, being rooted and established in love, may have power...to grasp how wide and long and high and deep is the love of Christ, and to know this love that surpasses knowledge...[133]

Receiving the Love of God

The Bible says that God loves each one of us, no matter who we are or what we have done. He sends His rain and His sunshine to both the just and the unjust, to those who acknowledge Him and to those who don't. *He loved us even when we were His enemies—when we rejected, denied, mocked, disobeyed, and perhaps even hated Him.* God loved us even in that wicked state.

We receive God's love more fully, however, when we choose to accept His gifts of salvation and eternal life—when we believe that Jesus, the Son of God, died for our sins. We must be genuinely sorry that we have caused God pain and that, in our self-centered rebellion, we have rejected and ignored Him. We must seek God's forgiveness and His help in turning from our sin. In this way, we can enter into a personal

---

[133] Ephesians 3:17b–19 (NIV).

relationship with God the Father, Jesus the Son, and the Holy Spirit (who will come to dwell within us after we enter into that relationship with the living God).

Once we are Christians, we can begin to cultivate the practice, each day, of *soaking* in God's love. It is so easy to get caught up in the stress, the rush, the hassles, and the problems of each day. I invite you to consciously stop, catch your breath, and choose to soak in God's love.

There are countless ways to do this. We can pause to enjoy daybreak as we get up in the morning. We can savor our cup of coffee. We can thank God for our piece of toast. We can appreciate the gifts of whatever clothing and shelter we have. We can treasure whatever measure of health, strength, and energy we have each new day. We can be thankful for the people that God has placed in our lives that care about us.

We can marvel at the beauty around us. Whether we live near an ocean, woods, mountains, desert, or ice-fields, all of us live in the midst of some kind of awesome beauty. Even if the landscape is bleak and barren, all of us can notice the sky—its ever-changing cloud patterns, the glory of the sunset, the starry nightscape. We can feast in this beauty and soak in the love of God as we do so.

David reveled in God's love expressed all around him when he wrote: "...the earth is filled with his tender love."[134] David wrote often about the heavens above, the birds of the air, the fish of the sea, mighty mountains, green pastures, and still waters.[135] We should not deify nature, but we can see its majesty and splendor as a gift from a loving God.

We can also close our eyes and think about God, talk to God, listen to God. We can bask in His presence as if we were basking in rays of sunshine. We can wait in His presence until we feel embraced by His love. We can thank God, praise God, worship God, and feel His Spirit covering us like a warm blanket. Our

---

[134] Psalm 33:5.
[135] See, for example, Psalms 1:3; 8:3, 6–8; 19:1; 23:2; 36:6; 65:12–13; 68:9.

deepest hurts can be healed. Our painful memories can be erased. Our anger can be calmed. Our fears can evaporate. Our burdensome worries can be handed over. Our sadness can be lifted. All of this can happen in the *loving presence* of God when we choose to close our eyes, shut out the world, seek His face, and reach out for His incomparably warm embrace.

If all of this sounds foreign to you, do not let another day go by without experiencing the intimate love of God! I invite you to enter into personal relationship with Him. Then, in prayer, ask God the Father to *show* you His love. In Psalm 17:7, David beseeched God: "Show me your strong love in wonderful ways..."

We can memorize all the verses that describe God's infinite love for us—words that have the power to strengthen and renew us. We can meditate on them, absorbing the truth that each one of us is so precious to God. He cherishes us. He treasures us. Choose to *believe* in God's love. Wait to *receive* it. Be alert to *perceive* it every day.

I enjoyed reading lawyer Charles Finney's description of his powerful encounter with God's love on the night after he became a Christian. He had fallen asleep, but could not stay asleep for long because of the "great flow" of God's love that was flooding through his heart. The flow of love so filled his being that he found it impossible to fall asleep again that night.[136] This intense awareness of God's precious love does not always come overnight, as it did with Finney, but it *will* come to those who seek God with their whole heart.

Finney had previously wrestled intellectually for a number of years, trying to discern whether the Christian faith was real. He finally decided that it was, indeed, real. Once he chose to enter into personal relationship with Him, he was so overwhelmed with God's love that Finney was thereafter able to leave his law practice behind without a second thought. He went on to spear-head the great spiritual revival that occurred in America in the 1800's.

---

[136] Bonnie Harvey, *Charles Finney*, quoting Finney's own words.

Once we become Christians, God truly becomes our Father. We become His children.[137] Jesus becomes our Lord and Savior, but also our Brother and our Friend. The Holy Spirit becomes our Comforter, Counselor, and Companion. All of this warm intimacy awaits us.

We shortchange our lives if we only accept God's forgiveness. Let's also receive the love that made the forgiveness possible in the first place.

Receiving God's Love in the Tough Times

The Christian life is not all green pastures and still waters. Troubles, illnesses, pain, and problems beset each Christian life. Yet the wonderful news is this: even in the midst of our darkest hours and stormiest times, we can still receive God's love.

In one of the most powerful letters that he ever wrote, Paul said this: "Who then can ever keep Christ's love from us? When we have trouble or calamity, when we are hunted down or destroyed, is it because he does not love us anymore? And if we are hungry, or penniless, or in danger, or threatened with death, has God deserted us?...I am convinced that *nothing* can ever separate us from his love. Death can't, and life can't. The angels won't, and all the powers of hell itself cannot keep God's love away. Our fears for today, our worries about tomorrow, or where we are—high above the sky, or in the deepest ocean—*nothing* will ever be able to separate us from the love of God demonstrated by our Lord Jesus Christ when he died for us."[138]

The Greatest Commandments

When we have received God's love, we are ready to obey the clear and simple words of Jesus: "'Love the Lord your God with all your heart and with all your soul and with all your mind.' This is the first and greatest commandment. And the second is

---

[137] See, for example, Romans 8:14–16.
[138] Romans 8:35, 38–39.

like it: 'Love your neighbor as yourself.' All the Law and the Prophets hang on these two commandments."[139]

Jesus makes it clear to us that these two commandments form the central core of Christian living. If we follow these simple instructions to love God, our own selves, and others, we have satisfied God's greatest requirements. Everything else hinges upon, and is secondary to, this call to love. We may never understand *every* passage in the Bible, but we can understand these two key commandments regarding love.

Returning God's Love

The first and greatest commandment (Matthew 22:37) tells us to *return* God's love. Once we grasp how infinite His love towards us is, this is not very difficult. As we learn to receive God's love, it will become increasingly natural to love Him in return.

We can express this love in many ways—by spending time with God in prayer, by worshipping Him, by reading what He has to say to us in His Word, by deeply desiring to obey Him, and by wanting to serve Him. We will exponentially feel God's warm embrace as we learn to express our love to Him in return.

We have to remain vigilant that our love for God does not cool or fade. I am always challenged by the words of Revelation 2:4–5: "…you don't love me as at first! Think about those times of your first love (how different now!) and turn back to me again…"

Loving Our Own Selves

Many Christians are wrongly taught that it is sinful and selfish to love themselves. I believe this kind of teaching is not scriptural.

Jesus taught in Matthew 22:39 that we are to love our neighbors *as we love ourselves.* This is part of the second love commandment. It is healthy, necessary, and important to love our own selves. We cannot truly love our neighbors *unless* and *until* we love our own selves.

---

[139] Matthew 22:37–40 (NIV).

Christian psychologist Dr. Richard Dobbins has observed that, too often, our worst enemy is the person we see in the mirror. If we are uncomfortable with the person staring back from the mirror, we can *do* something to change that.[140] With God's help, we can develop healthy self-love.

Battered Self-Esteem

Many Christians go through life with some measure of self-condemnation or self-loathing. We are not meant to have a poor self-image. We are, instead, meant to look in the mirror and love the person we see—not in a vain, self-centered, pompous, arrogant, proud, conceited spirit but in a gentle, kind, compassionate, and humble spirit. It is surely not sinful to be kind to ourselves or to extend compassion to ourselves. Christian humility does not require us to belittle, berate, or beat up on ourselves.

We can love our own selves because God loves us. He has accepted us just as we are. He has affirmed us, esteemed us, approved us, and adopted us as His very own children. If we are worthy of His love, because of the identity and the right-standing He gives us in Christ, then we are worthy of our own love. As I have heard many a pastor proclaim, we are not "worms in the dust." We are, instead, the beloved children of God!

And yet, many Christians continue to struggle with terribly low self-esteem. My husband, Sam, has a number of Christian patients who suffer with poor self-image—even those who have wealth, education, good looks, stellar careers, and wonderful families. They don't really like themselves. They can't imagine why anyone else would want to love them. They are their own worst critics. They come into my husband's office complaining of depression, fatigue, and all kinds of aches and pains. Dr. Sam tries to help them discern that their real problem is not physical in true origin. These patients suffer physically and emotionally

---

[140] Dr. Dobbins, pgs. 35–36.

because of a poor self-image. They have bullied themselves, and their bodies and souls bear the tell-tale bruises.

Sometimes this poor self-image is caused by *guilt*, arising out of actual sin. Perhaps they have cheated, stolen, or lied. Perhaps they have had an abortion, abandoned their family, or abused their children. The first remedy for a low self-esteem based on true guilt is to seek and to receive God's forgiveness—and then to choose to forgive themselves. The second step is to receive God's love and to thereby be able to love themselves. Confessed sins should never stand in the way of a healthy and positive self-image.

Low self-esteem is, in many other cases, rooted in hurt, rejection, and criticism inflicted upon undeserving individuals. This often occurs in childhood, but is just as painful in the adult years. Some children hear a steady stream of criticism from their mother or father: "You're so stupid!"; "Can't you do anything right?"; "You'll never amount to anything." Other children hear a barrage of taunts from peers in the recess yard or disparaging comments from teachers.

Many adults hear hurtful words from a husband or wife. Other adults hear negative feedback from a boss. No wonder the self-esteem of so many people withers and droops. All of us have, at one time or another, felt our spirits crushed and wounded by others.

How the World Bolsters Battered Self-Esteem

People deal with their battered self-esteem in a variety of ways. Wounded children might become shy, withdrawn loners. Or they might become bullies and rebels. As teenagers and adults, they might seek relief by: eating their favorite comfort foods; turning to drugs or alcohol; keeping their mind constantly numbed with the TV or the Internet; pursuing an increasingly desperate series of romantic or sexual relationships; or retreating into fantasy and daydreams.

Many adults think that buying a prestige car, achieving career success, being part of the right crowd, and living in the best neighborhood will somehow boost their image in the world and magically transform their self-image. If we choose to believe the media, even the right kind of deodorant or the perfect shade of lipstick will boost our confidence. Christians get sucked into all of this too.

Sadly, any of the above means of bolstering self-esteem only works for a while, in a very fleeting and superficial way. Some methods of emotional escape, such as over-eating or substance abuse (which are usually followed by guilt and shame), eventually cause self-esteem to plummet even further. Romantic relationships entered into to bolster a deflated ego come undone, leaving the ego even further crushed. The most enticing day-dreams don't make reality go away—they just make us ever more discontent with the reality that we actually live in.

The shade of lipstick goes out of style. Mr. or Ms. Career Success arrives at the office one day to find out they have been down-sized. The cool friends find someone more successful to hang out with.

Self-esteem anchored in looks, success, money, popularity, or human approval is built on very shaky ground—it is too dependent on unreliable circumstances and fickle relationships. Furthermore, this kind of self-esteem can never erase the words of the critical parents, peers, teachers, or mates that battered one's self-esteem in the first place.

The Christian Basis for Self-Esteem

Only a self-esteem based on God's love can withstand the test of time, difficult circumstances, and the critical voices of those who hurt us, reject us, put us down, and stomp all over our self-worth. Remember that alphabet of dysfunctional "love"? Only God's love is powerful enough to heal the hurts inflicted by that kind of "love." Only God's love fully enables us to deeply accept, approve, and affirm our own selves.

So let us settle in our minds, and believe with all of our hearts, that God *does* love us and that we are, on that basis, worthy of love. Let us see ourselves not as others might have seen us but *as God sees us*. In God's eyes, we are wonderful—full of potential—sons and daughters with confident access to the Father's throne. Let's look at ourselves that way too.

We can choose to constantly renew our minds in this area of self-esteem and let our thinking line up with God's positive view of us as His redeemed children, purchased with the blood of His Son Jesus. We are worth much because we cost much.

With the help of the Spirit, we *can* develop a healthy self-image. We can see that we have been given *some* measure of beauty, strength, intelligence, talent, or social ability. It does not matter whether we are *as* beautiful, strong, intelligent, talented, or sociable as our parents, siblings, or friends. We are who we are. God loves us just the way we are.

My Struggle to Love Myself

My greatest battle with self-esteem began when I was just nine years old. Until an unexpected curve ball came my way, I was generally enjoying my childhood. I did well in school. I had friends. I loved playing after school in the nearby playground. I could run fast, skip rope, hit a baseball, and toss a mean football.

Then, seemingly out of the blue, I developed an auto-immune disease. My muscle cells inexplicably began to attack each other, leaving my damaged muscles feeling weak and tired. Even the most everyday tasks became increasingly difficult. Trying to finish a math test, I struggled to push my pencil as fast as I could, but the day came that I was too weak to finish a test. My winter coat began to feel unbearably heavy on my shoulders. The short walk home from school felt like a marathon. I was frightened by this rapid onset of unfamiliar weakness and fatigue.

When I was finally diagnosed, after many weeks in the hospital, the treatment was a fairly high dosage of cortisone, which had various side effects, including some temporary weight gain. For some time I continued to feel weak and lethargic. I returned to school feeling "different" from the other kids. For the rest of that school year, I could not join in the skipping and ball games at school. At the recess break, while all the other children laughed and played (as I used to), I sat alone on the school steps.

Even during the next school year, when I did start to join the others, I was always the last person selected by any captain to be on their team. I fumbled the football, could not make it to first base fast enough, and let my team down over and over. I was the first person caught in the game of tag and the last one to finish any race. It was devastating.

Needless to say, my self-esteem plummeted. I felt weak, socially awkward, and on the "outside." I continued to struggle with these feelings as I entered my teen years, even long after I had stopped taking cortisone and my weight had returned to normal. In high school I was never a varsity athlete, but my muscles recovered enough so that I could skate, swim, play tennis, and walk. Although to all surface appearances I had thankfully recovered from both the disease and the effects of the medication, it took much longer for my *interior* world to recover.

Over the next few years, I tried to boost my self-esteem by seeking good marks in school, dying my hair blonde to attract the boys, becoming intoxicated enough at parties to amuse my peers, and learning to put on make-up by reading teen glamour magazines. These endeavors helped my self-image in a superficial sort of way, but on a deeper level they did not take away my pain. I lived with myself from day to day, but I would not say that I truly *loved* myself. No matter what level of popularity I achieved, I was somehow still the little girl sitting alone on the steps in the recess yard.

All that changed when I fully committed my life to Christ in my late teens and learned on a much deeper level how much God loved me. I began to realize that God had loved me even as a hurting nine-year-old girl. He had loved me in the hospital. He had loved me in the schoolyard. He had cheered for me in each race—even if I could not hear Him then, even if I finished last. It did not matter to Him one little bit that I never made a varsity athletic team. He had even loved me during my earlier teen years, when I had recklessly danced through a somewhat wild phase of partying and drinking.

A new chapter in my interior life began the day that I became a committed Christian. From that point on, I somehow grasped that God would love me *no matter what*—whether I earned straight A's, had a boyfriend, found a husband, excelled in a career, kept my friends, made lots of money, *or not*. With God, I was allowed to be weak, to stumble, to fall, to fail, to start afresh after giving in to some temptation, to make a fool of myself, and to lose *whatever* race I was in. All that mattered was that I come regularly into His loving embrace, confessing my sins and failures as need be, freely admitting my weakness. On that same awesome basis, I could love myself—*no matter what*.

I am deeply thankful that God taught me to love myself *even when* I am sick, weak, discouraged, and the last one to finish a race. What a great relief to know that *even when I am not strong* God loves me and I can love myself! I do not have to be an achiever, a performer, a superwoman, or a winner for God to love me or for me to properly love myself.

Loving Others

After I learned that I could truly love myself, exactly as I was, it became so much easier to love others. David Seamands, a pastor and author, once observed that the hardest people to get along with are the people who do not like themselves. Because they do not like themselves, they are not capable of genuinely liking others. They are the prickly, difficult people who create much friction in interpersonal relationships.[141] The converse is also

---

[141] David Seamands, *Healing for Damaged Emotions*, pg. 54.

true: the easiest people to get along with are those who truly like themselves.

The last half of Matthew 22:39 commands us to love our neighbors as much as we love our own selves. Loving those around us is not an option. It is not something that we do only when we are in the mood or when those around us deserve it. Once we have received God's love and have learned to love ourselves, the requirement to love others is actually not very onerous. We want to love others more and more as God's love bubbles up within us.

Jesus spoke of the great commandment to love others many times in the Gospels, as did the apostles Paul, Peter, and John in their letters:

"A new command I give you: Love one another. As I have loved you, so you must love one another." (John 13:34, NIV)

"My command is this: Love each other as I have loved you." (John 15:12, NIV)

"Do everything in love." (1 Corinthians 16:14, NIV)

"...serve one another in love." (Galatians 5:13b, NIV)

"...live a life of love, just as Christ loved us..." (Ephesians 5:2, NIV)

"...love one another deeply, from the heart....Above all, love each other deeply..." (1 Peter 1:22; 4:8, NIV)

"We love because he first loved us. If anyone says, 'I love God,' yet hates his brother, he is a liar. For anyone who does not love his brother, whom he has seen, cannot love God, whom he has not seen. And he has given us this command: Whoever loves God must also love his brother." (1 John 4:19–21, NIV)

"As you have heard from the beginning, his command is that you walk in love." (2 John 1:6b, NIV)

It is clear that our love is not to be based on mere feelings, (although it is certainly easier when the feelings are present). Our love is not to be shallow or selfish. Love in its purest form is a choice and a commitment we make—*whether or not* the other person is lovable at any point in time and *despite* their annoying habits, weaknesses, faults, and mistakes.

Who is my neighbor? My neighbor is anyone walking or living alongside me. My neighbor is my mother and father, sister and brother, husband or wife, son and daughter, friend, work colleague, fellow church member, and of course my literal neighbor next door. My neighbor can also be a stranger in need.

Hallmarks of Healthy Love

Here is an *alternative* "alphabet" of words, *this* time describing the Christian ideal of healthy love.

A: Love affirms and accepts. It tirelessly advances the best interests of the beloved.

B: Love blesses and builds up the beloved.

C: Love is compassionate, caring, and committed. It cherishes and comforts.

D: Love is devoted. It delights in the beloved. It defends them.

E: Love encourages, esteems, enjoys, and warmly embraces the beloved.

F: Love is forgiving and it is faithful. It values the freedom of the beloved.

G: Love is gentle, generous, giving, grateful, gracious.

H: Love honors the beloved. It is full of hope. It is honest. It hugs the other, holds their hand, no matter what.

I: Love invests in the beloved. It shows infinite interest in them.

J: Love is joyful. It is not jealous.

K: Love is kind. Love knits people together.

L: Love is loyal.

M: Love creates good memories.

N: Love is noble.

O: Love is open-hearted and open-handed.

P: Love protects and provides. It is patient and persevering. It is prayerful. It is neither proud nor possessive.

Q: Love is quick to restore and quick to overlook faults and mistakes. It offers both quantity and quality of time.

R: Love is responsible. It is never rude. It responds to the needs of the beloved. It rejoices in the success, blessing, well-being, and achievement of the beloved.

S: Love serves. Love shares. Loves sees the best qualities of the beloved. Love sacrifices and supports. The beloved feels sheltered, safe, and secure.

T: Love trusts. It is transparent. It treasures the beloved.

U: Love uplifts the other. It is unconditional and unselfish.

V: Love values the beloved. It validates their worth as a child of God. It is valiant, always ready to fight for the beloved.

W: Love is wise. It keeps no record of wrongs.

X: Love is excellent.

Y: Love yields to the valid needs of the beloved. Love forgets yesterday's hurts and grievances.

Z: Love zealously supports the beloved.

As Christians, we can exchange that old alphabet of dysfunctional, destructive "love" with this awesome new list of attributes. God can help us to love others with the kind of love that exceeds our human potential to love. We will never love perfectly, but Spirit-empowered love far surpasses mere human love. I am not just rhapsodizing about something abstract and ideal. I have been the recipient of this kind of love from my husband, children, parents, siblings, and some dear friends—how incomparably precious it is!

Human love that does not find its roots in divine love will be second-rate, incomplete, tough to sustain, too conditional, and often motivated by selfish expectations. It can develop many of the attributes of the alphabet of destructive *dys*functional love. Human love is a counterfeit of love that is divinely inspired and empowered. Divine love, flowing into us from Father God, Jesus the risen Son, and the indwelling Holy Spirit, is real and enduring!

The Benefits of Healthy Love

Those who are involved in healthy loving relationships with others enjoy many benefits. According to Dr. Sam, they usually suffer less from depression or anxiety. They tend to eat and sleep better. They are more socially engaged and less isolated and therefore more likely to be active and fit. They are less prone to tension headaches, indigestion, aches and pains, colds and flues, and many other ailments. Reporting a greater sense of well-being and overall enjoyment of life, they are able to bounce back better from life's curve balls. They grumble less, smile and laugh more. This increases the biochemical activity of their endorphins and serotonin, which further helps them to feel good. Not surprisingly, people in loving relationships statistically live longer and usually have a higher quality of life, especially in their later years.

Those who simply hold hands with someone on a regular basis have been shown to have better health and well-being than those who don't. Babies who are frequently held in someone's arms fare better than those who are not. Hugs, kisses, and verbal expressions of love positively impact our bodies and our souls.

According to the Mayo Clinic, those who have strong commitments to healthy marriages live longer, enjoy better mental and emotional health, and have lower rates of heart failure, cancer, and other diseases than those who are in unhealthy marriages.[142] Positive relationships with friends and family members are also beneficial.

Agape: The Christian Expression of Divine Love

In modern day English, we use only one word for love. At the time of Christ, the Greek language had four common words that all meant love: *agape, phileo, storge,* and *eros*.[143]

The word *agape* is the love word found most often in the original Greek language text of the New Testament. *Agape* is the ideal Christian love. It is what we are meant to express to *all* those we love, whether a parent, spouse, child, friend, or neighbor. It is the most selfless love—a love that focuses on *giving to* its object, not on what it can *get from* its object. It chooses to keep on loving the other person, even when they are unlovable. It is the kind of love that Jesus said we should have for even our enemies.[144]

Agape imitates the divine love that God bestows on us. It is empowered by the indwelling Spirit. *Agape* is an ongoing commitment and a sustained choice that God helps us to maintain. It is clearly distinct from ordinary human love—it is higher and nobler.

The word *agape* was used, for example, in the famous words of Paul in 1 Corinthians 13:1–8a,13 (NIV):

> If I speak in the tongues of men and of angels, but have not love, I am only a resounding gong or a clanging cymbal. If I have the gift of prophecy and can fathom all mysteries and all knowledge, and if I have a faith that can move mountains, but have not love, I am nothing. If I give all I possess to the poor and surrender my body to the flames, but have not love, I gain nothing.
>
> Love is patient, love is kind. It does not envy, it does not boast, it is not proud. It is not rude, it is not self-seeking, it is not easily angered, it keeps no record of wrongs. Love does not delight in evil but rejoices with the truth. It always protects,

---

[142] Mayo Foundation for Medical Education and Research article.
[143] C. S. Lewis, *The Four Loves.*
[144] Matthew 5:44.

always trusts, always hopes, always perseveres. Love never fails....

And now these three remain: faith, hope and love. But the greatest of these is love.

Let us briefly contrast *agape* love with three kinds of human love.[145]

Friendship Love

Phileo is another word meaning love that was used in the original Greek language version of the New Testament. It conveys the kind of affection we feel for friends.

Friendship involves a love that is merited and earned. We choose our friends because we *like* them. At least to begin with, they are nice to us. We have something in common with them. We share the same interests, values, and pursuits.

Friendship can be pleasant. We can enjoy being with our friends, sharing a meal, laughing at one another's jokes, attending a special event together. These are hours to be treasured, especially with friends we have known for years.

Many friendships eventually fade. Friends can be there for us in one season of life but nowhere to be found in the next season. Friends change. They move, they move on, they drift away.

Friendship is based on both what is given *and* what is gained. It is usually sustained over the long haul as long as the other person keeps giving back. Reciprocity is at its very core. If the friend never returns the dinner invitation, never takes their turn calling on the phone, never sends a birthday greeting, the friendship is destined to fade.

Christians can certainly enjoy rich friendships. But because friendship is based on our human feelings, likes, wants, egos, and needs, it is by nature too tainted with conditional and self-seeking qualities to be the equal of *agape*. The deepest level of friendship is only achieved when *agape* love enriches it.

---

[145] I am indebted to C. S. Lewis for his brilliant discussion of these human loves in *The Four Loves.*

Family Love

Storge was another Greek word for love that was commonly used at the time of the writing of the New Testament. This word was *not*, however, actually used in the New Testament in the context of the command to love others.

Storge connotes family affection—the kind of warm, familiar, comfortable love we might develop living together with our families of origin and, later on, the families we create when we marry. I have treasured family closeness my whole life.

Those who have not been blessed with a cosy and congenial family often seek out a new "family"—perhaps their buddies in college, their colleagues at work, or their team-mates at the hockey arena. Christians find new "brothers" and "sisters" at church. Everyone tries to find "family" that they can be warmly familiar and comfortable with.

Like friendship, family love can certainly be enjoyed by Christians. To survive and thrive, however, it needs to also be enriched by agape. Agape love requires that we choose to love our family members whether or not they always feel as comfortable as our favorite old clothes. We are to love them even when they annoy us, hurt us, or disappoint us. Family love must be undergirded by agape love if it is to weather all the changes and storms of our lives and the inevitable hurt that arises.

Romantic/Sexual Love

Eros was the fourth Greek word for love that was commonly used at the time of Jesus' life on earth and the subsequent writing of the New Testament. It was used to connote romantic/sexual love. The word *eros* was not actually used in the New Testament.

Let me clarify at the outset that Jesus and the early Christians did not frown on romantic/sexual love in the appropriate context of marriage. The physical act of sex itself was referred to in the New Testament and encouraged between a husband and wife.

God intends for a husband and wife to enjoy the romantic/sexual dimension of love, but this is not the same thing as *agape*.

Because *eros* is not referred to in the New Testament, we can once again assume that it is neither the ideal expression nor a true imitation of divine love. Romantic/sexual love has its rightful place in the Christian life, but it is, once again, a merely human expression of love.

Yet, quite strikingly, *eros* is the kind of love most deified by our modern Western society. It is the love most often elevated (and even worshipped) in Hollywood movies, popular music, and best-selling novels. Romantic/sexual love is pursued relentlessly (and sometimes elusively) by most people in the modern Western world.

Authentic Christian love should be higher and nobler than the plot of a movie, the pleasure of chocolate, the sparkle of a diamond, the sizzle of sex, or the exchange of gifts. It is so much more than warm and fuzzy feelings, the grip of physical passion, or the comfort of companionship. Yet we Christians are too often guilty of seeking and expressing love on the same plane as the secular world around us.

Eros is dangerous in its merely human dimension, without *agape* love to enrich and to undergird it. *Eros* has a strong element of being merit-based. Purely human *eros* can become jealous, possessive, obsessive, controlling, unpredictable, and too conditional. It is not strong enough on its own to sustain the focused, exclusive, fulfilling, faithful pursuit of one beloved for a lifetime. *Eros* can so easily become tangled up with pretense, illusion, false promises, and fantasy. It can seduce and amuse, but it can also manipulate and confuse. It can begin as a dream and end as a nightmare. Look back at the "alphabet" of dysfunctional "love"—many of the words in that list describe *eros* in its most distorted, selfish expression, without the presence of *agape*.

One set of my grandparents were married for more than seven decades. Their marriage lasted because they understood the *agape* dimension of love. Even the secular world understands this—those with longstanding marriages have learned to live by the principles of 1 Corinthians 13, even if they don't acknowledge the other truths of the Christian faith. This is one of the reasons that the "love chapter" of the Bible is so often quoted at secular weddings.

Most healthy marriages contain elements of friendship, family devotion, and romantic/sexual love, which add delightful human warmth, companionship, and pleasure to the marriage. To be a truly Christian marriage, however, distinct from the societal norm, *agape* love must be foundational.

A healthy marriage is nurtured and nourished, in good times *and* bad, by a thousand daily choices that are loving—when the other person deserves it and when they don't—in the very *midst* of hurt, indifference, boredom, fatigue, illness, meddling in-laws, financial setbacks, the challenges of aging, and a multitude of other problems.

In these present days, in which the Christian divorce rate does not lag far behind the secular statistics, the need to cultivate *agape* love is urgent. In our marriages we need to separate choice/commitment from our transient romantic/sexual feelings.

Substitution Will Not Satisfy

The three human expressions of love (friendship, family, and romantic/sexual love) can co-exist with *agape*, but they all have this in common: they are not meant to be substitutes for *agape*. Friendship, family, and romantic/sexual love (*without* the enrichment of *agape*) are nothing more than human love—the kind of love that men and women intuitively feel and aspire to, whether they are Christians or not. The love I have exchanged in marriage, family, and friendship relationships has been priceless, but it is the *agape* dimension of those relationships that has shone the very brightest.

God's Help

It is up to us to make the choice and the commitment to express *agape* love in our various relationships. God will not do that for us. But once we have made the choice and commitment to love, come what may, God is there to help us. It is impossible to fully and consistently live out *agape* love in our own strength. Been there, tried that. Human beings are by nature too intrinsically self-centered. We desperately need the empowerment of the Holy Spirit.

Galatians 5:22 tells us that love is a fruit of the Spirit. If we are full of the Spirit, then we become full of *agape* love. Whenever we are unable to love with the kind of love that Paul talked about in 1 Corinthians 13, we need more of the Spirit's empowerment.

Just before His death, Jesus prayed to His Father about us, asking that "…the mighty love you have for me may be in them, and I in them."[146] Jesus asked for the Father's love to be expressed through us. We can have the sacred privilege of being channels of God's love to this needy world.

Paul wrote: "May the Lord make your love increase and overflow for each other and for everyone else…"[147] For a change, Paul is not using an action verb requiring *us* to do something. This verse suggests that God will increase the love within us, adding His supernatural empowerment to our human efforts.

In another letter, Paul wrote: "The grace of our Lord was *poured out* on me abundantly, along with the faith and love that are in Christ Jesus."[148] In Romans, Paul stated: "…God has *poured out* his love into our hearts by the Holy Spirit, whom he has given us."[149] Paul later referred again to this Spirit-empowered love: "…because of your love for me—*given to you* by the Holy Spirit…"[150] Finally, in Colossians 1:8, Paul mentioned he had heard "…about the great love for others which the Holy Spirit has given you."

---

[146] John 17:26.
[147] 1 Thessalonians 3:12 (NIV).
[148] 1 Timothy 1:14 (NIV).
[149] Romans 5:5 (NIV).
[150] Romans 15:30b.

Many other verses demonstrate that God has a clear part to play in the development of *agape* love within us. The secular world may try to imitate *agape* love, but they can never achieve more than a pale counterfeit because they do not have the indwelling assistance of the Spirit.

The Danger of Deifying Love

Although we are commanded to love our fellow human beings, it is dangerous to love them so much that we *deify* or *idolize* them—making them "gods" in their own right—considering them our highest objects of love.

I confess that I have had my seasons of deifying human love without initially being aware of it. While dating my future husband, Sam, I fell under the powerful spell of romance—lingering candlelit dinners, sentimental cards, walks in the moonlight, the warmth of embrace. My world revolved around the excitement of being with Sam. I spent my time thinking about Sam—when I would see him next and how I could please him. Our relationship became all important.

I wanted us to have a "grand passion." I read about a couple who were so close that the wife could glance across a crowded room at a pair of unlit candles and her husband, noticing that glance, would immediately cross the room to light the candles. I wanted that kind of constant intimacy—being intensely *aware of* and *connected to* each other every single moment.

It was during this time that I first read C. S. Lewis's marvelous book, *The Four Loves*. I began to realize that my desire to have such an all-consuming grand passion was in effect deifying our relationship. Lewis cautioned that we can begin to confuse the notion that *God* is love with *love* being god. He warned that we can too easily grant our human loves the unconditional loyalty and supreme importance which we ought to reserve for God alone—that we can too easily become an idolater of human love.[151]

---

[151] C. S. Lewis, *The Four Loves*, pgs. 12 and 13.

When we elevate a human beloved to the status of a god, we set ourselves up for eventual grief, hurt, disillusionment, and disappointment.

In Matthew 10:37, Jesus said: "If you love your father and mother *more* than you love me, you are not worthy of being mine; or if you love your son or daughter *more* than me, you are not worthy of being mine." Of course we can still love our father, mother, spouse, son, and daughter. But we should never allow ourselves to love them *more* than we love God.

The idolatry of love seems especially to occur with romantic love. We are all a mixture of unmet needs, unresolved hurts, and *some* measure of inner emptiness and loneliness. We exchange vows at the marriage altar, believing that our loved one will surely meet those unmet needs, melt away the hurt, fill the emptiness, and take away all loneliness. Subconsciously, we think that our beloved will *bring* us happiness and fulfillment. Lovers can expect so much of each other that they are bound to be hurt when their partner does not meet their high expectations. They wake up one day and realize that the beloved they are deifying is no deity at all. Instead, the object of their love is human and all too capable of hurting them. Hurt paves the way for anger, which can turn into resentment, perhaps ultimately hatred. How strange that human beings have the potential to bitterly hate the very person they once loved as almost a god.

And so, over time, we naturally stop deifying our beloveds. We eventually recognize their human weaknesses, sins, and shortcomings. They do eventually wound us, neglect us, and disappoint us in some fashion. Inevitably, they fall off the pedestal we have put them on.

At this point, an even more dangerous deification of love might emerge. When we stop deifying the *object* of our love, we might begin to instead deify the *idea* of love. When the actual person fails to satisfy the image, the picture, or the dream of love we have carried within us, we might stop focusing on the person but hold on to the image, the picture, and the dream. If the real person does not satisfy our idea of the perfect partner, we might begin to daydream about *what could be,* imagining what our husband or wife could be, *if only they would change*—perhaps by losing a few pounds, dressing a little sharper, kissing with more passion, saying just the right words, or kicking that annoying habit.

It is easy to lapse into occasional fantasy, deifying whatever *idea* of perfect love we think is possible. Perfect love seems to exist in the movies, in poetry and literature, or in the untested promise of a flirtatious smile that we receive from someone else. We long to live out the *idea* of love that we have idolized in our minds. Sadly, this might lead one day to a foolish affair. At a minimum, it leads to a lot of inner discontentment and despair.

Similarly, we might create fantasies about what a perfect parent, child, or friend should be like and begin to deify those ideas. This is one danger of being saturated with (and heavily influenced by) television, movies, magazines, advertisements, and popular music. All of these cultural media deify certain ideas and images of what love in marriage or family or friendship is supposed to look like. They present the *illusion* that these perfect relationships are out there somewhere. They create an intense longing in our hearts for an idea of love we wish we could experience.

We can never enjoy true love with the *real* people in our lives—our spouses, parents, children, and friends—if we hold on to the fantasy idea of what a spouse, parent, child, or friend *should be.* As long as we live in a fantasy world, we will resent the real people we relate to every day because they fall short of this idea of love which we have set up as an idol in our hearts and our dreams. The only solution is to get rid of the idol.

Loving with true *agape* love protects us from the risk of idolizing love. *Agape* love is the only love that *expects* and *accepts* human weakness, failure, hurt, and disappointment— and endlessly commits itself to loving anyways. That is why *agape* requires, by definition, qualities such as patience and refusing to bear a grudge.[152] It is not based on feelings or on what it gets back. Because it does not require the other person to be lovable or to conform to some *idea* or *image*, it is not the stuff of fantasy or daydreams. It is *real*.

The Love Deficit

Instead of idolizing human love of any kind, we can soberly recognize that human love, no matter how wonderful it is at times, will always leave us with a *deficit* of love. The love of others can enrich our lives, but the love we receive from others is not meant to complete us.

I have been blessed with loving family and friends. I have received the full measure of the love they have each been able to give. I have tried to love all of them to the best of my limited ability. Friendship, family, and marital love have all graced my life as much as anyone on this earth can reasonably expect. And yet, a deficit of love remains, both in the love I give and the love I receive.

I cannot imagine how great this deficit of love must feel for those who have been abandoned or abused by parents, taunted by siblings, or rejected by a spouse. If, in the best of human circumstances, there yet remains a deficit of love—a hunger for *more* love—in the worst of human circumstances the deficit of love must be very painful. Imagine how Joseph felt when his brothers threw him in a pit and sold him as a slave.

Some people resign themselves to the deficit of love they feel. They go through the motions of their human relationships, feeling a vague emptiness, perhaps some indifference, yet a chronic sense that there must be more. They ride around in cars with bumper stickers that say things like: "We're staying together for the sake of the dog." Or they might withdraw to a lonely, near-hermit existence.

---

[152] 1 Corinthians 13.

Many do not realize that every human being feels a deficit of love as life progresses—not necessarily all of the time, but in some seasons of life. Everyone eventually feels some pain when they encounter inadequacy in the love that they receive from other people. So great are the needs of each one of us for love, affection, approval, intimacy, and embrace that no human being (or combination of human beings) can fulfill those needs. If you are feeling this deficit of love, welcome to the human race.

In this place of painful deficit, we might ratchet up the expectations we have of parents, spouse, children, and friends. We might be more demanding. Or, as we just finished discussing, we might turn to a life of fantasy and daydreaming.

The *best* choice we can make is to turn to God. We can seek and receive *His* love, which alone has the ability to ultimately fill up that deficit of love. We have come full circle in our discussion about love.

God's Unfailing Love

Only God's love is unfailing. Only God's love is ultimately enough. I invite you to meditate on these descriptions of His love:

"...he has shown me his *never-failing love* protects me like the walls of a fort!" Psalm 31:21

"...*abiding love* surrounds those who trust in the Lord." Psalm 32:10

"Yes, Lord, let your *constant love* surround us..." Psalm 33:22

"How precious is your *constant love*, O God!...Pour out your *unfailing love* on those who know you!" Psalm 36:7a, 10a

"My God is *changeless* in his love for me..." Psalm 59:10a

"...your love and kindness are better to me than life itself..." Psalm 63:3a

When we feel unloved by the rest of the world, we can turn to the constant, steadfast, changeless, unfailing, and everlasting love of

God. If we turn to God, He will not reject us, forsake us, or abandon us. He will never stop loving us. We all desperately yearn for the kind of true, permanent, unconditional love that only God can *perfectly* provide. Let's take our hungry hearts to God.

A Concluding Challenge

John wrote: "Dear friends, let us love one another, for love comes from God. Everyone who loves has been born of God and knows God....Dear friends, since God so loved us, we also ought to love one another. No one has ever seen God; but if we love one another, God lives in us and his love is made complete in us....God is love. Whoever lives in love lives in God and God in him. In this way, love is made complete among us..."[153] May we all grow in our understanding of what this means.

There are almost seven billion people in this world. And God is ever present. None of us need to be lonely or unloved. Abundant love *can* fill our days.

...we beg you, as though Christ himself were here pleading
with you, receive the love he offers you—be reconciled to God.
2 Corinthians 5:20b

....Christ's love controls us now...
2 Corinthians 5:14

... see to it that you really do love each other warmly,
with all your hearts.
1 Peter 1:22

The only thing that counts is faith expressing itself through love.
Galatians 5:6b (NIV)

Let love be your greatest aim...
1 Corinthians 14:1

---

[153] 1 John 4:7, 11, 12, 16bc–17a (NIV).

11
FEAR
The Frantic Soul

My heart is in anguish within me. Stark fear overpowers me.
Trembling and horror overwhelm me.
Oh, for wings like a dove, to fly away and rest!
...I would flee to some refuge from all this storm.
Psalm 55: 4–6, 8

Strengthen the feeble hands, steady the knees that give way;
say to those with fearful hearts,
'Be strong, do not fear; your God will come...'
Isaiah 35:3–4 (NIV)

Do not let your hearts be troubled and do not be afraid.
John 14:27c (NIV)

Our Frightening World

A FEW YEARS ago, I watched *Bowling for Columbine*, a documentary by the provocative film-maker Michael Moore. His film captured the spirit of fear that tightly gripped America, and the world as a whole, after the tragic events of 9/11. Fear is still the staple story of the morning papers and the evening news. Pervasive fear of the next terrorist attack, an avian flu pandemic, and catastrophic global warming seems to be everywhere. Even before 9/11, people were afraid of Y2K crashing their computers, of mad cow tainting their beef, or of the next economic downturn.

In the midst of this *societal* fear, individuals battle their *personal* fears—fear of heights, flying, failure, rejection, cancer, carbohydrates, needles, germs—and, of course, fear of dying.

We first begin to experience fear as infants. A baby wails when he realizes he is alone and his mother is not in view. As little children grow, they soon develop a further range of fears, some of them healthy and appropriate, others that are not.

Children *should* develop a fear of fire, snarling dogs, and sharp knives. These are prudent fears that protect them from danger. These fears transform into informed knowledge.

Many children also battle unnecessary fears, such as fear of the dark, fear of a monster in the closet, fear of spiders, and fear of being alone. Usually, these fears are simply outgrown. Unfortunately, they are often replaced by bigger fears.

As adults, we fear attacks on our health, our marriages, our pocketbooks, and our children. What will happen before the sun goes down? *Are we going to be okay?* The daily news keeps telling us that we are *not* okay, that the world is a dangerous place.

Sometimes what we fear is real. Other times, we fear something that does not actually exist. In the late summer of 2005, thousands of Sunni pilgrims were crossing a bridge in Iraq. A rumor spread that a suicide bomber was on the bridge. Mass panic ensued, creating a wild stampede. Everyone ran to get off the bridge. More than a thousand people were trampled to death, most of them women and children. In fact, there was no suicide bomber on that bridge. Fear can take just as terrible a toll as an actual physical attack. Fear has its own destructive power—whether or not there is real and present danger.

Fear of God

The Bible teaches that the *only* fear we are meant to have is the fear of God. King Solomon wrote: "The fear of the Lord is the beginning of knowledge..."[154] and "The fear of the Lord is a life-giving fountain."[155] The prophet Isaiah taught: "Don't fear

---

[154] Proverbs 1:7 (NIV).
[155] Proverbs 14:27 (NLT).

anything except the Lord of the armies of heaven! If you fear him, you need fear nothing else."[156]

Jesus told His followers: "I tell you, my friends, do not be afraid of those who kill the body and after that can do no more. But I will show you whom you should fear: Fear him who, after the killing of the body, has power to throw you into hell. Yes, I tell you, fear him."[157]

If we fear God, we need fear nothing and no one else. Psalm 46:7a exclaims: "The Commander of the armies of heaven is here among us." If God is on our side, then there is no reason to fear anything or anyone—not our strongest enemy, not even death itself.

Paul wrote about deliverance from the fear of death. When Jesus died on the Cross in our place, He broke the power of death, offering us eternal life instead. Only in that way, Paul wrote, could He "free those who all their lives were held in slavery by their fear of death."[158] When we are delivered from the fear of death, then we are freed from all lesser fears. If we are not afraid of dying, then we are not afraid of living life to its fullest, even in the midst of surrounding dangers. We can travel anywhere, confront anyone, tackle any problem, and do any thing—knowing that God is on our side.

The converse is also true. If we do *not* fear God, then we may fear our very shadow. Moses warned about what would happen to those who do not fear God and choose instead to live in disobedience: "they will live in constant fear. The sound of a leaf driven in the wind will send them fleeing as though chased by a man with a sword; they shall fall when no one is pursuing them."[159]

Those with rebellious hearts, who manage to maintain a brash, God-defying bravado throughout their lifetimes, will have great reason to fear on their deathbeds. Their bravery will melt

---

[156] Isaiah 8:13 .
[157] Luke 12:4–5 (NIV).
[158] Hebrews 2:15 (NIV).
[159] Leviticus 26:36bc.

when they come face to face with the living God. A man that I knew for decades received a terminal diagnosis a few years ago. Although he was not a Christian, he boldly and arrogantly said that he was not afraid to meet his Maker. As the months passed and his health deteriorated, however, he began to experience nightmares and panic attacks as he drew closer to death.

When we fear God, we are able to come boldly into His presence. A healthy fear of God involves having a reverent, respectful, humble attitude toward Him, recognizing that He is Creator and Sustainer of all. We do not need to have a cowering, anxious fear of Him.

Paul said to his fellow believers in Ephesians 3:12: "Now we can come *fearlessly* right into God's presence, assured of his glad welcome when we come with Christ and trust in him." I don't think Paul meant that we should stop having a reverent, respectful, humble fear of God. I think he meant that we do not need to fear God's wrath, God's punishment, or God's judgment. A reverent fear is fully aware of the consequences of disobeying and rebelling against God, but such reverent fear does not tremble in terror that God will capriciously squash them like a bug or strike them with lightning.

Reverent, respectful, humble fear of God is premised on God being a loving Father who wants the best for us—He will only "punish" us in the same way that a loving father punishes his errant child. In 1 John 4:18a, we are told: "We need have no fear of someone who loves us perfectly; his perfect love for us eliminates all dread of what he might do to us." Christians must *revere* God, with due awe and respect, but we do not need to *cringe* in fear of God's wrath.

Fear of Others

If we fear God, there is no need to fear men. And yet we sometimes do.

After God brought His people out of Egypt, Moses sent twelve men to spy out the Promised Land. Ten of them came back, reporting *in fear* that there were giants in the Land and that, in comparison, the Israelites were as small as grasshoppers. Only Joshua and Caleb had the faith to believe that the Israelites could, with God's help, go in to possess the Land.[160] Fear and faith are opposites in the spiritual realm.

Was Joshua superhuman? No, he battled fear like the rest of us. After the death of Moses, God told Joshua to lead the Israelites into the Promised Land. God also said this to Joshua: "Be strong and courageous....Be strong and very courageous....Be strong and courageous. Do not be terrified; do not be discouraged, for the Lord your God will be with you wherever you go."[161] Another translation of this last verse states: "...be bold and strong! *Banish fear and doubt!* For remember, the Lord your God is with you wherever you go!"[162]

Notice how many times, in the space of a few verses, God had to tell Joshua to be courageous and not afraid. Joshua must have been battling some fear. God needed to reassure him that He would be with him.

As Joshua obediently led the people into the Land, God had to keep reminding Joshua to not fear. In Joshua 8:1a, for example, God told him yet again: "...Don't be afraid or discouraged..." Joshua responded by choosing not to fear other men, but to instead obey in faith, whether or not his knees were still knocking.

David

David spent many years on the battlefield and many years running as a fugitive from King Saul. Sometimes David was remarkably brave; on other occasions, he struggled with his fears.

In Psalm 62:2 David sounded full of boldness as he expressed his faith and trust in God: "Yes, he alone is my Rock, my rescuer, defense and fortress. Why then should I be tense with fear when troubles come?" On another occasion, as he fled from his own son

---

[160] The full story is recorded in Numbers 13 and 14.
[161] Joshua 1:6, 7a, 9bc (NIV).
[162] Joshua 1:9 (TLB).

Absalom, David valiantly exclaimed: "I will *not fear* the tens of thousands drawn up against me on every side."[163] In the beloved Psalm 23:4, David prayed to the God he trusted: "Even when walking through the dark valley of death *I will not be afraid*, for you are close beside me, guarding, guiding all the way." In Psalm 27:1–3 David again courageously asserted: "The Lord is my light and my salvation; he protects me from danger—*whom shall I fear?*...Yes, though a mighty army marches against me, my heart shall know no fear! I am confident that God will save me."

Yet David had his weak moments. In Psalm 22:14b, David sighed: "My heart melts like wax..." In Psalm 143:4, he sounded in even worse shape: "I am losing all hope; I am paralyzed with fear." David was a *real* person, who bounced back and forth between faith and fear.

Peter

Peter was another very human character. We encounter one of his battles between faith and fear in the story of his attempt to walk on the water. In Matthew 14, Peter bravely got out of the boat and started to walk on the water towards Jesus. Jesus had invited him to do this and had told him not to be afraid. As long as Peter kept his eyes fixed on Jesus he was able to maintain his faith. As soon as he got his eyes off of Jesus and onto the waves, he became terrified. In his fear, he then began to sink. His fear was stronger than his faith at that point in his life.

Peter again struggled with fear on the night of Jesus' crucifixion. At the last supper, Peter confidently told Jesus that he would never deny Him. Soon after, however, when Jesus was taken into captivity, Peter was asked three times if he had been with Jesus. Three times Peter denied knowing Jesus, afraid to admit that he was a follower of Christ. At that point in his life, he was a confused coward.

---

[163] Psalm 3:6 (NIV).

Some weeks later, after he had spent time with the risen Christ, Peter waited in the upper room in Jerusalem—waited obediently until the promised Holy Spirit came to empower him and the others. The Spirit-filled Peter was a whole new man! We read in Acts about Peter's incredible courage and faith soon after this first encounter with the Spirit.

Thereafter Peter publicly proclaimed who Jesus was to large crowds. When Peter was imprisoned and questioned by the same authorities who had successfully sought to crucify Christ, those men noted Peter's courage and were astonished.[164]

The authorities released Peter but sternly commanded him not to speak or teach in the name of Jesus. Peter immediately replied to them that he could not stop speaking about what he had seen and heard. He was prepared to openly defy the very authorities who could arrange for his death.

Peter was no longer a timid man. Instead, he was remarkably fearless. He prayed to God: "Now, Lord, consider their threats and enable your servants to speak your word with great boldness."[165] He had no intention of cowering in the shadows. When told *again* by the authorities to stop teaching in the name of Jesus, Peter courageously responded: "...We must obey God rather than men!"[166] He knew that this would cost him dearly— but further imprisonment, suffering, persecution, and even death did not frighten him anymore.

Peter was ultimately able to face a martyr's death. Many historians believe that Peter was crucified, upside down, in Rome (probably at the hands of the Emperor Nero).

Peter learned that if he feared God he need not fear anything or anyone else. He became one of the ringleaders of the early Christian group that turned the world upside down. He was transformed from a coward into a man of commanding presence. This transformation is possible for all of us.

---

[164] Acts 4:13.
[165] Acts 4:29 (NIV).
[166] Acts 5:29 (NIV).

A Destructive Force

Fear undermines our spiritual, mental, and physical health.

In the *spiritual* realm, fear fosters doubt instead of faith. James tells us that a person who doubts is like a wave tossed in every direction by changing winds, unstable in all their ways.[167] Fear feeds anxiety and worry. Fear blocks our ability to receive the peace and joy that the Spirit wants to give us. In contrast, faith generates hope and trust. Faith is more powerful than fear if we are willing to give it a chance.

On the *mental* level, fear can create inner turmoil, confusion, loss of focus, loss of creativity, and depression. Fear can dominate our thoughts. When we are afraid, we need to *get a grip* on our thoughts. When we start to feel afraid, we can fill our minds with comforting Scriptures. We can also pray. These efforts invite God into the situation. Fear melts in the conscious awareness of a powerful, loving God.

On the *physical* level, according to Dr. Sam, fear triggers a powerful biochemical response known as the "flight or fight" response. The consequent chemical mediators increase heart rate and blood pressure, cause muscle tension and aches, bring on headaches, and interfere with the digestive process. This biochemical response to fear is not friendly to the body, particularly in the long term. Medical studies have correlated chronic fear with heart disease, gastro-intestinal dysfunction, skin disorders, insomnia, and various other maladies. This should motivate us to take our fears seriously and to resolve to do something about them!

Medical science is also exploring what happens when fear takes up residence in our brain. According to Dr. Sam, research in the field of neuroplasticity is discovering how neural pathways are created when the brain is subjected over and over to intense fear. These pathways allow fears and phobias direct access to certain parts of the brain, which become storage centers

---

[167] James 1:6.

for fearful memories. Small fears, which are normal, can grow into intense, irrational fears and phobias. These fears are pathological (disease) conditions that form over time.

Overcoming Our Fears

By consistently choosing to have faith, instead of fear, in response to a particular stimulus, the brain can, in time, form new pathways. The brain can be retrained. New memories can be stored with respect to a particular stimulus such as flying in an airplane or receiving needles at the doctor's office.

Psychiatrist Dr. Stephen Stokl has opined: "The only way to treat fear is to take action and face it....If we can change the way we think and correct our cognitive distortions and subsequently change the way we act, we can change the way we feel."[168]

Neuroscientist Dr. Mario Beauregard advises that we can even overcome phobias (which he defines as unreasonable fears). In Britain, for example, about one million people have spider phobia. Dr. Beauregard claims that spider phobia can be cured. Through a technique such as cognitive behavioral therapy, a person can learn some new facts about spiders that will help them to lose their old, irrational fear of spiders (which for many started in childhood). These re-educated spiderphobes can then, through gradual safe exposure to spiders, overcome their fear even to the point of voluntarily touching a large, live tarantula.[169]

My Fear of Speaking

One of the fears I have had to overcome in my life is the fear of speaking in front of others. I was quite shy and quiet as a child. During my elementary school years, when I had to speak in front of a circle of even just four or five classmates, my little hands would tightly clench into closed fists. My fingernails would dig

---

[168] Dr. Stokl, pg. 147–148.
[169] Dr. Beauregard et al, pgs. 136–138.

so deeply into my palms that my skin was marked with deep indentations. I dreaded the even worse nightmare of having to speak in front of the *whole* class. I still remember how traumatized I was presenting my dinosaur project at the front of my grade six classroom.

It is a miracle of sorts that I grew up to be a courtroom lawyer and a public speaker. How did I get from being a shy little school girl to a woman who can *enjoy* speaking in front of crowds?

The process of overcoming my fear of speaking began in my thought life. In my mid-teens, I read something that Eleanor Roosevelt once wrote. As a child, she had been painfully shy. Much later, in the spotlight as President Franklin D. Roosevelt's wife, she once again battled shyness, insecurity, and feelings of inferiority. She wrote about how she chose to overcome her social fears. Reading this was one of those thunderbolt moments for me. It was the first time it really occurred to me that I could choose *not* to be shy. Was my shyness really a choice, I asked myself? Could I *choose* to be more confident?

Eleanor suggested acting and speaking with confidence even when we don't *feel* confident. She further suggested focusing one's thoughts on other people—searching for something unique, interesting, and valuable in each person instead of obsessing about one's own insecurities, shortcomings, and imperfections. (Does my hair look okay? Do I have parsley stuck in my teeth?) She also shared how she discovered, after she learned to connect more with others, that *everyone* has inner insecurities, fears, and moments of social awkwardness—even the rich, the powerful, the beautiful, the successful, and the strong. She entertained many such people in the White House and realized, over and over, that other well-known people were often just as nervous as she was! Eleanor became a highly influential public speaker and one of the greatest advocates of social justice and reform during the past century.

So I began to change how I *thought* every time I entered a conversation, a social gathering, or a classroom discussion. I consciously stopped thinking about what I was wearing, whether I looked scared, or whether anyone noticed that I was blushing. I stopped mentally caring about what other people might think of my opinions or my ideas. I chose instead to be interested in how other people were feeling. Eleanor Roosevelt was right—many of them *did* feel just as shy and insecure as I did.

Over my lifetime, I have continued to learn the truth of what Eleanor so humbly shared. Lawyers, doctors, business executives, politicians, and even entertainers are all just human beings, battling their own doubts, fears, and uncertainties. Over time, I gradually became less shy speaking with one person or with a small circle of people. Being able to speak in front of a larger group came later.

I did not overcome my shyness all on my own. Changing my thinking was a good start, but it was not enough. There was clearly a *spiritual* dimension to my victory in this battle. This process did not occur overnight, although I must say that, like Peter, once I deeply encountered the Spirit's power within, as a young and freshly committed Christian, I felt an almost immediate new boldness, confidence, and authority that surprised me. Soon after I made my firm commitment to Christ, at the age of nineteen, I had to give my testimony to a packed church on the evening that I was baptized. As I told my story in that crowded room, I did not recognize my own voice. It was remarkably calm, clear, steady. I spoke much longer than I had planned. My old nervousness and self-conscious timidity were really starting to leave me. It was exhilarating!

I began to pray about my fear and learned to trust God each time I felt nervous opening my mouth. I meditated on what God said *about* me and *to* me in His Word. I sought deeper and deeper connection with the empowering Spirit.

God told Moses that he was to go and speak to Pharaoh. Moses tried to decline, because he was such a clumsy speaker. Moses said to God: "...I have never been eloquent....I am slow of speech and tongue."[170] God responded: "...Who gave man his mouth?....Is it not I, the Lord? Now go; I will help you speak and will teach you what to say."[171]

Was it possible that God wanted to help me too?

As I matured in my Christian faith, I realized that I have the incredible privilege of speaking words of truth, love, faith, hope, joy, blessing, encouragement, integrity, support, compassion, and empathy. These are *powerful* words. Recognizing this, I began speaking with increasing boldness, conviction, purpose, confidence, and authority—especially when I was communicating spiritual truths. As Christians, we have *words of life* to offer. The power of life and death are in the tongue.[172]

God's help was critical in overcoming my shyness and my fear of speaking in front of others. All the positive thinking of my teen years was of some benefit, but it would never have been enough to take me from where I once was to the place I am in now.

I also learned that God has a delightful sense of humor. As I developed my ability to speak in court, in professional meetings, before church groups, and in front of business women's groups, God had one further method to help me overcome my lingering fear of public speaking—He let my very worst fears come to pass! At times, I could identify with Job's statement: "What I feared has come upon me; what I dreaded has happened to me."[173] Whatever disastrous thing *could* happen *has* happened to me. Stumbling over a word or two or forgetting a particular point became the least of my worries.

Once, on a cloudless blue-sky day, I was on my way to a meeting which would include a number of older, more experienced lawyers. I was going to have to present my detailed position on a settlement proposal. I felt intimidated by this challenge

---

[170] Exodus 4:10 (NIV).
[171] Exodus 4:11–12 (NIV).
[172] Proverbs 18:21.
[173] Job 3:25 (NIV).

and by some of the legal giants I knew would be there. Just as I was approaching the office building where the meeting was taking place, a window-washer high above me tipped his bucket of water. I was promptly drenched! There was no time to change or dry off. I arrived at the meeting, my hair and my business suit still dripping wet, creating a puddle around my feet. Shivering in the chilly, air-conditioned room, I managed to somehow successfully present my case.

On another occasion, I was on my way to court and a gull flying overhead made me a target. Once again, I had no time to change. I had to clean the bird doo-doo off my suit jacket as best I could and carry on as if everything was normal.

Another day, I was eating Chinese food for lunch (foolishly using chopsticks while wearing a light pastel jacket). A sauce-covered piece of broccoli slipped from my chopsticks and bounced not once, but several times, down the front of my jacket. I hurriedly tried to clean it as best I could with soda water. My jacket still had tell-tale wet stains on it as my hectic afternoon began. You must understand that many of my meetings and courtroom appearances, involving sometimes dozens of other lawyers, had been set up months in advance. Canceling was not an option!

I have been in the middle of court appearances and, battling nasty flues or gastro bugs, have had to ask for emergency bathroom breaks. I have knocked a glass of water flying over my court documents while sweeping my arm in a dramatic gesture as I tried to make a persuasive point.

One morning, after a mere few hours of sleep, (I was the mother of two toddlers at the time) my mind went totally blank in the middle of the submissions I was making to a Judge. It felt like my mind froze for several minutes. In a complete daze, I looked down at my notes, having no idea where I had left off. I finally decided to pick *any* point to carry on with (not knowing, in my fatigue and confusion, that I was in fact repeating the very point I had just made). After that court argument, a fellow barrister came up to me and complimented me on how effective my sustained *pause* had been after making a crucial point. Then he said that it was particularly effective, the way I had *repeated* that point to give it emphasis!

These days, when I get up to speak, I always feel particularly calm if I *don't* have a run in my stocking, a stain on my jacket, a rumble in my belly, or a water glass within striking distance—and if I'm dry and halfway coherent. But I know that if some new kind of embarrassment comes my way, God will help me to laugh at myself and carry on. What is there to fear? I have *finally* learned the wonderful lesson that people like to laugh along with me. My best opening jokes have been my explanation for the reason why I'm wet or dirty or late on *that* occasion! I have lost my fear of being embarrassed and the underlying fears of failing and being rejected if I mess up. God has shown me that, even when my worst fears came true, it did not mean the end of the world. I always lived to tell the tale.

As I continue to speak publicly in my fifties, I am so grateful for how God has helped me to deal with my fear of speaking in front of others. While, of course, I still sometimes feel butterflies (and, truth be told, I looked like a startled deer caught in the headlights when I was recently on television), more often than not, I marvel at how calm I feel inside whenever I speak in front of others. I actually *enjoy* the privilege of speaking in front of many.

My Many Other Fears

I wish that I could say that fear of public speaking has been my only battle with fear. Not so! From childhood on, I feared spiders and snakes—in fact, almost any kind of bug or reptile. I feared being a victim of crime. After some childhood hospitalizations, I feared illness. God has graciously allowed unwanted confrontations with these other fears, in the midst of which He has shown me how to overcome my fears.

In my mid-twenties, for example, I spent some time traveling in India. During my first weeks there, a snake jumped out of a tree right in front of me. I rode in densely packed buses, physically pressed against people with wet leprosy, tuberculosis, and lots of other contagious diseases. One student-budget hotel room had giant cockroaches crawling on the floor and lizards climbing up the walls. I came down with an extreme fever and chills, which were later diagnosed as malaria. Because of the torrid summer heat, I had to keep the window of my hotel room open. A steady procession of strangers walked by outside, staring in on me. There I lay, sick and shivering in my bed. I was too sick to worry about being attacked or robbed if a stranger decided to climb in the open window. When I was well enough to go out, I *was* in fact robbed in a crowded marketplace.

In the midst of all this, God taught me much about the choice between faith and fear. I realized that I could collapse under the weight of so many fears, which assaulted me all at once in the space of a few weeks—or I could choose to have faith and trust that God would bring me out of all of those circumstances, healthy and alive and secure.

I battled my fear by praying. I meditated on helpful Bible verses. I kept my mind focused on God and His promises of protection and deliverance. While God often protects us and shields us from harm, it seems to me that there are far more verses in the Bible about God *delivering* us from harmful circumstances than there are verses about God *protecting* us from encountering harm. On those occasions in which God does not completely protect us from surrounding harm, I learned that He eventually delivers us.

Decades after my first trip to India, I was invited to travel there again as the guest of a Christian ministry. Initially, I had to battle fear of traveling in that nation and resist the strong inclination to decline the opportunity. I chose to overcome my fear. That second trip to India was an awesome experience.

Mary Slessor

While reading the biography of an 18th-century woman missionary to Africa named Mary Slessor, I felt a bond with her when I learned that she, too, had once feared insects, snakes, reptiles, and public speaking! Meditating on the Bible helped Mary overcome her fears. Her favorite verse was Psalm 27:14c: "Be brave, stout-hearted and courageous."[174]

If you chronically struggle with all kinds of fears, I encourage you to immerse yourself in prayer, in the Bible, and in good Christian biographies. You will soon discover you are not alone and you are not helpless!

Being Determined Not to Fear

Like Mary Slessor, we can saturate our minds with these kinds of verses:

Psalm 34:4b: "He freed me from all my fears."

Psalm 56:3–4: "When I am afraid, I will trust in you. In God, whose word I praise, in God I trust; I will not be afraid. What can mortal man do to me?"(NIV)

Psalm 112:7–8: "[The God-fearing person] does not fear bad news, nor live in dread of what may happen. For he is settled in his mind that [God] will take care of him. That is why he is not afraid, but can calmly face his foes."

Psalm 91:1, 5–6: "He who dwells in the shelter of the Most High will rest in the shadow of the Almighty....You will not fear the terror of night, nor the arrow that flies by day, nor the pestilence that stalks in the darkness, nor the plague that destroys at midday." (NIV)

Isaiah 12:2a: "Surely God is my salvation; I will trust and not be afraid." (NIV)

Isaiah 41:10: "So do not fear, for I am with you; do not be dismayed, for I am your God. I will strengthen you and help you…" (NIV)

Isaiah 43:1–2: "…Fear not, for I have redeemed you; I have summoned you by name; you are mine. When you pass

---

[174] Sam Wellman, *Mary Slessor.*

through the waters, I will be with you; and when you pass through the rivers, they will not sweep over you. When you walk through the fire, you will not be burned; the flames will not set you ablaze." (NIV)

Matthew 14:27: Jesus told His disciples in the midst of the storm: "...Take courage! It is I. Don't be afraid." (NIV)

Mark 5:36: "...Don't be afraid. Just trust me."

2 Timothy 1:7: "God has not given us a spirit of fear, but of power and of love and of a sound mind." (NKJV)

1 Peter 3:14b: "Do not fear what they fear; do not be frightened." (NIV)

There are apparently 365 verses in the Bible that encourage us not to fear! I invite you to become acquainted with them. There are *active verbs* in these verses, putting the onus on us to make a deliberate choice—do not fear, do not be afraid, trust, have faith. It is up to us to make the decision not to fear, no matter what circumstances we are in. Once we have made that decision, God will help us to live in faith.

Corrie

During Corrie ten Boom's years in the Nazi concentration camp, the crematorium (where the Nazis burned the bodies they had gassed or executed) was always in ominous view when she walked outside. But Corrie refused to give fear a foothold in her soul. She was later able to write about how she was not afraid, even though she knew she was walking through the valley of the shadow of death.[175]

Heather Mercer

Heather Mercer, who spent some time as an aid worker in Afghanistan, was one of eight Westerners who were arrested by

---

[175] Ten Boom, *Tramp for the Lord,* pg. 23.

the Taliban just before 9/11 and charged with the crime of sharing their Christian faith with Afghan Muslims. Heather was only twenty-four when she endured months of imprisonment and a trial under Sharia law. I have had the privilege of meeting Heather and of hearing her tell her story in person.

For some reason, Heather did not immediately feel fear after she was arrested. Instead, she initially felt peace. At some point, however, in the first three weeks of imprisonment, fear began to grip her. It became clear to her that the Taliban wanted to convict Heather and her seven fellow prisoners and make examples out of their punishment. Realizing that she might actually be sentenced to death, she began to cry every day. She was so afraid that her heart literally hurt. She sometimes felt as if she was suffocating.

While Heather was still in the Afghan prison, the 9/11 terrorist attacks occurred in New York City. Days later, Heather wrote in her journal about her struggles with this new reason to fear. It had gotten to the point that she felt fear every moment of every day.[176] Not long after, while Heather was still in prison and in the midst of her legal trial, the Americans started bombing Kabul. This gave yet further new reason to fear. Spending her nights hiding under her bed, Heather continued her downward spiral into ever deepening fear. The fear became so intense it filled her with chronic pain and made her feel continually exhausted.

Heather ultimately realized that she had to make a critical decision: was she going to focus on placing her faith in God (whether that meant living *or* dying), or was she going to continue to struggle with the debilitating fear? She made the decision to put her life (and possible death) into God's hands, to fully yield to faith and trust, no matter what.

This decision released more of God's power into her life. She no longer feared death. The Taliban still held her in a physical

---

[176] Dayna Curry and Heather Mercer, *Prisoners of Hope*, pg. 180; talk at Queensway Cathedral in Toronto, Canada, on February 28, 2002.

prison, but her spirit was no longer imprisoned behind bars of fear.[177]

Meditating on Bible stories helped Heather. David particularly encouraged her. We have discussed how David was sometimes a valiant leader but, at other times, David was paralyzed with fear. David's psalms gave Heather the motivation to frequently pour out her fear to God in prayer, asking Him to deliver her from her fear.[178] By the end of her ordeal, Heather was emotionally one of the strongest of the eight imprisoned Westerners.

While the Americans were still bombing Kabul, the Taliban decided to move the eight foreigners outside the city. The eight had no idea where they were going or what their fate would be. For all they knew, they could have been on their way to execution.

Her fellow American prisoner, Dayna Curry, marveled at Heather's transcendent courage and faith. As they rode along in the darkness into the terrifying unknown, Heather began singing. She sang the words: "There is a light in the darkness and his name is Jesus." Then Heather asked for a Bible. Heather pulled out her flashlight and began to read to her fellow prisoners, showing strong and confident leadership. After the singing and Bible reading, the prisoners actually began to laugh.[179]

Heather's dire circumstances had not changed. In fact, they had grown worse. But her inner choices regarding what she was going to think and to feel had changed dramatically.

After being relocated, the group of eight escaped from Taliban custody and ran for their lives. One night soon after, American helicopters flew overhead, trying to find the group, but it became obvious to the eight that the helicopters could not see them. The situation was becoming extremely perilous. With the choppers above them, the fugitive Westerners were becoming marked targets for Taliban ambush and recapture. It was Heather who

---

[177] Ibid., pgs. 226–227.
[178] Ibid., pgs. 114–117.
[179] Ibid., pg. 259–260.

was calm and clear-minded enough to think of the idea of burning the women's headscarves. The fire was bright enough for the helicopters to see them and to safely touch down long enough to rescue them.[180]

John Harper

John Harper was a passenger on the *Titanic* that night in 1912 when the luxury ship sank, taking 1522 lives with it. He was only thirty-nine years old, and a widower, with a six-year-old daughter on board with him. Harper was making the trans-Atlantic voyage because he had been invited to speak at the Moody Church in Chicago.

After the *Titanic* struck an iceberg, Harper and his daughter were initially two of the fortunate few who obtained life jackets before the supply ran out. They also had the opportunity to get into a lifeboat. (Although an adult male, Harper was allowed into a lifeboat because he was the sole parent of a very young girl.)

Fear, panic, and confusion gripped the thousands of people still on deck as the *Titanic* sank deeper and sea water rushed into its grand rooms and hallways.

People were doing anything to get a life jacket and a place in a lifeboat. They were pushing and yelling. One man dressed himself as a woman to increase his chances of securing a spot in a lifeboat. Rich men were desperately offering their millions in exchange for a seat.

While sitting safe and secure in the lifeboat, Harper made an incredible decision. A mature Christian, he was not afraid of death. He was not afraid to meet his Maker that very night. Seeing the terror on the faces of those rushing around, Harper started to call out to the people around him to let the women, children, and the *unsaved* into the lifeboats first. Making sure that his little girl still had a secure place and adults to watch over

---

[180] Ibid., pgs. 293–297.

her, he then gave up his place on the lifeboat *and* his precious life jacket. God gave him the ability to rise above all fear—even his fear for his daughter's future—to courageously lay down his very life for others.

Harper went down with the ship and tried to keep afloat in the ocean. Just before he drowned, Harper led another man in the water to Christ. That man survived to tell Harper's story. So did Harper's daughter. She grew up to become a strong Christian woman and to marry a minister.[181] She will see her father again one day. In the meantime, she can be proud of his incredible bravery in the face of mass fear and so much selfish cowardice.

I am encouraged by such stories to make the decision each day to rise above my fears, both small and large—to embrace faith and trust in God in all my circumstances. I do believe that if we fear Him, and Him alone, we need fear nothing and no one else. The challenge is to daily remind ourselves of this truth and to seek God's help in living it out. The world is a frightening place. But we *can* choose faith, and faith *will* overcome fear just as light overtakes darkness. We all know that even a tiny candle is always enough to light up a dark room.

Be strong! Be courageous! Do not be afraid
...For the Lord your God will be with you.
Deuteronomy 31:6a-d

The Lord is with me; I will not be afraid.
What can man do to me?
Psalm 118:6 (NIV)

You have been bought and paid for by Christ, so you belong to
him—be free now from all these earthly prides and fears.
1 Corinthians 7:23

---

[181] Moody Adams, *The Titanic's Last Hero.*

There is no need to fear when times of trouble come...
Psalm 49:5

He freed me from all my fears.
Psalm 34:4b

12
WORRY
AND
ANXIETY
Distracted and Disturbed

Woe to my people...They lie there sleepless with anxiety,
but won't ask my help.
Hosea 7:13a, 14a

Do not be anxious about anything,
but in everything, by prayer and petition,
with thanksgiving, present your requests to God.
And the peace of God, which transcends all understanding,
will guard your hearts and minds in Christ Jesus.
Philippians 4:6–7 (NIV)

THE YEAR THAT my husband and I spent traveling across Africa, I suffered from bouts of insomnia. Physical discomfort was part of the cause. Some nights, our ever-changing hotel rooms were stifling hot. Other hotel rooms were hyper-chilled by air-conditioners that rattled all night long. Some mattresses were too hard, some too soft, some just plain lumpy. In rural areas, mosquitoes buzzed by our ears from dusk to dawn. In the teeming cities, the African hotels were often very noisy for other reasons. No wonder I had trouble sleeping!

My insomnia could not, however, be totally blamed on physical discomfort. Many nights brought fitful sleep because of worry. I was anxious about our physical safety and security. We camped in some places. We had to get used to the proximity of wild animals and the possible presence of spiders, snakes, and scorpions (not to mention tics and tsetse flies). We sometimes slept in places known for violence, crime, and unrest.

And, of course, my mind sometimes wandered into the future. Would we be able to kick-start our careers again once we returned home? Would we be able to find an affordable place to live? Would we make enough to support ourselves? Both of us turned thirty on that year-long journey. Would we be able to start our family when we returned? Would I get pregnant right away? Were we ready to be parents? What extra finances would that involve? How would motherhood impact my hope of returning to my career?

Fortunately, we had some sleeping medication with us. How wonderful I felt those nights when the medication helped me fall into deep, unbroken sleep. I knew better than to allow myself to become dependent on this medication night after night, but I took comfort that once or twice a week I could count on a decent rest.

Then one day, in Nairobi, we attended a church service that really impacted me. In the midst of speaking on a totally unrelated (and quite dry) topic, the pastor suddenly started talking about sleeping pills. He reminded his flock that the Lord gives His beloved sleep.[182] The pastor challenged those who used sleeping medication to start taking their worry and anxiety seriously—to learn what God has to say about these kinds of thoughts and emotions—and to more consciously turn their cares and concerns over to God. I knew that the pastor was speaking to me. That very night, I resolved to stop taking sleeping pills so often and to search the Word for verses that I could meditate on in the middle of my sleepless nights.

Over the following months, I learned a lot about what the Bible says on the topics of worry and anxiety. Even before my year in Africa, I had been prone to fretting and worrying about matters both large and small. It was time to really address this issue.

---

[182] Psalm 4:8.

All of these years later, I still use the occasional sleeping pill. Hormonal fluctuations, unusual stresses, caffeine too late in the day, time zone changes, and jet lag all affect my ability to sleep from time to time. Medication can be a blessing when used appropriately. But I have learned that this kind of relief is no substitute for getting a good grip on life's daily worries and anxieties. With God's help, we can deal with our worries and anxieties in healthier ways.

The Scope of the Problem of Anxiety

Dr. Sam estimates that nearly 75% of the patients he sees every day struggle to some degree with anxiety and stress. Many of these patients are Christians. Some patients will respond to supportive therapy. Others will require mild anxiolytic medications or sleeping pills. Still others will only respond to stronger psychotropic, mood-modifying drugs combined with psychotherapy.

According to Dr. Sam, anti-anxiety medications neither cure anxiety nor address its causes. These drugs only help to suppress the bothersome physical symptoms by artificially manipulating neurochemicals. They do not *solve* the underlying deeper issues that caused the anxiety in the first place. These drugs simply numb the mind to the "noise" of anxiety. Their usefulness is that, in the short-term, they can give the patient a modicum of peace and clear thinking, allowing them to address their underlying issues.

Approximately 20 million Americans suffer from anxiety disorders. In Canada, where I live (where the population is just over 30 million), *tens of millions* of prescriptions are filled each year for tranquillizers, sleeping pills, and mood-enhancing drugs. Billions of dollars are additionally spent on alcohol and recreational drugs, on which some people also rely to blunt their anxiety.

Christian psychologist Dr. Dobbins observed that anxiety disorders are among the most common problems he has dealt with in his counseling of Christian patients.[183] Modern society is very stressed-out and we are all affected. The world is in a constant state of very rapid change—and change produces a lot of anxiety. Just when we get some of our ducks in a row, one of the ducks steps out of line! Most people are stressed to some degree about their job, their marriage, their children, their finances, their health, and their future. I read recently that every single minute someone in North America is having a heart attack. Anxiety and stress are major risk factors and contributors to the development of hypertension and heart disease.

Children are being diagnosed much more frequently with stress-related physical, mental, and emotional disorders. Children are worried about school performance, bullies in the recess yard, whether their parents will stay together, whether there is enough money for a new pair of running shoes, or whether there will be a shooting in their school. Bulletproof back-packs are now on the market.

Worry and anxiety rob too much of our time and our energy. We are not meant to live in tension, turmoil, unease, or a state of nervousness and dread.

Martha

My favorite biblical example of an anxious, fretting person is Martha. She was a classic worrier! One day, Jesus came to visit Martha and her sister, Mary. Martha started rushing around, cooking, cleaning, and playing the perfect hostess. In contrast, her sister, Mary, relaxed with Jesus, choosing to enjoy His visit. Martha complained to Jesus, asking Him to tell Mary to help her. I can just imagine Martha, fussing and fuming, resenting that her sister was not helping with the hospitality.

Jesus did not respond as Martha expected. Instead, He said to her: "Martha, Martha..., you are *worried and upset* about many things, but only *one* thing is needed."[184] Jesus approved of Mary's

---

[183] Dr. Dobbins, pg. iii.
[184] Luke 10:41–42a (NIV).

choice. Mary wanted to spend precious time with Jesus *more* than she cared about fixing the perfect meal. Martha was so needlessly anxious about fulfilling societal expectations that she missed out on the joy of the presence of Jesus.

I can relate to Martha. I used to be way too concerned about similar matters. I need to keep reminding myself that my relationship with God is far more important than perfecting anything else in this earthly life.

Biblical Commands about Worry and Anxiety

Jesus was well aware of the propensity of most people to fret and worry about life's details—and so He spoke these words in Matthew 6:25–34:

"Therefore I tell you, *do not worry about your life*, what you will eat or drink; or about your body, what you will wear. Is not life more important than food, and the body more important than clothes? Look at the birds of the air; they do not sow or reap or store away in barns, and yet your heavenly Father feeds them. Are you not much more valuable than they? Who of you by worrying can add a single hour to his life?

And why do you worry about clothes? See how the lilies of the field grow. They do not labor or spin. Yet I tell you that not even Solomon in all his splendor was dressed like one of these. If that is how God clothes the grass of the field, which is here today and tomorrow is thrown into the fire, will he not much more clothe you, O you of little faith? *So do not worry,* saying 'What shall we eat?' or 'What shall we drink?' or 'What shall we wear?'....But seek first his kingdom and his righteousness, and all these things will be given to you as well. Therefore do not worry about tomorrow, for tomorrow will worry about itself. Each day has enough trouble of its own." (NIV)

Jesus reiterated, in Luke 21:34, that we are to take care that our hearts do not become "weighed down" with the "anxieties of life. (NIV)"

Paul's well-known words regarding anxiety are found in Philippians 4:6–7: *"Don't worry* about *anything;* instead, pray about *everything;* tell God your needs and don't forget to thank him for his answers. If you do this you will experience God's peace, which is far more wonderful than the human mind can understand. His peace will keep your thoughts and your hearts quiet and at rest as you trust in Christ Jesus." Paul tells us that we should not worry about anything! We can instead pray about everything—even the smallest details of our lives.

Peter told his fellow Christians: "Cast *all your anxiety* on him because he cares for you." (1 Peter 5:7, NIV).

David said in Psalm 55:22ab: "Give your burdens to the Lord. He will carry them." The Bible describes worry and anxiety as heavy burdens we needlessly bear. On that note, King Solomon astutely observed in Proverbs 12:25: "Anxious hearts are very heavy..."

Notice all the active verbs in the above verses: "Do not worry"; "Do not be anxious"; "Cast all your anxiety"; and "Give your burdens." Clearly, *we* are expected to do something. Our worries and our cares will not be magically lifted off of our shoulders or out of our minds when we become Christians. *We* must stop ourselves from worrying and from thinking thoughts that generate anxiety. *We* must consciously, in thankful prayer, turn our cares over to Christ. *Then* the Spirit does His part. As Paul describes in Philippians 4, *after* we have decided not to be anxious, *after* we have prayed about our concerns, *after* we have thanked God for listening, *then* God will fill us with His peace and help to guard our hearts and minds. We need to get our focus off of our problems and onto God and His greatness. I have heard many pastors say that our problems may be big, but our God is bigger.

Do you know the old hymn, "What a Friend We Have in Jesus"? As a child, I used to love these lyrics:

What a Friend we have in Jesus,
All our sins and griefs to bear!

What a privilege to carry
Everything to God in prayer!
O what peace we often forfeit,
O what needless pain we bear,
All because we do not carry
Everything to God in prayer....
Are we weak and heavy laden?
Cumbered with a load of care?
Precious Saviour, still our refuge,
Take it to the Lord in prayer.[185]

Worry Runs in Families

I used to worry about almost everything. I have identified with what Jesus talked about in Luke 8:14—being "choked" by life's worries. That is why I have always loved the hymn I just quoted.

My daughter showed, very early in her life, the same tendency to worry that I have battled. When Samantha was a preschooler, she invented a new word: 'wuff.' It was her shortened version of "what if." When we talked about going on a picnic the next day, she would ask, "But wuff it rains?" If we planned to go over to play at a friend's house in the morning, she would question, "But wuff she's sick tomorrow?" Any plan or proposal was immediately greeted with "wuff this or that." I recognized that, even as a young child, she was feeling worry and anxiety. Her bright and creative young mind could so easily imagine all of the negative possibilities!

So I helped her the same way I had helped myself. I taught her some Bible verses about worry, anxiety, and fear. Before she could even properly read, I helped her to underline verses in her own little Bible: anything that started with "Do not be afraid," "Do not fear," or "Do not worry." We prayed together whenever she said "wuff." I helped her to think more about all of the positive possibilities. She learned that most of the time it did not

---

[185] Joseph Scriven, "What A Friend We Have in Jesus," (1855, Public Domain); author's italics.

rain on our picnics and on most days her best friend was not sick. And when these things *did* happen, she learned that worrying about them ahead of time did not prevent them from happening.

I am proud of Samantha. She has grown up to be a mature Christian woman. Of course, she has her moments of being worried and concerned like everyone else, but she has conquered her frequent use of the "wuff" word and its adult equivalents. She is generally an optimist. She has learned to choose faith, trust, and hope—and to make *new* plans when obstacles, challenges, and difficulties come. She has been unusually mature in this area through her later childhood and teen years. In the present, as she faces tough university exams and essay deadlines, she is learning afresh the power of meditating on God's words about choosing not to be anxious.

Worrying About the Future

The majority of our worries are focused on the future. The Bible's advice on this is quite simple. In Matthew 6, Jesus emphasizes that we are to live *one day at a time*. Jesus concluded His remarks about worry with these final statements: "Therefore do not worry about tomorrow, for tomorrow will worry about itself. Each day has enough trouble of its own."

We are not given the divine resources and empowerment to deal with *tomorrow's* problems *today*. Each day, we are meant to tackle that day's problems and challenges, doing whatever we can reasonably do. If we have a health problem today, we can pray and do whatever else might help instead of worrying about what will happen to our health tomorrow. If we have bills to pay today, we can partner with God in finding a way to pay them without wasting energy wondering what state our finances will be in next year. If we have outstanding issues in our marriage today, we can work at resolving them instead of worrying about whether or not our spouse will walk out on us tomorrow.

If we can only get a handle on this, the *weight* of our worries and anxieties will certainly lessen. But I know this is much easier said than done.

Perfectionists

It has been my experience and observation that the greatest worriers are often perfectionists. I have struggled with tendencies towards perfectionism. The perfectionist has a mind that speeds ahead on all cylinders, thinking a stream of these kinds of thoughts: What if the boss doesn't like the third page in my sixty page report? Does this paint chip *really* match this fabric? Why is that little patch of grass not as green as the rest of the yard? What will happen to the roast beef if my guests are late? Did I remember to put the right shade of lipstick in my purse?

Can you feel the anxiety in these questions?

Perfectionists like me need to re-read the chapters on how God forgives them of *all* their sins, mistakes, and failures—how God loves them just as they are, with all their humanity, their weaknesses, and their *imperfections*—how they can forgive themselves and love themselves *now* (not when they finish the task, improve, change, or mature). Chronic anxiety so often flows from an underlying sense of: I'm not good enough unless I'm perfect; I might fail; I might prove unworthy of love; I might be rejected again; someone else might do a better job.

Unrealistic expectations, standards set too high, and constant perfectionism all breed chronic worry and anxiety. Life becomes far more complicated, complex, competitive, and exacting than it needs to be. God knows we are a work-in-progress. He is not finished with any of us yet!

We need to develop practical strategies in our daily lives, such as rotating the holiday occasions that will get the *most* attention each year. No one can "go all out" for every birthday, anniversary, Easter, Thanksgiving, Christmas, and New Year's without making it full-time work. Do we really need to make a gourmet meal, eat out at an expensive restaurant, buy a gift, or decorate the house for every single celebration?

A few years ago, my husband (who usually puts up quite a magnificent display of Christmas lights) decided to take one year off and *not put up any at all.* He said that it was quite liberating. Normally he enjoys this activity, but that particularly busy year he valued knowing that he does not *have* to make this effort *every* year unless he feels up to it. And the world did not stop revolving on its axis just because our house did not have Christmas lights one year. I am personally trying to apply this kind of lesson to more areas of my life.

Controllers

Psychologists say that people who worry are often trying to control people and circumstances that are outside of their control. Worrying becomes their way of exerting some measure of present control over the future. Some people have to be "in control" of everything. Unfortunately, this kind of person often has trouble giving up control to God. They think they can do everything themselves and turn to God only as a last resort. (Been there and done that too.)

It takes humility for a person to give control of their lives and their problems to God. Casting our cares on God is an admission that we cannot fully handle them all on our own. Proud people resist doing this. Submitting to God, seeking His will and His timing, waiting patiently, having trust and faith in Him—all of this takes humility.

Controlling people pay a huge price. Aside from missing out on a healthy relationship with God as *Lord*, these people hold on to more than their problems—they hold on to the worries and anxieties that accompany the problems. The buck stops with them! If the plan does not work, they feel that it is totally their fault.

God wants to liberate us from our needless burdens. He wants us to give up control to Him—*not* because He is a vain and dominating puppet-master in the sky or a giant cosmic control freak, but because He knows it is good for us to release control to Him.

Chronic Worry and Anxiety: Some Insights from Dr. Sam

According to Dr. Sam, some people worry so habitually that they eventually develop chronic anxiety disorder. Feeling anxious all of the time, they have forgotten what it feels like *not* to be anxious. They often have no idea what they are actually anxious about. Every day feels stressful. Life constantly feels burdensome.

Dr. Sam warns that chronic anxiety can ultimately lead to: high blood pressure, heart disease, insomnia, gastro-intestinal problems, skin rashes, or a compromised immune system. Anxiety has also been linked to depression, asthma, and arthritis.[186] Chronic anxiety is a frequent cause of headaches and sleep disorders.

About 5% of the population in Canada will experience *generalized anxiety disorder* at some point in their lives. Generalized anxiety is diagnosed: when a person experiences overwhelming worry on most days for at least half a year; when the anxiety is far greater than the likelihood of the actual event or problem occurring; when the person never feels rested or relaxed; and when there is constant muscle tension.

Social anxiety disorder is diagnosed: when a person fears social events or performance situations, avoids them if possible, or endures them with a high degree of distress; and when a person worries excessively about what others think. Between 3–13% of Canadians experience this disorder for some time period in their lives.

Panic disorder is characterized by recurrent sudden onset of feelings of terror or panic, accompanied by physical and emotional symptoms such as a racing heartbeat, rapid breathing, the sensation of suffocating, excessive sweating, nausea, the urge to escape, dizziness, fear of fainting in public, and feeling out of

---

[186] See articles by: Kubzansky et al; Raikkonen et al; Fredrickson and Levenson; Kiecolt-Glaser et al.

control. Those with a severe form of this disorder often develop agoraphobia—a fear of being in public places, especially in situations where immediate escape is difficult in the event of a panic attack. About 1–2% of Canadians experience this crippling disorder during their lifetime.

An intensive look at anxiety-related psychiatric disorders is beyond the scope of this book. If you think that you suffer with one of these disorders, you would be wise to visit your doctor.

Treatment for Anxiety

According to Dr. Sam, the following are the three most commonly recommended kinds of treatment for anxiety:

Self-help

Healthy diet, regular exercise, and adequate sleep are all helpful in keeping anxiety under control. Exercise will actually lower the levels of harmful biochemical mediators in the bloodstream. Reducing the consumption of caffeine and other stimulants will accomplish this same goal. Spending time in the company of supportive family and friends will have a similar effect. Active, sociable people are less anxious than those who lead more idle, isolated lives.

In addition, we can practice focusing on faith-filled, peace-generating, positive thoughts. We will discuss this further in later pages.

Medication

Medical research suggests that some people with anxiety disorders have an imbalance in brain biochemicals called neuro-transmitters. Common anti-anxiety medications are used to readjust the levels of serotonin and norepinephrine (two brain biochemicals that might have become imbalanced). Those with uncontrolled anxiety or severe anxiety should not delay in getting a professional opinion as to whether medication would be helpful. Christians need not feel ashamed of taking anxiety medication—in some cases it is vital.

The use of appropriate medication, under the watchful monitoring of a caring physician, can be invaluable in some situations. Medication can help to restore a healthy biochemical balance in the brain, allowing the patient to think more clearly. They are then better able to understand the causes of their anxiety. They can more effectively learn new coping strategies and healthier thought patterns.

Therapy

Medication is often combined with psychotherapy. Cognitive behavioral therapy (CBT) is a common form of professional therapy used to treat chronic anxiety. This therapy recognizes that some people have predominantly negative, anxiety-producing thought tendencies. The therapist attempts to help the patient become aware of these thought tendencies and to begin replacing these negative thought patterns with positive thoughts about oneself, others, and life in general. The patient is shown how their negative thought patterns have led to negative feelings such as worry, fear, and hopelessness.

According to psychiatrist Dr. Stephen Stokl, the goal of CBT "is to identify distorted unrealistic harmful thinking, and replace it with healthier, more adaptable, and realistic reasoning."[187] CBT, under the care of a doctor, psychologist or psychiatrist, can be very useful for some people. Dr. Sam recommends that, if possible, Christians seek out professionals who are also Christian. These professionals can augment the CBT with references from the Bible.

Those of us with occasional worry and anxiety (as opposed to an anxiety disorder) can consider this: cognitive behavioral therapy is very similar to what the Bible teaches. Secular professionals sometimes act as if they invented it, when actually it is

---

[187] Dr. Stokl, pg. 148.

premised on what the Bible has prescribed all along. In a sense, this book presents a Christian version of cognitive behavioral therapy.

We *can* learn to rule over our own thoughts. We *can* choose positive thoughts and learn to reject negative, self-defeating, destructive, and pessimistic thoughts. We can find new mental strategies for coping with our most frequent areas of anxiety. We *can* renew our minds by: meditating on (and memorizing) helpful Scripture; by thinking thoughts consistent with sound biblical principles; by editing or reframing our negative memories; and by focusing on God's promises to help us. These ageless biblical strategies really do work. And we have the power of God to assist us.

This is not meant to discourage anyone from seeking professional help. It is useful, however, to know that successful therapy for worry and anxiety is not some mysterious magic that occurs *only* in a professional's office. Not everyone needs to rush to professional therapy. Even professional therapy only works insofar as the patient is able and willing to take personal responsibility for controlling and repatterning their own thoughts.

Stormie

Best-selling author Stormie Omartian has been helpfully honest and open about her history of chronic anxiety. Years ago, during her first career in Hollywood show business, she suffered frequent panic attacks.

On one occasion, for example, she suffered a severe panic attack just after she finished taping a television show. She felt irrational fear and noticed pressure in her chest. Pain seemed to rise from her stomach up to her throat and she had trouble speaking. Her breathing felt labored, and she had the sensation that she was suffocating. She felt the sudden urge to rush to a bathroom, dressing room, or other private place.[188]

---

[188] Omartian, see especially pg. 24.

Stormie ultimately overcame her battles with chronic anxiety and panic attacks by a combination of prayer, faith, acquiring biblical knowledge, counseling, and emotional healing. The story of her emotional battles and her encouraging victories are related in fascinating, instructive detail in her autobiography *Stormie*.

Some Other Success Stories

I have been close to a few Christian women who have battled debilitating panic attacks and/or quite serious anxiety over a period of years. Each of these women eventually overcame their panic attacks and habitual anxiety. They attribute their victories to a combination of several strategies: rejecting fear-filled, worried, anxious thoughts (one thought at a time); consciously choosing faith, trust, and hope; memorizing Bible verses about worry, anxiety, faith, and trust; much personal prayer; the intercessory prayer of others; and the empowerment of the Holy Spirit. One of them benefited from some counseling. Another took medication for a period, until her symptoms were under control, but has not been on medication for the past few decades.

All of them are living very victoriously at this time. They were determined to overcome their crippling anxiety attacks. It was not easy. It took time. Most importantly, they relied on God's help. He added His empowerment to their practical resolve to deal with their anxiety issues.

Prayer

We most effectively cast our cares on God in our prayer time. I have developed a non-negotiable habit of praying daily for a certain period of time. I do not do this because I am super-spiritual. I am an ordinary Christian. One of the reasons I do this (and have grown to *enjoy* it so immensely) is that it really does help me to manage my worries and anxieties. As I spend time focusing on God's presence in prayer (and on His love, His unlimited power, His Sovereignty over the universe, His promises, and His faithful answers to so many past prayers), I can feel my worries and anxieties melting away. I discovered that it takes no more time or emotional energy to pray about an issue than it does to worry about it.

What a privilege to go before the throne of God Most High, with Jesus (our Advocate, our Savior, our Brother, and our Friend) seated beside Him, and to *hand over* all of my cares and concerns. When I still feel anxious after prayer, it's because I'm sometimes still holding on to my worries—I need to truly let them go.

God knows how to work through any problem, meet any need, provide any resource, or change any heart. After more than three decades of Christian commitment, I can say unequivocally that God has helped me to eventually solve or cope with every problem that has crossed my path. He has met all of my needs. I have survived all of these years with more than sufficient clothing, food and drink, just as Jesus promised in Matthew 6. In light of this, it's amazing that I still battle worry as often as I do.

Prayer is an integral component of all emotional management, but it is especially important in the process of casting our cares on God. As Paul so aptly taught in Philippians 4, prayer is the key antidote to anxiety.

Focusing on Freedom

Peter wrote: "May God bless you richly and grant you *increasing* freedom from all anxiety and fear."[189] Freedom! That is my desire and my prayer for you and for me. I know that it is possible. I have already personally experienced so much release and deliverance from my tendency to worry and fret—and I know others even further down the road to freedom.

To successfully reject thoughts of fear, worry, and anxiety, we must instead choose thoughts consistent with faith, trust, and peace. Fear is the opposite of faith. Worry is the opposite of trust.

---

[189] 1 Peter 1:2c.

Anxiety is the opposite of inner peace. Every hour we have the choice between these powerful opposites. So let's move on to focus in more detail on the *positive* mental and emotional choices we can make, with God's help.

I have been through some terrible things in my life,
some of which actually happened.
Mark Twain

When anxiety was great within me, your consolation
brought joy to my soul.
Psalm 94:19 (NIV)

Don't fret and worry—it only leads to harm.
Psalm 37:8c

In all you do, I want you to be free from worry.
1 Corinthians 7:32a

13
FAITH
AND
TRUST
The Unshakable Soul

...all we need is faith working through love.
Galatians 5:6

Anything is possible if you have faith.
Mark 9:23b

MY HUSBAND, SAM, has always been fit. He loves to play tennis a few times a week and can run for a few hours without shortness of breath. You can imagine his shock when he learned, a few years ago, that he had to undergo urgent open heart surgery. His actual heart was in great shape, according to the gold standard tests—but a large, ominous aneurysm was sitting in the aortic root, just above his heart. Sam's cardiac specialist told him that, if the aneurysm was not removed, it would burst sometime within the year—likely resulting in sudden death. The cardiac surgeon compared Sam's aortic wall to a balloon blown up too large and stretched too thin.

Open heart surgery of any kind has all kinds of risks. From the moment we learned about the aneurysm, both of us had to battle fear, anxiety, and worry. Everything we have been discussing in the last few chapters became all too gut-wrenchingly real. We had daily, sometimes even hourly, choices to make as to whether or not we would dwell on thoughts of fear or faith, worry or trust. I wish I could report that we always made the right choices, but that would not be honest.

Our son and daughter were still in their mid-teens. I had retired from my law practice just six months prior to Sam's devastating news. The financial safety net of that second income was gone. I had recently committed myself to some short-term, unpaid projects with Christian organizations. From my perspective, the timing of this crisis was terrible! Having to face this situation seemed cruel and unfair. We had to believe that God was in control of it all and that He knew what He was doing.

Remarkably, as we struggled to choose faith over fear and trust over worry, God did supply both of us with a divine measure of faith that was clearly greater than any faith our human thoughts and feelings could generate.

Surgery was booked for the end of that summer. In the meantime, Sam and I decided to proceed with a trip we had planned to Russia and Scandinavia. Crossing Red Square in Moscow, I remember feeling really vulnerable. What if Sam suddenly collapsed? Would I be able to find a phone? I carried the phone numbers of English-speaking hospitals for all the cities we were going to. But what if the operator did not speak English? In the back of my mind, I was aware that our travel insurance would not cover the risks we had chosen to take. Most importantly, would Sam be able to get the medical help he might need?

On so many levels, I was not ready to be a widow and a single mom. I was not ready to say good-bye to the love of my life and my best friend. As soon as these kinds of thoughts surfaced, I made the choice *to believe* that God was with us and that Sam would live through that summer, that trip, his surgery, and beyond—and that even if the unimaginable happened, God would be with me in those circumstances too. We *had* to proceed forward in faith or we would have crumbled under the weight of the fear that was waiting to crush us if we let it.

God kept giving me strong assurances, as I read the Bible that summer, that this was all going to turn out for our good. I will share further, in the next chapter, a few particular verses that God brought across my path over and over again that never failed to calm my spirit and strengthen my faith. Thankfully, the surgery and recovery went well.

This is not, of course, the only time that Sam and I have had to exercise faith instead of fear. Over the years, we have each had to have faith that God would help us to get through all of our university courses and exams (some required more faith than others!), to survive many difficult situations in our careers, to overcome many other medical challenges, to work through various issues in our marriage, to pay our bills, and to raise our children.

Daily, we *still* have to trust that God will guide us and help us in all of life's ever-changing circumstances. The Bible tells us that God loves it when we exercise our faith in Him and His Word. In Hebrews 11:6, Paul said that without faith it is impossible to please God.

The Basis for our Faith and Trust

It has often been said that we all have faith in something and someone. We exercise faith every day, whether we are Christians or not. Everyone has implicit faith that the sun will rise every day, that spring will follow winter, and that tomorrow will follow today. We generally have faith that our alarm clocks will wake us up, that our morning cups of coffee will *really* wake us up, that our seatbelts will work, that our banks will safeguard our money, that fellow motorists will stop at red lights, and that our e-mails will reach their destinations.

We generally choose to trust our families, neighbors, friends, and work colleagues. Eventually, some of these people will let us down. They will, in some cases, prove to be untrustworthy. We will have reason to lose faith in the integrity and the word of those who abuse our trust.

Only God is truly trustworthy. Only God does not break His promises. He alone has the power, ability, and steadfastness to honor the covenants that He made with us the moment we turned our lives over to Him. We can safely place our faith in

Him. He may not always do what we *want* Him to do or *ask* Him to do—nor is He governed by our timetable. Yet, even when we do not understand what is happening to us, He remains worthy of our faith and our trust.

As Christians, we begin by having faith that God exists. Most of us need look no further than the majesty and glory of the sun, stars, clouds, birds, flowers, trees, mountains, lakes, and oceans.

If you are one of those who can look at the miracles of nature and still not believe that God exists, I challenge you to pray a simple prayer: ask God to *show* you that He exists. Dare to make that request. If you are sincerely looking for Him, I promise that you will find Him—and He will show Himself to *you* with great delight.

But it is not enough to merely believe that God exists. The Bible says that even the Devil—even demons—believe that God exists, and they tremble.[190]

There are further layers to Christian faith. Christians believe that God has spoken to us through His Word. Christians choose to believe that Jesus is who He says He is—the Son of God. Christians believe that Jesus died for our sins, that He rose again, and that He is now seated beside Father God in the heavens. Christians have faith that this is true, simply because God has said so.

How do we develop faith along these lines? The Bible tells us that faith comes from hearing the Word. So read the Bible, even if you begin doing so with some skepticism. Start by reading the New Testament. Ask yourself: is it true, what it says about the human heart, about *your* heart? Is it true, what is says about the affairs of this world?

At a certain point, we must step out in faith to *believe* and to *trust*. We do not have to wait until our every last question is answered. Paul wrote in Galatians 3:11: "…God has said that the only way we can be right in his sight is by faith. As the prophet Habukkuk says it, 'The man who finds life will find it through trusting God.' "

---

[190] James 2:19.

Once we become Christians, committed to believing in God's existence and in salvation through His Son Jesus, then we can have faith in *much* more: faith that God forgives our sins every time we sincerely ask Him to; faith that God will provide for all of our needs; faith that God will strengthen, heal, help, and sustain us; faith that God will give us the indwelling Holy Spirit to be our Conscience, Counselor, Companion, and Comforter; faith that God will honor all His other promises; and faith that, at the end of it all, there is eternal life.

We all have the choice. We can have faith in our own abilities, our own strength, and our own resources. We can place our faith in others. We can have faith that our money will solve all of our problems. We can have faith in our intelligence and our education. We can place our faith in human philosophies. We can have faith in the goodness of our fellow men and women. *Or* we can have faith in God, His Word, and His promises.

I have personally discovered that my own abilities are limited. My strength sometimes fails. My resources run dry. Others disappoint me from time to time. Money cannot solve everything and the stock market is not always on the uptick. My own intelligence does not know all of the answers. The many human philosophies I once deeply explored ultimately left me empty, frustrated, and in despair. My fellow human beings are not good all of the time.

I have personally discovered that God is the only worthy Object of my faith and trust. I heartily agree with what one of Job's friends said: "A man without God is trusting in a spider's web. Everything he counts on will collapse."[191]

There comes a point, in all of our lives, when *all* that we really truly have is our faith in God. Joseph, Peter, and Paul discovered this during their time in prison. Moses discovered this as a young man on the backside of the desert after fleeing for his very life and leaving all that he had behind. Job discovered this after he lost his wealth, his health, and his family. David

---

[191] Job 8:14.

discovered this while hiding in caves, a fugitive from a powerful king trying to kill him. There are times when God—and God alone—is all that separates us from disappointment, despair, destruction, and perhaps death itself.

There is a lot of power in positive thinking, but even that power has its limits. Christians can know the even greater power of positive *believing*. With faith in God, nothing is impossible![192]

Abraham

Abraham has often been described as the "father of faith." He believed everything that God told him. He and his wife Sarah were already very old, beyond their natural child-bearing years, when God told them they would have a son. In fact, God told them that their descendants would be as numerous as the stars in the sky and the grains of sand on the seashore. Against all odds— against the very laws of nature—Abraham chose to believe God.[193] At the age of one hundred, Abraham became the father of Isaac, who became the father of Jacob, who had twelve sons that became the patriarchs of the twelve tribes of Israel.

God also promised Abraham that He would give his descendants a land flowing with milk and honey. Abraham chose to believe God. Thousands of years later, the Jewish people are dwelling in that very land.

Joshua and Caleb

After reaching the edge of the Promised Land, Moses decided to send twelve spies into the land to see who was living there. Ten of the twelve spies came back with a negative report, advising that the people living in the land were like giants and the Israelites were like "grasshoppers" in comparison.

Only Joshua and Caleb returned with a positive report, having *faith* that, with God's help, the Israelites could go in to possess the

---

[192] Matthew 17:20, Mark 9:23; Mark 11:22–24.
[193] Genesis 15:6; Romans 4:18–20.

land. Caleb encouraged the people with enthusiasm: "Let us go up at once and possess it...for we are *well able* to conquer it!"[194]

The Israelites chose to believe the negative majority. As a result, God did not allow that generation to enter the Promised Land. They died in their unbelief. Only Joshua and Caleb, the two men of positive faith, were allowed to go into the Promised Land. Sure enough, God did help them to conquer the land that He had long before promised to Abraham and his descendants.

Paul

Paul spoke about faith and modeled faith through all the trials and hardships of his life. No matter what he went through, he did not lose his faith in God. After days of a terrible storm, for example, while on board a ship that faced certain shipwreck, Paul told his frightened shipmates: "...take courage! *For I believe God.*"[195] God had told him that, although the ship would be lost, not one person would lose their lives. Not one person did.

In another letter, Paul wrote to the church at Corinth: "We walk by faith, not by sight."[196] Paul had learned how to have faith and trust in God no matter how dismal, dangerous, or difficult the circumstances appeared.

Near the end of his life, Paul wrote the young Timothy: "I have fought the good fight, I have finished the race, I have kept the faith."[197]

Many Heroes of Faith

There is not enough space in this book to list all the great heroes of faith in the Bible. I invite you to spend time in Hebrews 11, where Paul describes the greatest men and women of faith—everyone

---

[194] Numbers 13:30b; read the rest of Numbers 13 and 14 for the full story.
[195] Acts 27:25ab, author's italics.
[196] 2 Corinthians 5:7 (NKJV).
[197] 2 Timothy 4:7 (NIV).

from Abel to Noah, from the prostitute Rahab to the various prophets.

After describing these great men and women of faith, Paul then wrote in Hebrews 12:1–2a (NIV): "Therefore, since we are surrounded by such a great cloud of witnesses, let us throw off everything that hinders and the sin that so easily entangles, and let us run with perseverance the race marked out for *us*. Let us fix our eyes on Jesus, the author and perfecter of our faith..."

The Fruit of Faith

I encourage you to consider these verses, which describe the fruit that follows when we put our faith and trust in God:

"'If your faith were only the size of a mustard seed,' Jesus [said], 'it would be large enough to uproot that mulberry tree over there and send it hurtling into the sea!' " (Luke 17:6a)

"You can get anything—*anything* you ask for in prayer—if you believe." (Matthew 21:22)

"*Anything* is possible if you have faith." (Mark 9:23b)

"...If you only have faith in God—this is the absolute truth—you can say to this Mount of Olives, 'Rise up and fall into the Mediterranean' and your command will be obeyed. All that's required is that you really believe and have no doubt! Listen to me! You can pray for *anything*, and *if you believe, you have it*; it's yours!" (Mark 11:22–24)

"...dearly loved friends, if our consciences are clear, we can come to the Lord with *perfect assurance* and *trust*, and get whatever we ask for because we are obeying him and doing the things that please him." (1 John 3:21–22)

"And we are *sure* of this, that he will listen to us whenever we ask him for anything in line with his will. And if we really know he is listening when we talk to him and make our requests, then we can be *sure* that he will answer us." (1 John 5:14–15)

Many more great promises are contained in the Bible for those who believe in God and in salvation through His Son. We can know that *all things are possible*—and *nothing is impossible*, if we simply believe. In this realm of faith, our lives have unlimited potential. We must, however, note the fine print in the above verses—we must also have clear consciences and obedient hearts that want to please God and fulfill His will for our lives.

Putting on Faith

Paul exhorted his fellow Christians: "...let us be self-controlled, *putting on* faith and love as a breastplate..."[198] In 2 Timothy 2:22 Paul said to *pursue* faith. Once again, notice these active verbs. God expects *us* to actively choose to have faith.

I love what Hannah Whitall Smith wrote about this choice in her classic book, *The Christian's Secret of a Happy Life*:

> I do beg of you to recognize...the extreme simplicity of faith; namely, that it is nothing more nor less than just *believing* God when He says He either has done something for us, or will do it; and then trusting Him to keep His word...
>
> How continually we are...trusting our health and our lives, without a thought of fear, to cooks and coachmen, engine drivers, railway conductors, and all sorts of paid servants, who have us completely at their mercy, and who could, if they chose to do so, or even if they failed in the necessary carefulness, plunge us into misery or death in a moment. All of this we do and make no demur about it. Upon the slightest acquaintance...we thus put our trust in people, requiring only the general knowledge of human nature and the common rules of human intercourse as the foundation for our trust, and we never feel as if we were doing anything in the least remarkable.
>
> You have done this yourself, dear reader, and are doing it continually....But yet you do not hesitate to say, continually, that you cannot trust your God! And you excuse yourself by the plea that you are "a poor weak creature" and "have no faith".

---

[198] 1 Thessalonians 5:8 (NIV).

I wish you would try to imagine yourself acting in your human relations as you do in your spiritual relations. Suppose you should begin tomorrow with the notion in your head that you could not trust anybody because you had no faith. When you sat down to breakfast you would say, 'I cannot eat anything on this table, for I have no faith, and I cannot believe that the cook has not put poison into the coffee, or that the butcher has not sent home diseased or unhealthy meat,' so you would go starving away. When you went out to your daily avocations, you would say, "I cannot ride in the railway train, for I have no faith, and therefore I cannot trust the engineer, nor the conductor, nor the builders of the carriages, nor the managers of the road." And you would be compelled to walk everywhere and would grow unutterably weary in the effort....

Just picture yourself such a day as this and see how disastrous it would be to yourself and what utter folly it would appear to anyone who would watch you through the whole of it....And then ask yourself the question, if this want of faith in your fellowmen would be so dreadful and such utter folly, what must it be when you tell God that you have no power to trust Him, nor to believe His word; that it is a great trial, but you cannot help it, "for you have no faith."

Is it possible that you can trust your fellowmen and cannot trust your God; that you can receive the "witness of men" and cannot receive "the witness of God"; that you can believe man's records and cannot believe God's record; that you can commit your dearest earthly interests to your weak, failing fellow creatures without a fear and are afraid to commit your spiritual interests to the Savior who laid down His life for you...?

Put your will, then, over on the *believing* side. Say, "Lord, I *will* believe; I *do* believe.", and *continue* to say it. *Insist* upon believing in the face of every suggestion of doubt that intrudes itself...

You must therefore *put your will* into believing. Your faith must not be a passive imbecility but an active energy...Set your face like flint to say, "I *will* believe and I know I shall not be confounded."[199]

---

[199] Hannah Whitall Smith, pgs. 66–72, my italics.

Let's choose to put *our* will over on the believing side! No matter what, let's choose to have faith. Let's decide, this very day, to trust the Creator and Sustainer of the whole universe.

Gladys Aylward

Gladys was a missionary in China during World War II. At one point, in the midst of fierce fighting between the Chinese and the Japanese, Gladys took one hundred children (many of them toddlers) on a one-month journey across steep mountains. They had to cross the Yellow River—a river known for so many drownings that it had been nick-named "China's Sorrow." Gladys, the only adult caring for all those children, had to have enormous faith as she trusted God to provide daily food, water, warmth, safety, and shelter for her and the one hundred orphans. On top of all the hardships she faced, she was traveling without any money. Amazing.

The war raged around her. Gladys often had to hide the children from Japanese dive bombers and foot patrols. Heightening the danger, the Japanese were offering a reward for her capture. So she avoided the main trails across the mountains, making the journey all the more difficult for the little ones. Along the way, Gladys personally battled typhus, pneumonia, and malnutrition. Yet she pressed on.

The perilous journey ended at an orphanage in Sian, where Gladys delivered the children into their relatively safe new home. Her faith had sustained her through the long, arduous days and nights—and was rewarded with divine aid, provision, and protection.

As I was writing this, I recalled some birthday parties that we had arranged for our son and daughter as they grew up. For about two hours, on each successive birthday, my husband and I would watch fifteen or sixteen children run around and play at indoor playgrounds, laser gun mazes, or mini-golf courses. We had to make sure that no one got hurt, lost, kidnapped, or sick from too much pizza and pop. We were pretty stressed after just a few *hours* of this responsibility. I simply cannot imagine what Gladys Aylward's journey was like, taking solo care of one hundred children for so long under such dangerous, difficult circumstances. How pathetic that many of us actually struggle to have faith in much more ordinary moments. When I read about women like Gladys, I am personally challenged to pull up the socks of my faith.

William Carey

William Carey, considered by many to be the "father" of the modern missionary movement, traveled as a pioneering missionary to India in the seventeenth century. He left his home in Britain to travel halfway around the globe with an unsupportive wife and four young sons. Despite suffering from depression, dysentery, extreme poverty, malaria, the death of a son, the debilitating mental illness of his wife and her eventual death, Carey remained in India for four decades.

In that time, he translated and/or published the Bible into forty-four languages and dialects (in itself an unfathomable achievement!), established a number of mission stations in India and surrounding nations, started Christian schools, and advanced agricultural practices in India. Nothing could make him lose faith in the God he so bravely and sacrificially served—not even the fire that destroyed most of his translation work.[200]

At the end of it all, Carey was able to say these words, which have echoed down through the centuries as the motto of his remarkable faith: "Expect great things from God, attempt great things for God."

Olympic Figure Skater Paul Wylie

In the 1988 Olympics, figure skater Paul Wylie took a bad fall in front of the watching world. Unfazed, he pressed on in competition. At the World Championships in 1991, he took another bad

---

[200] Petersen, supra, chapter 16; Vishal and Ruth Mangalwadi.

fall. He still did not give up. But these falls, on the world stage, had led to him developing a fear of triple axel jumps.

At the age of twenty-seven, he was the oldest competitor slated to skate in the 1992 men's Olympic events. He knew he was going to have to once again perform triple axel jumps before millions of viewers all over the globe and he felt intimidated. He decided ahead of time that he was going to have to change the way he thought about the dreaded triple axel.

He worked at developing faith that God would help him with the triple axel—that God would help him to overcome his fear and to skate his best. He knew that it was not enough to simply have faith in his own ability. Armed with this new attitude, as he prepared for the 1992 competition, he actually began to enjoy performing the triple axel. At the 1992 Games, he was able to give the best performance of his life and won a Silver Olympic Medal. His faith triumphed over his fear.[201]

Former President Jimmy Carter

I have always admired the faith of former U.S. President Jimmy Carter. When he declared his bid to run for President in 1976, he did not initially have the backing of his own party leaders. His chance of winning without their support seemed next to impossible. At the starting gate, few people were betting on this racehorse.

Carter maintained an unswerving faith that God was going to help him in the election, even if powerful men did not. He demonstrated this faith in many ways. The year *before* he had announced his candidacy, he had already made five miles of television commercial film. Before he ran in even a single primary, he asked for the zoning bylaws in Plains to be changed so that, once he was in the White House, his beloved little home town (population 683) would not become a tourist zoo. He further

---

[201] Kelly Monroe (ed.), *Finding God at Harvard*, facts from article by Wylie.

stepped out in faith by putting his own financial resources on the line during the election.

At the beginning of 1976, he began his campaign with only 4% of the support of his own party, the Democrats, and with obviously no support from the opposing Republicans. With a calm and gentle demeanor, Carter criss-crossed America over the following months. When asked at one point to summarize the theme of his campaign in a single word, he chose the word faith.

To the surprise of many, Carter won the election that year. The story of his unusual and unexpected rise to the Presidency of the United States remains one of the most interesting political campaign stories of modern history.[202]

Lisa Beamer

Within a month of her husband losing his life on a United Airlines flight to San Francisco, widow Lisa Beamer flew on a United Airlines flight to that same city to settle some insurance issues. Can you imagine the faith that required?

We have already talked about Lisa's decision to choose forgiveness instead of anger, bitterness, and hatred. She had learned, through circumstances earlier in her life, that negative emotions of any kind were a waste of time and a drain of energy.

After 9/11, Lisa also made the quality choice to choose faith over fear. She could not deny that terrorists had taken her husband's life. But she resolved that they would not cause further harm to the lives of herself and her children. She firmly decided that her little family was going to *move on* with their lives, overcoming the fear of the future by placing their faith and trust in God.[203]

---

[202] Howard Norton & Bob Slosser, *The Miracle of Jimmy Carter.*
[203] Beamer, pg. 270.

Patience and Perseverance

I have learned, both in my own faith journey and from reading many Christian biographies, that faith must go hand in hand with two other godly virtues: patience and perseverance. God seldom answers prayers overnight. The Bible is full of verses that counsel us to *wait* on God and, in the meantime, to have courage and good cheer. Most people hate having to develop patience, but it is unavoidable in the Christian journey.

Paul wrote: "fight the good fight of faith, *holding on* to faith and a good conscience. Some have rejected these and so have shipwrecked their faith."[204] We hold on to our faith by exercising patient perseverance—unwavering faith in the face of whatever life throws at us. Paul told the early Christians: "Do not let this happy trust in the Lord die away, *no matter what happens.*"[205]

Peter gave the same advice when he told the early Christians to *stand firm* in their faith.[206] We must dig in our heels and stand our ground if we want to prevail in the battle of faith.

Peter and Paul certainly knew what it was to persist and persevere through thick and thin. In 2 Corinthians 4:8–9, Paul described their patient endurance: "We are pressed on every side by troubles, but not crushed and broken. We are perplexed because we don't know why things happen as they do, *but we don't give up and quit.* We are hunted down, but God never abandons us. We get knocked down, *but we get up again* and *keep going.*"

Praying for Healing

Praying in faith for healing especially requires patience and perseverance. I can bear testimony that on a few occasions I have been healed overnight. But on more occasions, the healing has taken weeks, months, or even *years* of patient, persistent prayers

---

[204] 1 Timothy 1:18–19 (NIV).

[205] Hebrews 10:35a.

[206] 1 Peter 5:9 (NIV).

of faith. To this day, there are physical needs that I am *still* praying about for myself and others. I will press on with these prayers for as long as I live! I continue to pray each day, even though I have not been healed *yet* in some ways. We are all growing older and cannot expect to maintain perfect, youthful bodies. Thankfully, we are promised new bodies in the next life. But we can have patient faith that God can and does heal in this life too.

I wrote in an earlier chapter about being diagnosed, at the age of nine, with a serious auto-immune disease. My muscle cells were attacking one another, causing my muscles to weaken. I vividly recall my pastor and my Uncle Phil coming to pray over me. I did not fully understand what they were saying, but did grasp that they were asking God to heal me. Something within me leapt up in response. I was so young, not even a fully committed Christian yet, and so very immature in my spiritual understanding. But I chose to have faith anyways—the faith of a child—the kind of faith the Father loves best!

After the powerful prayer was spoken over me, I often prayed alone in the quiet of my hospital room, and somehow trusted that God *would* heal me. And, in time, He did. At that tender age, I learned something valuable about *not giving up*. It seemed to take forever, but my prayers and the fervent prayers of my pastor and others were eventually answered. Although the auto-immune disease that had afflicted me can be chronically debilitating for many, in my case I fully recovered and have thankfully not had symptoms in the four decades since. I encourage you to *press on* in faith regarding your own physical needs, no matter how much time passes, and to have the courage to pray out loud over receptive loved ones.

Selling Our House

My husband and I learned fresh lessons about patiently waiting for God to answer prayer a few years ago. After living for fifteen years in our second home, we made the decision to sell it. We bought another home before the first one was sold. The real estate market was hot. (Or so we had been told—it seemed to be hot for everyone else but us!) Ultimately, it took us ten grueling months to sell our home and another few months until the deal closed.

About halfway through this ordeal, we moved into our new home and began bearing *double* the usual expenses for insurance, taxes, snow-clearing, electricity, and heating costs during a brutal Canadian winter. Our faith was really tested as we kept paying all those duplicate bills, but we chose to patiently persevere in faith. Every day, we believed that we were one day closer to the unknown date that we would sell our home. Eventually that day came.

Let me encourage each one of you. Whatever you are going through—whatever is pressing down on you, knocking you over, taxing your strength, beating you up, making you doubt, wearing you out—whatever it is, I encourage you to *hold on, cling tightly,* and *stand firm* in your faith. Be patient, persistent, persevering! You are one day closer to God intervening in your situation—one day closer to the healing, the guidance, the provision, the financial help, or the solution you are seeking. *You are one day closer....*

You might believe that you have already lost the battle. Your goals and dreams may feel unattainable. How do you think Joseph felt about his dreams during the years he served an unjust prison sentence? How do you think David felt while running from Saul after David had supposedly been anointed as King? The Bible talks about how a kernel of wheat must fall into the ground and die before it can produce further seeds.[207] There is life beyond your apparent short-term failure, disaster, or defeat. Perhaps there are new dreams to pursue. God has not abandoned you. Have faith that you are *one day closer* to brighter, better circumstances.

---

[207] John 12:23–24.

God's Ways are Not Our Ways

The prophet Isaiah declared that God's ways are not our ways.[208] God might not answer our prayers and respond to our faith exactly the way that *we* want Him to. We must remember that He is God and we are mere men and women.

My favorite story in this regard involves well-known missionary Amy Carmichael. As a child, Amy kept praying for her brown eyes to turn blue.[209] Her eyes never did turn blue! But God *did* marvelously answer her lifetime of prayers regarding her work with orphans and others in India.

Sometimes we have to let go of our requests to turn our brown eyes blue. Let us never abandon our faith in a loving God—just our misguided prayers. Faith is not meant to be presumptuous. We are not entitled to tell God the exact nuts and bolts of what He must do for us. We must ultimately have faith that God loves us and that, in His sovereign control and in His timing, with our best interests dear to His heart, He will answer our prayers *His* way. Earlier, I recited several verses that talk about how we can receive *anything* that we request in faith-filled prayer—but remember the caveat in 1 John 5:14 that these prayers need to be in accordance with God's will. All prayer requests must line up with the general principles of right living and right relationship with God that are outlined in the Bible.

God has not answered all my prayers exactly as I wanted Him to. He has not always responded to my faith as I expected, no matter how persevering I was. Although I do not understand all of God's ways or His timing, I do know this: God has so specifically, marvelously, incredibly, and even miraculously answered so many of my prayers over so many years that I remain excited and enthused about the life of faith. God has helped me reach mountaintops, climb out of distressing pits, survive dark nights of the soul, awaken to new dawns, emerge

---

[208] Isaiah 55:8.
[209] Sam Wellman, *Amy Carmichael*, pg. 7.

from frightening medical situations, finish races (sometimes in first place, sometimes in last place), fulfill dreams, obtain prizes, and overcome adversities *enough times* that I trust Him and want to keep living on in faith.

I have decided that I will not waste time trying to figure out the "why," "why not," and "why didn't He" situations in life. God will one day explain all that to me, if not in this life than in the next. I will not let life's unexplained mysteries deter me from living a life of faith.

Keep It Simple

On that note, I need to keep reminding myself to keep faith simple. Jesus Himself said to His followers: "…the Kingdom of God belongs to men who have hearts as *trusting* as these little children's. And anyone who doesn't have *their* kind of faith will never get within the Kingdom's gates."[210]

We must never be held back by thinking we need to understand more about faith, or strive for a greater faith, or compete with someone else's faith, or wait until we are spiritual giants— before we simply step out in faith to believe what He says.

My children taught me so much in this regard as they grew up. On one occasion, when our son, Darrin, was three, we were returning from a store where we had bought him a little motorized jeep that he could "drive" himself. He was so excited to try it out! But very dark rain clouds and loud thunder told me that he was going to have to wait until another day. With uncomplicated faith, he announced that he was praying that God would blow the rain clouds away. When we arrived home fifteen minutes later, the large mass of black clouds had moved to the far horizon and the sun was shining! God had responded to a child's simple faith. As he grew into adulthood, my son had his fair share of tough times, but I deeply admire his ongoing faith whether the clouds are ominously dark *or* the sun is brightly shining.

---

[210] Luke 18:16c–17.

Our daughter, Samantha, had an interesting faith experience in her mid-teens while participating in a Habitat for Humanity project in El Salvador. Her suitcase was lost on the flight there. She had several discussions with a close friend as to whether her suitcase would show up that week. Samantha kept praying about it and believing that God would find that suitcase for her. Her friend queried whether God really cared about these little details of our lives. Samantha insisted that He did. Sure enough, the suitcase did turn up. God not only provided that answer to prayer—He also answered the friend's query—He does indeed care about the small details of our lives.

God, Help My Unbelief!

Thankfully, having faith is not all up to us. One of my favorite Bible stories is told in Mark 9. A father asked Jesus to heal his son, for his son was unable to speak and suffered from seizures that threatened his life. The father asked Jesus to help them, *if* He could. The father had some measure of faith to approach Jesus with this request, and Jesus responded by saying that anything was possible, if the man had faith. The father replied: "I *do* have faith; oh, help me to have *more!*" In another translation, the father states: "I do believe; help me overcome my unbelief! (NIV)"[211]

From the moment we become Christians, we all have some measure of faith. We also struggle with doubt and uncertainty. Numerous letters written by the late Mother Teresa demonstrate that even she struggled with doubt.[212]

When our measure of faith is not sufficient, God is there to supply more. He can increase our measure of faith. We only need to step out, with whatever faith we have, and God will do the rest. He will help us overcome whatever amount of unbelief hinders us. We need only ask Him. Remember the verse we quoted earlier that says all we need is faith the size of a mustard

---

[211] Quotes from Mark 9:24.
[212] David Van Biema article in TIME magazine (Canadian edition), September 3, 2007.

seed? Imagine faith the size of the period at the end of this sentence—that is all the faith we need to move forward in our circumstances.

In Psalm 80:18b, Asaph wrote: "Revive us to trust in you." We do not need to exhaust ourselves by trying to "conjure up" more faith than we actually have. There comes a point when we must "let go" and "let God."

Peter also spoke of this. He said: "How precious it is, and how just and good he is to *give* this same faith to each of us."[213] God *gives* us more faith as we need it. The catch is that we must be stepping out, in action, with whatever faith we already have, however meager it may be.

God sometimes uses other believers to boost our faith. In Romans 1:11–12, Paul wrote: "For I long to visit you so that I can *impart* to you the faith that will help your church grow strong in the Lord. Then , too, I need your help, for I want not only to share my faith with you but to be encouraged by yours..."

This is one of the reasons I encourage you to attend church and become involved in regular fellowship with Christian friends and mentors. God can *impart* faith from seasoned, stronger Christians to newer, weaker Christians—or from those enjoying a time of rest and renewal to those in the thick of the fight.

That we all have a different measure of faith at any point in time can be seen in Paul's words at Romans 12:3: "...Be honest in your estimate of yourselves, measuring your value by how much faith God has given you." This further corroborates the principle that, while *we* are expected to choose faith and trust, God adds to that whatever divine measure of faith *He* chooses to give.

There are other scriptural references to this divine gift of faith and trust. Let us look at one more. In Ephesians 2:8, Paul wrote: "Because of his kindness you have been saved through trusting Christ. And even trusting is not of yourselves; it too is a gift from God."

---

[213] 2 Peter 1:1d.

So do not despair if you feel your faith and trust are weak, maybe almost non-existent. Ask God to supply you with a greater measure of faith and trust. Exercise what you have and wait for more. Surround yourself with other Christians who are full of faith. Do your part, however humble, and expect God to do the rest.

A Few Further Musings On the Fruit of Faith

I love what Jeremiah 17:7–8 promises: "...blessed is the man who *trusts* in the Lord, whose confidence is in him. He will be like a tree planted by the water that sends out its roots by the stream. It does not fear when heat comes; its leaves are always green. It has no worries in a year of drought and never fails to bear fruit. (NIV)"

Real faith and trust always result in tangible fruit. Some of this fruit is the *good* that we do in this life. James wrote that we know we have faith when our lives bear good fruit. Faith that does not eventually result in good works is not really faith at all.[214] Although we are not saved by our "works," genuine faith always compels us towards fruitful, godly words and actions.

Through faith, we can receive what we need, regain our strength, get through each storm, win the battle, achieve our God-given dreams, move mountains, prosper in all that we do, and mightily bless others, thereby fulfilling all of God's wonderful purposes for each of our lives.

In Conclusion

Faith is one of the great keys of the Christian life. It is a critical foundation to everything else that we have been discussing. Faith brings the supernatural into the natural realm. It transforms us and our circumstances. The impossible changes into the possible.

My husband and I grew stronger in faith that summer when he was diagnosed with a life-threatening aneurysm. As we

---

[214] James 2:17.

brought faith to bear in our scary circumstances, God helped us get through the weeks of waiting for the surgery, the day of the surgery, and the weeks of recovery. In spite of our fears and worries, we chose to exercise faith and trust—and God supplied a gift of divine faith that helped us rise even higher in our spirits. I learned afresh that we can trust God—He is indeed completely trustworthy.

In every battle you will need faith as your shield
to stop the fiery arrows aimed at you by Satan.
Ephesians 6:16

Now faith is being sure of what we hope for
and certain of what we do not see.
Hebrews 11:1 (NIV)

Faith is like radar which sees through the fog—the reality of
things at a distance which the eye cannot see.
Corrie ten Boom[215]

Fight the good fight of faith.
1 Timothy 6:12a (NIV)

---

[215] Corrie ten Boom, *Tramp for the Lord*, supra, pg. 12.

14
PEACE
Settled and Still

...I have stilled and quieted my soul...
Psalm 131:2 (NIV)

Lord, grant us peace...
Isaiah 26:12

Peace I leave with you; my peace I give you.
I do not give to you as the world gives.
Do not let your hearts be troubled and do not be afraid.
John 14:27 (NIV)

O VER THE YEARS, I have sometimes wondered how I would feel if I knew that death was suddenly imminent. Would I be paralyzed with fear? Would I feel an ounce of courage? Would I have sudden doubts about my faith? Would I joyously anticipate leaving this world for my eternal home? Would I panic? Would my heart pound and my mind spin? Would I cry, rage, faint, or pray?

In the spring of 1981, I learned the answer to those questions in the middle of a five-week journey through Egypt and Israel. One very eventful night, my sister and I were staying in a room on the fifth floor of a grand old hotel in Cairo.

Around mid-evening, we started to smell smoke. It was soon clear that a fire had started somewhere nearby. We decided to leave our room and go down to the lobby.

The hotel's electricity was off. Moonlight, streetlights, and neon lights from adjacent buildings gave us some light in our room. When we entered the wide hallway, however, which had no windows, it was completely dark. We had to grope our way along one of the walls, feeling carefully for the side hall that led to the only staircase. As we stumbled along, I noted with apprehension that there were no fire alarms ringing and no sprinklers in the ceiling.

Nearing the staircase, the smoke thickened. We started to cough. It was terribly acrid. We tried to go down the stairs, but the smoke in the stairwell was too thick. We simply could not breathe. We had no choice but to return to our room.

At that point, our room was not yet too smoky. We dampened some towels and soon began to breathe through those, filtering some of the smoke. We opened the very narrow windows, allowing some fresh air into the room. Looking outside, we could see dense smoke billowing from lower windows. We could also see fire trucks arriving on the street below. They did not hook up to hydrants; the trucks had their own water tanks, with an obviously limited supply of water. I remember the thought crossing my mind that Cairo is a city located in the desert. I prayed that there would be enough water available in the row of trucks to fight this fire.

Gut-wrenching fear and a sense of panic began to creep over me. The fear increased as we noticed the smoke in our own room getting thicker, despite the open windows. My sister and I sat down on the edge of one bed and decided to pray out loud together. It was at that point that it occurred to me that I might actually die that night. I had read enough to know that people often die of smoke inhalation long before the flames of a fire reach the room they are in.

I began to wonder if, that very night, I would face eternity. I remember feeling a little ripped off. I had just passed the ten rigorous qualifying exams required at that time to enter the legal profession. *If* I returned from this trip, I would be "called to the Bar" in a ceremony a few days later. I remember thinking that all of my law studies could have been for naught. With each passing moment, the stark reality of our situation looked more grim and the possibility that we might actually die loomed larger in my mind.

As we prayed out loud together, however, an amazing peace began to enter that room. The peace felt as thick as the smoke. There seemed to be more light in the room (that just moments before had seemed so depressingly dark). The peace began to flow through my mind and heart and I began to personally understand why some old hymns compared peace to a river. As I focused on praying—and on thinking about verses that assured me of my salvation and eternal life—faith, trust, and joy were superimposed onto the supernatural peace that washed through me.

I realized that I was not afraid of death! I was not afraid of meeting God that very night. In fact, I *wanted* to meet God the Father and Jesus face to face. What I felt in those moments has impacted the rest of my life. I will never forget how the fear and panic drained out of me—and how peace, calm, assurance, certainty of faith, and strength of trust flowed into my soul.

God's presence was tangible. I knew that I was experiencing the peace that surpasses understanding that Paul wrote about in Philippians 4:7. This peace was not rational. It certainly did not flow from my circumstances! It was too powerful to have been merely mentally conjured up. It was so beautiful, so gentle, so unexpected, that I recognized that it came from the Spirit.

My breathing began to relax and slow down. I knew that, live or die, all was well with my soul. There is no peace more infinite than the deep awareness that I had that night—live or die, all *was* well with my soul.

The firemen were able to put out the fire before the acrid smoke became too dense. We did not get much sleep over the next hours, but at least we lived to tell the tale.

That night was a precious gift to me. I have remembered it over and over when fear has tried to grip my soul on other occasions. I have hungrily sought that same level of peace in many a subsequent crisis—because I learned that it is truly real and available, just a prayer away.

Making Choices Consistent with God's Gift of Peace

The finest and deepest peace that Christians can know is a *gift* (also described as a *fruit*) of the Spirit. We do not earn this gift. We cannot pay for it. It is freely received from God. It is supernatural, transcending the kind of peace we can create within our souls by positive thinking and stress management tools.

Having said that, God does expect *us* to do something at soul level before we can receive His peace. As we mentioned at the start of this book, we cannot be fretting, stewing, fussing, and expecting the worst—and then wonder why *God* is not bestowing His peace upon us. We cannot be entertaining fear, worry, and anxiety and expect that the Spirit will override the negative thoughts and feelings we are choosing to allow in our soul.

Of course, in many circumstances, we will initially feel fear, worry, and anxiety. These are normal human responses. But whatever the circumstances, we can try to rein in whatever thoughts are giving rise to these feelings. In that hotel room in Cairo, as fear began to grip me, I had to consciously start turning my thoughts to God—to His power, His love, and His ability to intervene in my circumstances. I had to choose to remember some Bible verses that helped to immediately calm and comfort me. I had to initiate the process of sitting still—getting my focus off of the fire trucks and the smoke—then concentrate on praying. My will had to get a grip on my mind, which in turn had to bring my feelings under control. *Then* my soul was ready for the Spirit to pour in His peace.

There are some wonderful verses that articulate this process. In Isaiah 26:3, the prophet said: "You will keep in perfect peace him whose *mind* is steadfast, because he trusts in you. (NIV)" Notice that *before* God does His part (keeping the person in perfect peace), the person has to *first* have a mind steadfastly focused on God and their trust in Him.

Philippians 4:6–7 describes the same process. Paul exhorts Christians to not be anxious about anything. Instead, Paul tells Christians to *pray* about everything, with thanksgiving. Being thankful before the prayer is even answered shows that the person has faith, trust, and hope that God will answer the prayer. *Then*, God bestows the peace that passes understanding. *Then* the Spirit guards the heart and mind of the person who is in Christ Jesus.

How can God's peace find room in a heart or mind that is overflowing with stress, worry, turmoil, anger, or negativity? The Holy Spirit is a gentleman. He does not crash down the doors of our hearts or minds and impose His presence. He waits to be invited by a *willing*, receptive heart and mind—in other words, where the person has exercised their will to sweep out (as best they can) any negative focus, fear, worry, panic, or the imagining of worst-case scenarios.

Peace With God

This whole process involves more than our reaction in the midst of sudden crisis. We make choices, with our free wills, every moment of every day of our lives. Whether we are cognizant of it or not, we have made some choices today that impact whether we are at peace with God, our fellow beings, and our own selves.

The most important of these three states is, of course, peace with God. Until we make the commitment to become a Christian, we are not at peace with God. In fact, we are enemies of God. If we are not at peace with God, then we cannot have deep enduring peace within. Isaiah 48:22 states: "...there is no peace, says the Lord, for the wicked."

Those who do not have right standing with God are destined to have inner turmoil in the depths of their soul. They may try to ignore it by drinking enough alcohol, taking mood-altering medications (legal or otherwise), working until they fall exhausted into bed, or keeping their mind steadily occupied with entertainment. But when they wake up in the middle of the night, alone in a quiet room, they risk coming face to face with that inner turmoil.

Jesus came to be the mediator between God and man so that there could be *peace with God.* Those who accept Jesus as the Son of God—confessing their sins as self-centered people who have rebelled from God's reign in their lives—can call God their Father. Paul affirmed this in Romans 5:1: "...since we have been made right in God's sight by faith in his promises, we can have *real peace* with him, because of what Jesus Christ our Lord has done for us."

I love Charles Finney's description of the peace he felt after he became a Christian. Finney was the 18th-century American lawyer who eventually spear-headed the great revival of Christian faith in his nation in that era. He wrestled intellectually for years regarding who God was, who Jesus was, and what it meant to become a Christian. He maintained an *unsettled mind* for a long time, and in that indecisive state, he felt restless and disturbed inside.

One day, in the woods alone, Finney struggled for hours in prayer. In a life-defining moment, he chose to believe that he was a sinner and that Jesus had died for him. He finally settled in his mind that Jesus was the Son of God. He committed his life to God. This is his description of how he felt leaving the woods that day: "I found that my mind had become most wonderfully quiet and peaceful....The repose of my mind was unspeakably great. I can never describe it in words. The thought of God was sweet to my mind, and the most profound spiritual tranquility had taken full possession of me."[216]

Famed singer Ethel Waters, who lived a turbulent and painful life, had an encounter with God at the age of eleven. She grew up with various relatives, amidst alcoholism, fighting, prostitution, and drugs. Not surprisingly, as a child she was angry at God, thinking He was not taking very good care of her.

One night, Ethel went up to the front of a church during a special children's service and experienced a great sensation of peace. It was the peace that had been eluding her up until that time. It was the peace she had been so desperately looking for.

---

[216] Bonnie Harvey quoting Finney, pgs. 38–39.

She knew that she had found God and that He was a Friend. She knew that she was no longer alone and would never be alone again, no matter what.[217]

Waters encountered further turbulence in her life, spiritually and otherwise, as the years passed, but she had tasted the magnificence of the transcending peace of God. Some years later she became a singer for the Billy Graham Crusade ministry and learned much more about resting her soul in the peace of God.

This deep inner peace can become richer as time passes. Peter advised: "Do you want *more and more* of God's kindness and peace? Then learn to know him better and better."[218]

We can maintain and increase our peace as we remain in fellowship with Him. Our peace will wax and wane, depending on our relationship with God. It does *not*, however, have to wax and wane with our changing circumstances.

We keep in right standing with God by daily acknowledging where we have slipped up. God wants nothing more than to be at peace with the men and women He has created—but the great prerequisite, on our parts, is to live in right relationship with God by maintaining a clear conscience. We can only have peace if we have unbroken fellowship with God, available if we remain ready to confess and turn from known sin in our lives.

If you have not entered into this peace with God, I invite you once again to turn to Appendix A at the end of this book. You can pray a simple prayer that will bring you into right relationship with God. He longs to grant you the peace that transcends understanding. It is not enough to have "religion." God wants intimate relationship. You might already have been religious for years, but have you entered into intimate personal relationship with God through His Son? Are you *settled in your mind* regarding this? Can you relate to the deep peace that Charles Finney described?

---

[217] Waters, pg. 54.
[218] 2 Peter 1:2.

Until we have true peace with God, we cannot hope to have lasting peace with our fellow human beings and within our own selves.

Peace with Our Fellow Human Beings

Solomon observed: "Fools start fights everywhere while wise men try to keep peace."[219]

Over and over, we are instructed in the Bible to do our best to live at peace with one another. In Psalm 34:14b David urged: "Try to live in peace with everyone; work hard at it." In 1 Thessalonians 5:13 Paul similarly exhorted Christians to live in peace with one another. In 2 Timothy 2:22 Paul further instructed Christians to *pursue* peace. Peter said "Try to live in peace even if you must *run after it* to *catch* and *hold* it."[220]

Notice the action verbs, the commands, the imperative instructions to *do* something. It is up to each one of us to *take steps* to live in harmony with our fellow human beings. God will not do this for us. The Spirit within will not compel us to do this against our wills. It is trite to say that we will not have peace within if we are living in outer discord, disharmony, strife, and conflict.

If we do seek peace with our fellow human beings, God then bestows His peace-giving Presence. Paul exhorted Christians to "live in peace." He then said: "And the God of love and peace will be with you."[221] Notice the order that this occurs in. First we do our part, then God does His.

Disharmony and conflict rob us of the well-being we could feel. Solomon so wisely said in Proverbs 17:1: "A dry crust eaten in peace is better than steak every day along with argument and strife."

Easier said than done—as a litigator for twenty years, I daily encountered the level of intense conflict that permeates modern society. I am thankful that the legal system has been placing an

---

[219] Proverbs 29:8.
[220] 1 Peter 3:11b, author's italics.
[221] 2 Corinthians 13:11bc (NIV).

increased emphasis on mediation and alternative dispute resolution. I was always keenly interested in being part of the peace-making process. Peace was never achieved, however, unless the parties to the dispute were willing to end the conflict.

At Peace with Ourselves

God wants us to have peace with ourselves. As we have mentioned in earlier chapters, God wants us to *love ourselves* and to *forgive ourselves*. He wants us to look in the mirror and see the face of a beloved friend. Once we have found peace with God and men, we can choose to silence self-criticism and stop all self-condemnation.

Peace in All Circumstances

God wants us to have inner peace *despite our circumstances*. Any of us can feel peaceful at the beach on a perfectly sunny day with our children beside us happily building sand castles. Anyone can feel peaceful in a soothing spa—with water trickling from a fountain, soft music playing, skilled hands massaging sore muscles, and aromatic scents filling the air. (Sadly, there are some people who cannot feel at peace even at the beach or in the spa!)

God wants us to have peace *in the storm...in the battle...in the night...in the hospital...in the valley of the shadow of death*. We are meant to have peace while still in the midst of trials, tribulations, problems, pain, and persecutions. Life is full of problems. Now that I am in my fifties, I have finally accepted the fact that, as soon as one problem is solved, a new problem surfaces. We are blessed if we have the chance to catch our breath in between problems. We should not wait until all of our problems are fixed before we seek peace within.

And so in all kinds of weather, we must watch our thoughts and feelings, lining them up with the kinds of thoughts and feelings the Bible teaches us to have. In Colossians 3:15, Paul said to let the peace of Christ *rule* in our hearts. So we must put off (get rid of, cast away, uproot, and reject) all the negative thoughts and emotions that interfere with peace in our hearts—anger, resentment, bitterness, hatred, unforgiveness, fear, anxiety, worry, despair, discouragement, depression, grumbling, discontentment, jealousy, and so on. These negative thoughts and feelings are the enemies of peace. Peace cannot dwell alongside any of these. Let's be ever vigilant as to what is ruling in our hearts and minds. We clean our kitchens after every meal. Why are we less vigilant with our souls? We can "clean house" in our minds and hearts a few times a day too.

Biblical Promises Regarding Peace

I invite you to spend some moments meditating on this sampling of God's numerous promises regarding peace:

> Great peace have they who love your law, and nothing can make them stumble. (Psalm 119:165 NIV)

> I have told you these things, so that in me you may have peace. In this world you will have trouble. But take heart! I have overcome the world. (John 16:33 NIV)

> ...Peace be with you! (John 20:19b NIV)

> ...the mind controlled by the Spirit is life and peace. (Romans 8:6 NIV)

> But when the Holy Spirit controls our lives he will produce this kind of fruit in us: love, joy, peace... (Galatians 5:22)

> May the Lord of peace himself give you his peace no matter what happens. (2 Thessalonians 3:16a)

> ...Grace and peace be yours in abundance. (1 Peter 1:2 NIV)

> But all who listen to me shall live in peace and safety, unafraid. (Proverbs 1:33)

> But all who humble themselves before the Lord shall be given every blessing, and shall have wonderful peace. (Psalm 37:11)

> May God our Father and the Lord Jesus Christ give you all his blessings, and great peace of heart and mind. (1 Corinthians 1:3)

One of my favorite Bible passages is found in the magnificent Psalm 23, where we are told that the Lord is our Shepherd and that He will lead us to green pastures and still waters to restore our souls. I sometimes ask God to place me in the midst of *actual* green pastures and still waters. God has faithfully done that for me on many occasions. In fact, I now live beside a beautiful golf course. My daily walk includes spending some moments on the stone terrace behind the clubhouse, overlooking a very green valley and a few serene ponds, with some lovely woods and colorful perennial gardens thrown in as extra blessings. (Because I live in Canada, my green pastures and still waters are sometimes white pastures and frozen waters, but they are nonetheless beautiful even on those days!)

God longs to bring us to green pastures and still waters— although there are times when the green pastures and still waters are not physical, geographical places, but calm places in our souls (no matter what rages around us).

David

David knew what it felt like to experience peace, even while enemies pursued him, even while in the heat of battle. No matter what was going on, David did not have a problem with insomnia. In Psalm 3:4–6, David wrote: "I cried out to the Lord, and he heard me...Then I lay down and slept in peace...for the Lord was watching over me. And now, although ten thousand enemies surround me on every side, I am not afraid." He continued this theme in Psalm 4:8: "I will lie down in peace and sleep, for though I am alone, O Lord, you will keep me safe." Thinking of these verses when I am too worried or anxious to sleep is better than taking a sleeping pill.

Rees Howells

During World War II, God granted His peace to those who sought Him in the midst of that storm. Rees Howells, famous for his intercessory prayer life, regularly gathered a group of over one hundred other intercessors at his college in Wales throughout the War. These were men of radical faith. During the years that the Nazis conquered and then dominated much of Europe, and in the years of the frightening air raids over the British Isles, these men persisted in passionate prayer.

They learned how to experience peace *in the battle*. Howells and his intercessors had deep peace and conviction that God would ultimately triumph in the War, that Hitler would not set foot in the British Isles, and that Hitler would be defeated. They maintained their peace even during the tough years when circumstances were not lining up with their faith.[222]

Lisa Beamer

As events unfolded on 9/11, Lisa was concerned about her husband Todd, who had left on a United Airlines flight to San Francisco earlier that morning. When she first starting watching television that morning, she did not know that her husband was already dead. When she eventually saw the charred remains of his United Airlines plane on the news, she withdrew to her bedroom. Although the horror of it all began to hit her, Lisa knew that God was with her. In that very bleak hour, she reached out to God. Despite the terrible images she had just seen, God began to give her a very real inner peace and an assurance that she and her little children (one still unborn) were going to make it through that day—and the days to come. Of course, she was also feeling an immediate sense of heart-wrenching loss and grief, but God's peace was there to help her carry on that day.[223]

When a United Airlines representative later called to confirm that her husband had in fact died on the flight that had crashed in Pennsylvania, Lisa was able to remain calm. Even the confirmation and the certainty of his death could not destroy her God-given peace.[224]

---

[222] Norman Grubb, *Rees Howells Intercessor*.

[223] Beamer, pgs. 10–11.

[224] Beamer, pg. 166.

Lisa visited the crash site with the families of other passengers who had died. She struggled with many emotions. But God's peace continued to help her through it. At one point, she looked upward and noticed a hawk gliding and soaring in the sky above the crash site. At that moment, she felt another clear sense of the peace that passes understanding washing over her. The soaring hawk reminded her to focus on the words of Isaiah 40:30–31—words that promise that those who wait upon the Lord will renew their strength and mount up on wings as eagles.[225]

In the months following 9/11, as Lisa cared for her two young children and gave birth to a third, she still had peace within that defied human explanation.[226]

Horatio Spafford

Horatio Spafford, a Chicago lawyer, saw his real estate investments plummet in value when the great Chicago fire of 1871 burned down a large section of the city. The significant losses did not affect his faith in God. Instead, he was grateful that all of his family survived the devastating fire.

Two years later, Spafford decided to take his family on a trip overseas. Because of business obligations that held Spafford up, his wife and four daughters boarded the ship without him. He intended to catch up with them later.

On November 22, 1873, the vessel carrying the Spafford women was hit by another ship at sea. It sank quickly and all four of the Spafford daughters drowned. Only Mrs. Spafford survived.

Horatio Spafford crossed the ocean on the next ship. Summoning every ounce of courage he had, he allowed his ship's captain to show him the very place where all his daughters had died at sea. Many people would have been too overwhelmed with anger at God, bitterness, self-pity, or despair to look at the

---

[225] Beamer, pg. 232.
[226] Beamer, pg. 310.

cruel waves. In stark contrast, it was on that *very voyage* that Spafford penned the famous words of an enduring hymn:

> *When peace like a river attendeth my way*
> *When sorrows like sea billows roll*
> *Whatever my lot, Thou hast taught me to say,*
> *"It is well, it is well, with my soul."*[227]

Above the Storm

Recently I heard a televangelist quoting Spafford's hymn. The pastor went on to give the following illustration of how *we* can have peace in the midst of the storm. He talked about a plane taking off during stormy weather and passing through the turbulence of thick grey clouds. He said that it is difficult to be at peace in the midst of the storm. The plane always rises above the storm, however, emerging into blue skies and sunshine. He said that if we are not experiencing peace *in* the storm, we need to go up higher, to rise above it, where the sun is still shining. The storm still exists but we can spiritually rise *above* its turbulence. All is peaceful *above* the storm.[228]

My Own Flight above the Storm

Before I heard that particular sermon, I had my own experience with that kind of peace, that kind of rising up *above* the storm. I shared, in the last chapter, about my husband's unexpected open heart surgery to remove an aneurysm located perilously just above his heart. We were both stunned to receive the news of his life-threatening medical condition and his urgent need for serious surgery. I have already shared how we both naturally faced an immediate battle with fear, worry, and anxiety.

---

[227] Horatio Spafford, "It is Well with My Soul," (1873, Public Domain).

[228] My paraphrase of an illustration from the sermon of Joel Osteen, broadcast on or about April 9, 2006.

Almost from the outset, however, God spoke to me through the same verses from Isaiah 40:30–31 that had comforted Lisa Beamer at the scene of her husband's plane crash. God also told me that I could rise up, as if on eagle's wings, *above the storm.*

God kept bringing these same comforting verses across my path—through the cards, calls, and spoken prayers of friends. I knew that God was giving me a very personal message. So I began, in my mind and in my own prayers, to imagine myself soaring up in the sky and looking down at our lives and our problem. Sam's need for surgery did not go away, notwithstanding our fervent prayers for healing. But somehow God generally kept my spirit *above the storm*, above the constant temptation to fear and to worry. This was especially remarkable because, as I have also shared earlier, I am prone to worry and anxiety over much smaller matters.

If you are going through a raging storm right now, I encourage you to meditate on Isaiah 40:30–31. This image of eagle's wings comes from another part of Scripture, in addition to Isaiah 40. In Exodus 19:4, Moses described how God had led His people out of Egypt "on eagle's wings."

Rise up *above* your storm, and be assured that it *will* pass. Don't stay in the turbulence of the clouds. We cannot control all of our physical circumstances, but in our spirits, we *can* choose to fly above the clouds. It does not matter if you imagine yourself as an eagle or as a passenger in a plane—just steadfastly maintain the image of rising above the storm, into the sunnier skies above.

Clinical Comments from Dr. Sam

When we choose peace, and consequently receive the transcendent peace of God, we are blessed in many ways. Dr. Sam confirms that our health is, in fact, positively impacted—physically, mentally, and emotionally. Being quietened and peaceful within helps to turn off the flow of all the powerful hormones and biochemicals that are secreted into the bloodstream in response to the stress of emotions such as fear or anger. As a result, we are more likely to sleep better and to eat normally. Our blood pressure lowers. Our muscles relax. Our digestive system and our immune system function better. We have more energy. Our mind focuses more clearly. Our outlook improves. We enjoy our lives more.

Long before medical science confirmed this, Solomon wrote in Proverbs 14:30a: "A peaceful heart leads to a healthy body. (NLT)"

The Challenge

So let's choose to be at peace with God, with others, and with our own selves. Let's decide to *rise up* above the storms of life to that place where the skies are blue and the sun is shining even while the storm still rages *below*.

Even in a burning building, wondering if eternity is just moments away, we can be in remarkable peace.

Following after the Holy Spirit leads to life and peace...
Romans 8:6

...God wants his children to live in peace and harmony.
1 Corinthians 7:15b

Let the peace of God rule in your hearts.
Colossians 3:15 (NKJV)

15
DISCOURAGEMENT
AND
DESPAIR
Wave Upon Wave

...your forces come against me wave upon wave.
Job 10:17 (NIV)

...all your waves and breakers have swept over me.
Psalm 42:7 (NIV)

I N EARLY 1999, wave upon wave of discouragement crashed over me. Just as soon as I would get my head above the rough waters of one circumstance, a fresh crisis would knock me back underwater.

It began with the Sunday afternoon that I returned home to find an urgent message on our answering machine. I soon learned that a close family member had suffered a massive heart attack in another city. I took the first flight there.

Back at home again, days later, I continued preparation for a complex trial. Over the following month, as I raced against time to get ready for trial, a series of strange events occurred in my home.

One morning my husband and I awoke, in the midst of the Canadian deep freeze of winter, to discover one of our front windows had been broken. My neighbor phoned to say hers had been broken too. It was obviously an act of vandalism. With sub-zero air rudely invading our home, I scrambled to find someone who could replace the window as soon as possible.

That same week, one of the glass walls of our shower cracked and also had to be replaced. Then our brand new dishwasher stopped working. A service technician was literally in our home, fixing the broken dishwasher, when our washing machine started leaking water all over the laundry room floor. The washing machine was no sooner fixed than the garage-door-opener went on the fritz *and* the roof started leaking.

As the repair people kept coming in and out of our home, I tried to press on with the trial preparation. Around that same time, my daughter developed sinusitis, and then I came down with a nasty cold. Day after day, I struggled to get my work done. Night after night, I sat on the couch, hand-sewing hundreds of sequins on my daughter's skating costume, barely having the strength to lift needle and thread.

In the midst of all this, there were snowstorms and icestorms, computer problems, and a very contentious meeting between parents and administrators at the school our children attended. How much I related to David and Job, who both talked about being submerged under wave upon wave.

And then came another huge blow. Another close family member went through a difficult hospital stay for eleven days.

All of these waves crashed relentlessly over my head, leaving in their wake much discouragement and despair. In those few months of my life, I learned deeper lessons about how we must make a daily (sometimes hourly!) choice between faith and fear, hope and despair, giving up or pressing on. Day after day, I prayed as often as I could and saturated myself with encouraging Bible verses. I found shoulders to cry on, sympathetic ears, and neighbors and colleagues who could help on both the home front and the work front. I tried to take care of my own physical health.

Every time I thought I could not rise above a fresh wave of discouragement, I somehow found the strength to carry on. As time passed, I was quite frankly amazed at the stamina God poured into me—and at the resources He provided to help me through this season of crisis. The discouragement and despair were enormous—but God was bigger.

A World in Despair

Our modern world is full of discouragement and despair. In fact, the prevailing worldview of many is that of intellectual despair.

For a few years, in my late teens, I was fascinated by many of the world's great secular philosophers who lived in recent centuries. I began to realize that most of them shared one thing in common—despair! Their philosophies were not based on hope. They were based on the premise that there is no absolute truth and no ultimate meaning to life. Most of them also concluded there is no God and that life is random, the product of pure chance. Because they believed that divine design, divine help, and divine destiny are non-existent, they concluded that humankind is left to struggle *all on its own* in a world full of pain, conflict, confusion, uncertainty, disease, and death. How depressing!

Many of the authors, poets, and artists I studied were just as gloomy. I read Hemingway, Fitzgerald, Woolf, Plath, and others. I discovered that Hemingway took his own life. Virginia Woolf stuffed her pockets with heavy rocks, walked into the river near her home, and deliberately drowned. Sylvia Plath stuck her head into a gas oven. Van Gogh cut part of his own ear off before he also committed suicide. Fitzgerald drank heavily to escape his despair and his wife ended up institutionalized after she lost her sanity.

I began to notice how many of the modern philosophies, novels, paintings, and poems were affecting me. I wrote my own poems and short stories full of despair. One poem ended with the line: "Afraid of the day I pull the trigger, creating my own small black dot of a period." How thankful I am that I became a Christian not long after this immersion into despondent art, philosophies, and worldviews.

Many in our modern world have adopted these worldviews of despair. In an address to Harvard graduates, actor and film-maker Woody Allen spoke out of such a secular worldview. He talked about mankind facing a crossroads. On the one hand, there is a path that leads to despair and complete hopelessness.

The other path leads to total extinction. What a choice! Allen shared his conviction that human existence is totally meaningless.[229] Ironically, Woody Allen is considered one of the great modern comedians.

Every day the media inform us of the breaking news—of wars, murders, suicides, rapes, riots, robberies, accidents, fires, floods, famines, earthquakes, bankruptcies, moral failures, celebrity divorces, government corruption, and the latest cancer statistics. No wonder too many people struggle to simply get out of bed in the morning.

A few years ago, I read an article about Christine Onassis. As the only surviving heir of shipbuilding tycoon Aristotle Onassis, she inherited *billions* of dollars. She could buy anything in the world. She could live in luxury and never have to work a day of her life. Yet she lived a life of despair and hopelessness, eventually overdosing on barbiturates and amphetamines at the young age of thirty-eight.

Even Mother Teresa, working for five decades with the poor of Calcutta, was well acquainted with despair. Letters kept in Jesuit archives until after her death reveal that she sometimes struggled with loneliness, angst, despair, and a sense of inner darkness.[230]

Despair. All around us. Sometimes within us.

The Destructive Effects of Discouragement and Despair

Discouragement and despair affect us spiritually. Hannah Whitall Smith once wisely wrote: "Sin makes an easy prey of a discouraged soul."[231]

Discouragement and despair affect the rest of our emotions. If we don't learn how to keep afloat when the waves of despair wash over us, we will perhaps find ourselves battling further

---

[229] Monroe, pg. 66, from *My Speech to the Graduates* by Woody Allen.

[230] David Van Biema article, TIME magazine, (Canadian edition), September 3, 2007.

[231] Smith, supra, pg. 113.

dark emotions such as anger, bitterness, self-pity, jealousy, and discontentment. In the next chapter, we will study the particularly distressing progression of despair into depression.

Discouragement and despair will compromise our physical health too. Dr. Sam advises that these emotions are associated with fatigue and lethargy. In a discouraged state, perhaps we will sleep too much. We will then have trouble falling asleep or staying asleep on future nights. We might eat too little or too much. We will not likely feel in the mood for exercise or for socializing. Imagine what all this does to the heart, lungs, muscles, brain, and digestive system. Proverbs 17:22 advises: "A cheerful heart does good like medicine, but a broken spirit makes one sick."

It is worth making whatever efforts we can to stay afloat in discouraging periods of our lives: prayerfully asking for God's help, meditating on God's word (especially searching for encouraging verses), talking to sympathetic listeners, maintaining good health habits, and staying engaged in positive activities—even if we don't feel like doing any of these things.

David

David understood what it felt like to be submerged under wave upon wave of difficulties and to almost drown in discouragement and despair. David had been anointed by Samuel, while still a teenage shepherd, to be the next King of Israel. More than a dozen years passed, however, between his anointing by Samuel and his actual possession of the throne. He went through *years* of fleeing from the jealous and murderous wrath of King Saul. He hid in caves, camped out in the wilderness, and even chose to live for a while in the enemy camp of the Philistines.

David wrote many psalms recording his discouragement and despair. In Psalm 42:7, he moaned to God: "...all your waves and breakers have swept over me..."(NIV). David groaned about being weary, worn, alone, distressed, weighed down—spiritually, mentally, emotionally, and physically.

David sometimes mustered the strength, however feeble, to cry out to God—to seek His help, to seek hope. In Psalm 40:2–3a David wrote: "He lifted me out of the pit of despair, out from the bog and the mire...He has given me a new song to sing..."

Job

Of course we have to mention Job in this chapter! God allowed Job to lose pretty much everything in this world that he valued. Understandably, after these grievous losses Job sat miserably in the dust, weighed down by profound discouragement and despair.

Job moaned to God: "...I am utterly helpless, *without any hope*....My life drags by—day after hopeless day....I am weary of living."[232] Have you ever felt this low?

Yet Job, like David, did not give up on God. He kept in dialogue with Him. He chose, in the worst of his circumstances, to say that *though* God was slaying him, *yet* would he trust in Him. Of course you remember the end of the story—as Job struggled to rise above his despair, God delivered him out of the wretched waves.

Paul

Paul also struggled with discouragement and despair while he suffered hunger, thirst, beatings, imprisonment, threats to his life, and sickness. After a shipwreck, he had to swim through literal wave upon wave in a stormy sea. (We should be thankful that, however rough our circumstances, we are not usually battling *actual* waves crashing over our heads like Paul!)

On one occasion, Paul wrote: "We were under great pressure, far beyond our ability to endure, so that we despaired even of life."[233] Paul was so discouraged he thought that he was going to die.

---

[232] Job 6:13; 7:6; 10:1a.
[233] 2 Corinthians 1:8b (NIV).

Yet, just a few sentences later (1:10b, NIV), Paul was able to write: "On him we have set our hope..." Paul refused to be defeated by the waves of discouragement and despair. To the very end, though buffeted and battered by many stormy waves, Paul never abandoned his hope.

More Stories

I noted, as I read dozens of biographies while writing this book, that most Christians encounter seasons of deep discouragement and despair, when "wave upon wave" crashes over them, submerging them in heavy discouragement and despair. Here are just a few examples.

Charles Spurgeon

One of the lowest points in Spurgeon's life occurred while he was still in his early twenties. He was already a well-known Christian preacher. One night in London, about 12,000 people packed a music hall to hear him speak. A further 10,000 waited outside, unable to get in.

During the evening, a foolish mischief-maker yelled "Fire" and mass panic ensued. As people tried to stampede out the doors, seven people died and a few dozen more were seriously injured. Spurgeon wept for a week. He had trouble sleeping. He entered a season of feeling intense discouragement and despair.

Like David and Job, however, he eventually chose to fight his despair by occupying himself again with his ministry and his relationship with God.

John Bunyan

John Bunyan was in and out of British prisons because of his faith. He used his personal encounters with *dis*couragement and despair to *en*courage many. By seeking to encourage others, he encouraged himself.

In Bunyan's much loved book, *The Pilgrim's Progress*, the main character Pilgrim encountered a Giant named "Despair" and the "Slough of Despond." The Slough of Despond was a deep, muddy pit. Pilgrim sat in the dark pit until someone reached in to pull him out.

We can only imagine the dark pit that Bunyan himself must have been in as he sat in various miserable prison cells a few centuries ago. How awesome that, in those surroundings, he could write a great work—a book that would bless millions of readers encountering discouragement and despair on their own Christian journeys—a book that could reach into dark pits to pull others out of their despair.

Various Missionaries

If you read the biographies of missionaries such as William Carey and David Livingstone, you will note that they, too, went through seasons of discouragement. As they labored in India and Africa, respectively, their spirits hit lows as a result of illness, marriage issues, financial pressures, stressful living conditions, spiritual malaise, and lack of fellowship. For some time, Carey lived in a malarial swamp. Livingstone and his family had to sometimes survive on caterpillars and locusts. Their mission efforts often seemed futile.

As they struggled to overcome their despair, they resolutely trusted God and pressed on in their relationships with Him. God reached down to help them out of their "Sloughs of Despond." Carey stayed in India for four decades, publishing the Bible in forty-four languages and dialects and establishing a number of mission stations, among other amazing accomplishments there. Livingstone became one of the most famous explorers who helped to map the continent of Africa. Although both men clearly *struggled* with discouragement, they did not allow it to *overwhelm* or *defeat* them.

Charles Colson

Charles Colson was inside President Richard Nixon's inner circle when the Watergate scandal broke. Later indicted for his role in various misdeeds of the Nixon administration, Colson served time in prison. His book, *Born Again*, chronicles many of the times he felt himself slip into despair during those difficult years.

In the days after being indicted, for example, Colson understandably felt a deep despair. Although he was a fairly new Christian (having become one after the Watergate waves crashed over him), he knew enough to turn to God in the midst of his darkness. Although he dreaded what lay ahead at that time, he chose to keep focused on God. As a result, on some days, he could go to his office with a surprising measure of serenity.

Later, while in prison, despair continued to drag him down from time to time. He learned *this* about darkness and light in the Christian life: the greater the darkness of the world around us, the more desperate our circumstances, the more light God gives us, and the more we can appreciate the empowerment of the Holy Spirit.

Sometimes the collective despair of others around him pulled Colson's spirit down. He especially noticed this after he was transferred to a federal prison in Alabama. Instead of succumbing to the pervasive despair, however, Colson ultimately chose to rise above it by starting a prison ministry. He decided to reach out to his fellow prisoners with the love, forgiveness, compassion, and mercy of Christ that he himself had so recently come to know. The light of Christ lit up the darkness for Colson and many others. Colson's personal choice to embrace hope, joy, singing, laughter, fellowship, and friendship changed the atmosphere around Colson.

His prison ministry has continued over the past few decades, reaching into many prisons in America and beyond.[234] I am

---

[234] Charles Colson, *Born Again*.

deeply impressed with what I hear about the work of this prison ministry in my own country, Canada.

Selling Our First Home

Permit me to share another stressful wave-upon-wave season of my life. Sam and I had a lot of difficulty selling our very first home in the late 1980's. During that same time period, a number of other discouraging events occurred. A beloved nanny quit on short notice. My grandfather died. On the day of his funeral, I received the news that I had basal cell carcinoma on my neck. (Fortunately, this is one of the least serious skin cancers and was completely treatable because it was caught early.)

Trying to sell our first home was especially difficult because our children were toddlers—it was tough to keep the house continuously clean. Unfortunately, most prospective purchasers dropped by on short notice.

I remember one occasion when the purchaser's agent did not even call in advance at all. It was early evening and I was already in my oldest, most comfortable (but frumpiest) bathrobe. I sheepishly answered the doorbell to find the real estate agent with an immaculately-dressed professional couple.

The house was a mess! The sink was piled high with dirty dinner dishes. Beds were not made. The couple walked into the kitchen and found my daughter, in her high chair, with a bowl of spaghetti tipped upside down on her head. Samantha thought that was funny! It was a scene that is only supposed to happen in movies. Not surprisingly, those potential purchasers did not even bother asking to see the second floor of our home.

On another day soon after, we did receive ten minutes warning that more potential purchasers wanted to come through our home. Our three-year-old son was trying to help quickly clean up. Darrin came running around the corner, his arms full of toys, with an angelic smile on his face. I had just washed the kitchen floor but did not have time to warn Darrin. He slipped on the wet floor, then fell on his back and started to cry, surrounded by the scattered toys. I slumped down beside him, gathered him in my arms, and started to cry too! I could not stop. We had a good cry together. I felt at the very end of my rope. When the potential purchasers arrived, the toys were still strewn about, but at least the floor was dry. I had reached my darkest hour in this house-selling nightmare. All I could do was cry out to God.

Just when I thought I could not bear another wave of discouragement, Sam and I found out that those very two people were offering to buy our home. By God's mercy, the tide began to turn. A much brighter season of life began that very day. Thankfully, our house sale closed soon after without a single problem and we happily moved into our second home.

Selling Our Second Home

Fifteen years later, I found myself struggling with despair *again* because we had even worse trouble trying to sell our second home. This second home had already been on the market for many months when we had to pay the full purchase price of our present home. As described earlier, we were then carrying the expenses of two homes for several more months.

I had to keep visiting the old home to vacuum, dust, tend the yard, and rotate the lights we were leaving on for security. During a major snowstorm, a tree toppled over. One day (also in the midst of the Canadian deep freeze of winter), we discovered our furnace had stopped working in the vacant home.

And then we sold our home—only to find out, about a week later, that this initial purchaser's financing had fallen through. The house went back on the market. This was a crushing disappointment. I found myself sinking deeper beneath the familiar waves of discouragement.

One of the ways I battled to keep my head above water was to read encouraging Scriptures and uplifting Christian books. One author urged me to simply make the decision to put a spring back in my step—to just *get on* with my life despite my problem. He made me realize that my life was bigger than this unsold home. I had other blessings, opportunities, and challenges to focus on. And so, I *resolved* that I *was* going to put a spring back in my step.

So, with what little strength I had, I started to rigorously reject discouraging thoughts every time they entered my mind. I knew that it could take further months to sell our home (especially in the middle of winter), but I *determined* that I was not going to waste those months. In fact, it was during those very months that I wrote most of my first book. Like Bunyan, I chose to shake off my own discouragement by putting my best energies into trying to encourage others in their Christian faith.

It did, in fact, take further months before our second home sold. I'm glad I decided to change my outlook long before our house sold. Those interim months were far happier and more productive than they would have been if I had allowed myself to get stuck in discouragement.

God's Command: Do Not Be Discouraged!

Throughout the Bible, God's voice tells us *not* to be discouraged, dismayed, or in despair. These emotions will wash over us, but we can choose to rise above them.

For example, after God promised to take the Israelites from Egypt to their Promised Land, they were told: "Do *not* be afraid. Do *not* be discouraged." Through Joshua, God re-affirmed this same message: "Have I not commanded you? Be strong and courageous. Do not be terrified; *do not be discouraged*, for the Lord your God will be with you wherever you go."[235]

God's Helping Hand

We all encounter times when it is not that easy to stay above the waves in our *own* strength. When we are feeling waves of despair and discouragement, we often do not have the strength to deal

---

[235] Deuteronomy 1:21c (NIV); Joshua 1:9; (NIV).

with our dark thoughts and emotions. We feel too weary, too down, too overwhelmed, and too weak. That is how I had felt the day my son and I cried together on the wet kitchen floor.

When Pilgrim was in the Slough of Despond, that is how he felt. On his own, he could not have climbed out of the pit. Thankfully, Help came along (a symbol of the Holy Spirit). Help reached down a hand. Help pulled him out.

If we turn to Him, God promises that He will bestow on us "a garment of praise instead of a spirit of despair."[236] God graciously does this when He knows that we do not have the strength to rise above our despair all on our own.

Psalm 34:18 tells us that "the Lord is *close* to the broken-hearted and saves those who are crushed in spirit." (NIV)

Isaiah 42:3b promises: "He will *encourage* the faint-hearted, those tempted to despair." Isaiah 42:7 further assures us that He will "release" those who sit in the "prison" of "darkness and despair."

Paul later echoed this in 2 Corinthians 7:6 when he referred to how he and his companions were "refreshed" by their fellow Christian Titus and the "God who cheers those who are discouraged." If you are weary and worn with your discouragement and despair, choose to *look up*. Help *is* on the way.

Sometimes it is God Himself who comes to personally offer His strong hand. Other times, He sends one of our fellow human beings. At the end of World War II, the German people were in despair. They had been defeated. Many of their homes had been damaged or destroyed. Many had lost loved ones. Some soldiers came home alive, but they were injured, scarred, or disabled. The German people began to hear the grisly details, and the scope and gravity, of the Nazi's horrendous crimes against the Jewish people. Waves of defeat, discouragement, disillusionment, and despair washed over post-war Germany.

We have talked earlier about Corrie ten Boom, who was unjustly imprisoned during the war in a German concentration

---

[236] Isaiah 61:3a (NIV).

camp. Can you believe that, after the war, God sent *Corrie* to help the German people? Obediently, she went to help the very nation that had brought so much pain, suffering, and tragedy to her own family during the war. God had given Corrie hope during her war-time season of despair. Now He wanted Corrie to give the German people hope too.

Corrie was given permission to take over a former German concentration camp. She fixed it up and made it a more hospitable, cheerful place. It became a shelter for 160 displaced German refugees. She wanted it to be a place where people could find life again.[237]

Be Encouraged

God is willing to help anyone who cries out for His help in the stormy waves of life. Whoever you are and whatever your circumstances, God will extend His helping hand to you if you make the choice to cry out to Him. When you have done whatever you can in your difficult circumstances, God is ready to carry you in His arms for a while. Despair may drag us down for a season, and it may threaten to engulf us, but with God on our side it will not swallow us up.

The Lord lifts the fallen and those bent beneath their loads.
Psalm 145:14

And let us not get tired of doing what is right,
for after a while we will reap a harvest of blessing
if we don't get discouraged and give up.
Galatians 6:9

---

[237] Corrie ten Boom, *Tramp for the Lord*, pg. 47.

16
DEPRESSION
Tsunami Waves

...I am saying to the prisoners of darkness,
"Come out! I am giving you your freedom!"
Isaiah 49:9a

A CCORDING TO RECENT World Health Organization statistics, depression affects more than 120 million individuals around the globe. By 2020, WHO predicts that depression will be the second greatest disability affecting people worldwide.[238] Medical professionals often describe it as the "common cold" of mental and emotional health.

About twenty million Americans are affected by clinical depression each year; some estimate that the *real* number of sufferers per year is closer to fifty million. In 2005, there were almost 150 million prescriptions in the U.S. for antidepressants like Prozac, Zoloft, and Paxil, making this the second most frequently prescribed class of medication. In 2006, almost half a million Americans were treated in emergency rooms for self-inflicted injuries and more than 30,000 committed suicide.[239]

An Ipsos Reid poll, surveying over 4,000 Canadian employees in November 2007, found that one in four working Canadians suffers from depression, with 18% having been formally diagnosed.[240] Recent Canadian studies further show that depression is the second most prevalent reason for patients to visit their family doctor.[241]

---

[238] Brooke Smith article, pg. 38.
[239] Statistics from the website of the Centers for Disease Control and Prevention (2006).
[240] Gordon article.
[241] Smith, pg. 38.

Dr. Armand Nicholi, who has been an associate clinical professor of psychiatry at Harvard Medical School and an editor and co-author of *The Harvard Guide to Psychiatry*, has written about the alarming increase of serious depression in modern society. Dr. Nicholi has noted an epidemic of suicides among depressed children and adolescents.[242] One out of every ten teenagers suffers from depression.

Dr. Nicholi has blamed some of these statistics on the secular roots of despair I discussed in the last chapter. Many people are rejecting spiritual resources.[243] Instead, they are embracing secular philosophies, worldviews, and artistic expressions that are full of hopelessness.

Books promoting atheism are making bestseller lists in Western countries. With the prevailing philosophies of many leading intellectuals being anti-God, it is no surprise that there is so much hopelessness and depression in secular society.

Unfortunately, depression is all too common amongst Christians too. Ann Graham Lotz has noted that counselors of all types have been dealing with a tidal wave of depression these days, even within the church.[244] Over the years, my husband, Sam, has treated many Christian patients suffering from depression. Christian churches can no longer sweep the epidemic of depression under the rug—it touches too many in their own pews.

All of us will likely experience at least a mild form of transient depression at some point in our lifetimes.[245] I have had my share of mornings when I really did not want to get out of bed and on with my day. Although I have never experienced prolonged or severe depression, I have certainly known days full of weariness and heaviness.

---

[242] Monroe (ed.), *Finding God at Harvard*, pg. 112.

[243] Ibid. pgs. 112–113.

[244] Ann Graham Lotz, *The Vision of His Glory*, (U.S.: W Publishing Group, 1996).

[245] Dr. Dobbins, pg. 145.

The High Cost of Depression

Depression can leave much destruction in its wake. According to Dr. Sam, long bouts of depression can make people more susceptible to physical illness. A 2007 study by the World Health Organization found that depression produces the greatest negative impact on health compared to chronic diseases such as angina, arthritis, asthma, and diabetes.[246] Chronic depression is linked to increased risk of heart disease, cancer, osteoporosis, asthma, and arthritis.[247] Without treatment, depression has the tendency to become either chronic or recurrent and to result in increasing disability.[248]

People suffering from ongoing depression often do not eat enough *or* they overeat for emotional pain relief. Some with chronic depression sleep poorly, while others cannot get out of bed. They are usually not very active, paralyzed by the inertia, lack of motivation, fatigue, and indecisiveness caused by their depression. They are at a higher risk for substance abuse and addictions. These harmful behaviors negatively impact their cardiovascular, immunological, and endocrinological systems.[249]

Depression also hurts relationships. It reduces the quality and enjoyment of life. Depression costs the economy billions of dollars in treatment and in lost productivity.

Perhaps most tragically, depression often undermines a person's relationship with God because depressed people sometimes lack the emotional and physical energy to pray, read their Bible, or attend church.

Biblical Examples of Depression

There is no shame in experiencing depression (although, sadly, the disease of depression is often accompanied by irrational thoughts

---

[246] See article by Moussavi et al.
[247] See articles by: Rozanski and Kubzansky; Kiecolt-Glaser et al.
[248] See article by Moussavi et al.
[249] See article by Kiecolt-Glaser et al.

of guilt and shame). Suffering from depression does not make a person less saved, less spiritual, or less worthy. Some of the most loved Bible characters experienced significant depression.

Jacob

After he was told that his young son Joseph was dead, Jacob experienced depression. He wept and wept. He grieved and grieved. He tore his garments and put on sackcloth. Refusing to be comforted, he said he would die in mourning.[250]

Even *years* later, when his sons came to tell him that Joseph was in fact alive, Jacob's heart was "like a stone."[251] He was so emotionally numb that he could not take in the news at first. Do you relate to a heart that feels *that* heavy and *that* lifeless?

David

David sometimes felt submerged in the rough waters of depression. In Psalm 42:6, for example, David complained that he was "depressed and gloomy." In Psalm 6:2–3, he moaned: "Pity me, O Lord, for I am weak. Heal me, for my body is sick, and I am upset and disturbed. My mind is filled with apprehension and with gloom. Oh, restore me soon."

In Psalm 69:1–2 David cried out: "Save me, O God, for the floodwaters are up to my neck. Deeper and deeper I sink into the mire; I can't find a foothold. I am in deep water, and the floods overwhelm me."(NLT)

In fact, almost fifty Psalms deal with depression. Most of them were written by David.

Job

Like David, Job did not just experience discouragement and despair. With each successive blow, Job became more and more

---

[250] Genesis 37:34–35.
[251] From Genesis 45:26c.

depressed. At one point, Job said: "My heart is broken. Depression haunts my days...I waited for the light. Darkness came. My heart is troubled and restless. Waves of affliction have come upon me."[252] There were times when Job wished that he had never been born and times when he wished he was already dead.

Elijah

Although Elijah was a powerful and authoritative man of God on most occasions, at one point he was severely depressed. As he lived alone in hiding from his enemies, the world looked so dark to him that he was sure he was the only man left on the face of the earth who still believed in God. He sank so low that at one point he asked God to let him die.[253]

In Further Good Company

A number of well-known Christians have suffered from significant depression in various seasons of their lives.

Martin Luther, father of the Protestant Reformation, experienced an unhappy childhood, partly because of a very rigid, strict, religious upbringing. Although he later enjoyed family life as a married man and also enjoyed socializing with his students, Luther battled bouts of depression and low self-esteem throughout his adult life.

John Newton, who would later write the beloved hymn, *Amazing Grace,* had at one point seriously considered suicide. He was a young sailor at the time, living a life of sinful excess. He reasoned that suicide "would put a period to all my sorrows at once," but fortunately, he would later say the "secret hand of God restrained me."[254]

Hudson Taylor, who started the China Inland Mission and placed hundreds of other missionaries in China during his

---

252 Job 30:16; 26cd–27.
253 1 Kings 19:3–4, 10c, 14c.
254 John Newton. *John Newton: His Autobiography,* pg. 36.

lifetime, also once contemplated suicide while in the throes of deep depression.

William and Catherine Booth, the couple who started the Salvation Army, struggled with periods of depression. William called it "a dark column" marching within. Catherine said that a dark "horror" seemed to come over her from time to time.[255]

C. S. Lewis married late in life to Joy, a woman he loved deeply. Joy died tragically early in their marriage. Understandably, Lewis went through a long period of depression after her death.

Common Roots of Depression

Depression has many possible roots: emotional, familial, circumstantial, physical (hormonal or biochemical), and spiritual. Understanding the main root cause of the depression is helpful in bringing it under control.

(a) Buried Emotions

According to Dr. Sam, people who allow negative emotions to fester for a long period of time will increase their risk of developing clinical depression. Anger, bitterness, hatred, unforgiveness, anxiety, fear, despair, jealousy, and discontentment will all potentially breed depression if they persist over months or years.

Dr. Helen Roseveare, a medical missionary to the Congo who battled depression, sometimes also struggled with anger, bitterness, fear, and doubt. Whenever Dr. Roseveare deliberately dealt with those latter emotions, she felt her depression lift. She grew in her understanding of the correlation between her depression and those other troublesome emotions.[256] If you suffer with depression, it is worth asking yourself whether you have unresolved anger, resentment, unforgiveness, worries, or areas of discontentment in your life.

---

[255] Petersen, quoting the Booth's own words on pgs. 80 and 84.
[256] Dr. Helen Roseveare, especially pgs. 54, 108–109, 112–113.

(b) Rejection

Depression can also develop out of the unresolved emotional pain of rejection. Jesus understood rejection. Imagine how He felt on the Cross. For a period of time, He even felt rejected by God the Father.[257] Every day God faces being rejected by billions of people in this present world.

For Christians, the good news is this: even if all others reject us, God will never reject a person who seeks after Him. Psalm 27:10, for example, assures us that even if our own mother and father reject us, God will never forsake us. God, who is full of empathy and compassion, wants to heal our feelings of rejection.

(c) Family History

Depression tends to show up in successive generations of a family. Adding to the possible genetic predisposition to depression, children intuitively learn emotional patterns from depressed parents.

(d) Situational Depression

Depression is often a response to circumstances that are emotionally overwhelming, such as divorce, serious illness, hospitalization, death of a loved one, loss of a job, financial setbacks, abuse, and virtually any other kind of difficult situation. Mental health professionals call this *situational* depression.

This kind of depression tends to lift once the circumstances improve. Circumstances do not always improve overnight, however, so the feelings of depression often need to be addressed in the midst of the difficult situation. If the depression is not dealt with, it just becomes worse if the difficult situation drags on and chronic stress ensues.

---

[257] See Isaiah 53 and Matthew 27:46.

(e) Low Self-Esteem

Depression can originate with chronic low self-esteem, which can have its own origins in myriad places: in rejection; unresolved guilt; the repeated negative messages of parents, friends, teachers, or others in a position of influence; failing to acknowledge and to receive God's forgiveness and love; or failing to forgive and love one's own self.

(f) Physical Factors

According to Dr. Sam, mild or moderate depression can be sometimes attributed, at least in part, to mismanagement of physical health. If a person does not get enough sleep or enough exercise, after a while they are likely to feel depressed. Similarly, if a person has a poor diet, the cumulative depletion of essential nutrients will eventually negatively affect their mind and their moods.

Those battling serious diseases can also be prone to depression. The depression can worsen the course of their disease, which only deepens the depression. This becomes a vicious cycle. The depression aspect of this cycle needs to be dealt with separately and compassionately.

In some cases, depression is primarily caused by hormones or abnormal biochemistry (as opposed to life's stresses and traumas). Clinical postpartum depression, for example, sometimes sets in after the birth of a baby.

A certain percentage of those suffering from depression have an imbalance in brain chemicals called neurotransmitters. We will discuss brain chemistry in more detail below.

(g) Chronic Guilt

Depression can also be caused by chronic repressed guilt. My husband has treated some women, for example, who have struggled with guilt since having an abortion. If their feelings are not dealt with in a healthy way, such as by receiving appropriate counseling, they will often also struggle with depression. This is also true of Christians who have indulged in "secret sins" such as pornography, sexual immorality, or excessive drinking. If their feelings of guilt are buried, they will potentially surface as depression.

To remain emotionally healthy, Christians need to always address their pangs of guilt. God will forgive any act, but it must first be admitted and, with a repentant heart, prayerfully brought into the light of His Presence.

Diagnosing Clinical Depression: Comments from Dr. Sam

There are various kinds of depression. Christian psychiatrist Dr. John White once observed that depression wears many masks.[258]

There is a clinical distinction between *unipolar* and *bipolar* depression. A discussion of bipolar (also known as manic/depressive) depression is beyond the scope of this book. Most depressive illness tends to be unipolar.

In its commonest form, depression is characterized by a number of symptoms: weariness, fatigue, loss of energy; loss of interest in usually pleasurable relationships and activities; lack of joy; feelings of worthlessness, sadness, and hopelessness; change in appetite (the person eats a lot less or a lot more than normal); change in sleep habits (the person sleeps a lot less or a lot more than normal); difficulty concentrating; lack of motivation; uncontrollable weeping; isolation from family and friends; and preoccupation with death or suicidal thoughts.[259] Depression might also show up as chronic pain with no medical explanation.

---

[258] Dr. John White, pgs. 75–76.

[259] For those interested in more detailed diagnostic information, please refer to the current *Diagnostic and Statistical Manual (DSM)*; Beck's Inventory for Measuring Depression; Zung's Self-rating Depression scale; and the Hamilton Rating Scale for Depression and other clinical tools used by medical practitioners, psychologists, and psychiatrists.

For someone to be diagnosed with clinical depression, they must have a few or more of these symptoms for at least a few weeks. Feeling blue for a day or two is normal and does not amount to clinical depression. Feeling constantly blue for several weeks is considered clinical depression.

Depression can vary in its severity. The more severe the depression, the more urgent the need for professional help. Anyone who thinks they are depressed should consult with their family doctor. This book is not meant to be a substitute for medical advice. It is important for a person to get a grip on depression as soon after it onsets as possible.

Depression is a stubborn and recurrent disease, and it has the ability to "dig in" to both body and soul. Once a person has one episode of clinical depression (at least a few of the symptoms described above for at least a few weeks), the chance of a recurrence is 50% even after the person has achieved a full remission. After two episodes, the odds of a recurrence increase to 70%.[260]

Changes in Biochemistry and Brain Circuitry

Before discussing the many ways we can deal with depression, it is worth spending a moment considering what effect depression has on our biochemistry and brain circuitry. According to Dr. Sam, feeling depressed over many weeks and months will result in physiological changes in our biochemistry and brain circuitry.

There are one hundred billion neurons in the brain. Innumerable electrochemical messages are transmitted between these neurons every second. Recent research in neuropsychiatry is discovering that, when a person is depressed for a sustained period, the brain biochemistry becomes altered on a molecular level. The neurotransmitters do not function in the usual way. Nerve pathways begin to change. The circuitry of the brain eventually changes as negative thinking patterns become more deeply entrenched. The greater these physiological changes, the

---

[260] From article *Stalking a Silent Killer* (Maclean's Magazine, November 14, 2005 issue), pg. 112.

greater the likelihood that the depressed person will need either medication and/or professional counseling to undo the bio-chemical changes and the habitually unhealthy thought patterns.

What Can We Do?

(a) Mental, Emotional, and Spiritual Choices

From the moment we wake up each morning, our minds begin to think of the day ahead. We can anticipate the day with faith and confidence that God will help us through it, hope that all things will turn out well, joy in remembering that God loves us with an unfailing love, and gratitude for all the blessings He has given us, or we can allow our minds to immediately focus on outstanding problems (and there will *always* be some problems on our present horizon), some recent hurt, some task ahead that we dislike or dread, the sound of rain outside, the lengthy list of what has to be done that day, or any disheartening issues in our relationships or circumstances.

Whatever choices we make will have a strong impact on the type of day we will have. If we choose to start thinking about our problems, we can become discouraged, defeated, and depressed before we even get out from under the covers. We can wallow in a negative mindset before we have our first cup of coffee. And reading the morning newspaper will not help that negative state of mind one bit!

From our very waking moment, and throughout the day, we need to pay attention to what we are thinking and feeling. For most of us, the onset of depression can be dealt with at a *very early stage* by better disciplining our thoughts and emotions. We can choose positive thoughts instead of negative ones. This choice becomes increasingly difficult, of course, after the depression has become more established.

Depression can grow if we let our thoughts and feelings go unchecked. Depression begins somewhere—with a single thought, a particular mood, a certain trigger. Depression is always easier to beat sooner rather than later.

When depressive thoughts *first* appear on our horizon, we can choose to change the channel of our minds. We can instead choose to: meditate on encouraging passages from Scripture; pray; talk to a trusted friend or family member; listen to uplifting music; recall some special moments from the past; count our present blessings; anticipate good events planned for the future; or focus on a meaningful task.

Let's revisit David's depression for a moment. Notice what he did. In Psalm 42:6–8, David said: "Yet I am standing here depressed and gloomy, but I will *meditate* upon your kindness....All your waves and billows have gone over me, and floods of sorrow pour upon me like a thundering cataract. Yet day by day the Lord also pours out his steadfast love upon me, and through the night I *sing* his songs and *pray* to God who gives me life."

David did not deny his feelings of gloom and depression. They were real. He acknowledged them. But he did not allow himself to sink deeper. He chose to *occupy his mind* in several ways: he meditated on the ways God had been kind to him in the past; he deliberately focused on God's love; he chose to sing, even while it was still the middle of the night; and he chose to pray. When a person is consciously meditating on God's goodness, singing, and praying, they are *busy* and *engaged*. Gloomy thoughts are eventually displaced.

It is important to realize that improvement in depression is often not easily achieved. It can take a long time for the depression to lift. Clinical psychologist Dr. Dobbins has opined that the usual pattern for most people involves gradually emerging from their depressed state.[261] We will only emerge, however, if we continually choose to take steps to help ourselves. We must persist in taking those steps even if we don't feel like it. People who are depressed generally don't feel like praying, reading their Bible,

---

[261] Dr. Dobbins, pg. 155.

talking, or singing. But the depressed person must start to take even small steps in this direction as early as possible.

(b) Improving Physical and Social Health

In addition to employing some of David's mental and spiritual disciplines, strong *defenses* against emotional lows can be created by regular exercise, good nutrition, and positive social activity. These choices can also help to elevate our mood.

When I was home on maternity leave with my infant son, I went through a period of lonely "cabin fever" while adjusting to a new neighborhood in the Canadian winter. Far from old friends and without a car for a few months, it was easy to feel down. Some days, I could not motivate myself to get out of my bathrobe. Other days, I more constructively decided to battle my low mood by dressing us up in warm clothes and getting outside for some fresh air. On those days, I deliberately chose to notice sunshine, blue skies, and sparkling snow drifts. I did everything I could to make friends in my new community. (For a while, my "friends" were the check-out cashiers I tried to chat with at the grocery store.) These positive efforts helped to prevent me from slipping into a deeper emotional low and to instead enjoy my motherhood.

In the present, when I catch myself thinking gloomy thoughts on a mundane day, I force myself to get up off the couch, make myself a cup of tea, and perhaps e-mail family and friends. (By encouraging someone else, I encourage myself.) I might then deliberately get out for a walk or spend some time gardening. I make even more effort than normal to eat regular meals—nutritious food feeds both body and soul.

Whether it's getting some exercise, fresh air, an energy-boosting meal, a dose of nature's beauty, a few moments of uplifting human contact, or a comforting beverage, we can take small steps to battle the *emerging* blues *early on*, before they become more established and overwhelming.

Just as depression can affect our brain's biochemistry in a negative way, some of the healthy steps mentioned above positively affect our brain's biochemistry. Brisk exercise, for example, causes an increase in the concentration of endorphins in our brain, enabling a sense of well-being. According to Dr. Sam, many studies show that exercise alone can be very helpful in combating mild or moderate depression. Simply getting out for a daily half-hour walk can make a big difference.

Laughter increases the levels of serotonin in our brain. In the same manner, fun activities with others are natural mood-lifters that positively impact our brain chemicals. (Conversely, lack of activity and social isolation make depressive states worse.) Keeping busy, being active, and connecting with a supportive group of family and friends all help us to battle the early stages of depression.

Seeking Help

Christian psychiatrist Dr. John White noted that, in most cases, Christians *do* have the inner resources to manage their own depressive moods, but for some people there are times when the darkness is too overwhelming to manage on their own. This becomes especially true once the brain's biochemistry has undergone significant changes.

In the spiritual realm, deepening depression can lead some Christians to begin to question whether they are saved, whether they have committed some unpardonable sin, or whether God has rejected and abandoned them.

What then? God can provide resources *outside* of our own selves. Dr. Sam recommends that when depressed feelings of any origin continue to bother us for more than two to three weeks, or if we begin to experience physical symptoms along with the sad feelings, it is time to turn to someone for help.[262] If

---

[262] Dr. John White, pg. 77.

family or friends cannot provide enough help, we must seek out qualified professionals.

The nature of the help will depend on whether the roots of the depression are primarily physical, mental, emotional, or spiritual.

(a) Medical Doctors

Medical doctors have been trained to recognize, diagnose, and treat depression. They can diagnose possible physical factors such as poor nutrition, lack of exercise, and sleep deficit. They can rule out or diagnose organic (purely physical) causes such as hormonal or biochemical imbalances or various illnesses. They can give insight into possible psycho-social issues that may have caused or contributed to the low mood. They can offer medication and/or counseling and/or referrals to specialized mental health professionals.

(b) Psychologists and Psychiatrists

Psychologists and psychiatrists are trained to provide counseling therapy to treat depression. There is no shame in seeking help from these educated individuals when we want help sorting out our emotions. If possible, Christians should seek out professionals who, besides being capable clinicians, share the same general values and belief system.

(c) Pastors and Lay Church Counselors

When feelings of depression result from violating one's conscience, anger against God, or uncertainty about one's spiritual standing, it is best to seek the counsel of a pastor or a properly trained lay counselor at church.

There has been a trend in churches to refer people with emotional problems to mental health professionals. Dr. White expressed concern regarding what he perceived to be the overuse of psychologists. He noted that, while it is legitimate to sometimes refer parishioners to mental health professionals, in some cases psychological help is no substitute for spiritual counsel.[263]

Dr. White commented on the limitations of experts such as psychologists and psychiatrists. Even if they are Christians, they do not necessarily incorporate spiritual counsel into their therapy. If there is a strong spiritual dimension to the depression, then a pastor would be the preferable counselor. Pastors are more equipped to deal with issues such as sin, guilt, assurance of salvation, God's forgiveness and grace, forgiving others, and trusting God.

Treatment with Medication

In the course of treatment for depression, medication *may* ultimately be required. Antidepressants can correct the levels of serotonin and norepinephrine in the brain and also address the depletion of other neurotransmitters in the brain.

Christian psychiatrist Dr. White commented that the worse the depressive illness becomes and the more its pathophysiology is established, the more important drug intervention becomes.[264] In other words, the more that the physiology of the brain has been affected, the greater the need for medication to address the biochemical abnormalities.

According to Dr. Sam, the treatment goal is not to simply numb the mind or provide chemical relief from emotional pain. The *primary* goal should be to gain insight into the root causes of the depression. Medication can assist in the treatment of the depression while the root causes are being addressed. To that end, it is important to note that antidepressants do not cure depression. Instead, they help to manage it. Antidepressant medications can be used to help relieve the painful, disabling physical and emotional symptoms that are part of this disease and that often cause the patient to feel too helpless and too paralyzed to take even the first steps toward recovery. When these symptoms are

---

[263] Dr. John White, pg. 59.
[264] Ibid., pg. 187.

more controlled with the help of medications, those suffering with depression are better able to look after their physical, emotional, social, and spiritual health and to start addressing the issues that may have precipitated their depression in the first place.

For example, a person might become depressed because of a difficult marriage, a disease condition, social isolation, or guilt feelings from inappropriate behavior. Over the long haul, this person should not rely solely on medication while ignoring the marriage, the disease, the loneliness, or the gnawing guilt. Medications that treat depression can eventually lose their effectiveness if the underlying causes of the depression are not addressed and treated.

Dr. White stated that you can't just tinker with brain chemistry and leave it at that. Because depression ultimately affects the *whole* person (spirit, body, and soul), then all of these dimensions must eventually be considered and treated appropriately.[265] Drugs are seldom a complete solution.

Having said that, it should be noted that *some* affective disorders originate from hormonal and other purely physical imbalances/changes in the body and not from spiritual, emotional, social, or circumstantial roots. The brain houses our thoughts and feelings, but it is also a physical organ. It is subject to physical dysfunction. Dr. Sam advises that depressive states arising from purely physical causes will likely need drug therapy as the primary treatment as soon as possible after the onset of clinically significant depression.

Cognitive Behavioral Therapy (CBT)

One of the most common forms of counseling therapy used in the treatment of depression is called cognitive behavioral therapy (CBT). Those suffering with depression tend to dwell on negative, pessimistic, self-defeating thoughts that affect the way they view life. They tend to have negative views on: their own selves and

---

[265] Ibid., pg. 139.

their worth; their circumstances and experiences; and the kind of future they expect to experience. With CBT, the goal of the therapist is to help the patient become aware of these negative, defeatist thought patterns and then to help the patient begin to think in a more positive way.

Many patients also need to realize that not all of their negative thoughts are based on fact. Imagine, for example, a person who goes out on a disastrous date. Their date does not want to see them again. This person could conclude that they are unlovable. The therapist would try to help this person recognize that one disastrous date does not mean that they are unlovable or that love will forever elude them. CBT helps a person recognize the kinds of conclusions they have drawn about themselves or their circumstances that are not grounded on true facts.

With CBT, patients learn to better identify the types of negative thoughts they are thinking when they feel they are slipping into depression. They can learn how to cope with (and to ultimately change) their worst habitual thoughts.

CBT is a short-term, time-limited psychotherapy of up to twenty sessions, usually over a ten- to twelve-week period. To the extent that depressed patients can learn to perceive life more optimistically and begin to have positive expectations, their depression will lift.[266] No one sees life with perfectly accurate perception all the time, but it is always better for a person's psychological health to see the glass half-full instead of half-empty.

CBT has been very effective in treating depression for many individuals and in preventing relapses. CBT has been shown to have the same efficacy for some people as medication has for others.

Doesn't CBT sound a lot like what we have been discussing throughout this book? We have been talking about choosing to think, for example, thoughts of love and forgiveness instead of thoughts of anger, resentment, bitterness, hatred, and

---

[266] Dr. John White, pg. 198.

unforgiveness. In a sense, this book provides a form of self-administered cognitive behavioral therapy from a Christian point of view.

Simply speaking, CBT teaches a person to take authority and control over their thoughts and to substitute positive thought patterns for negative thought patterns. CBT came into vogue in the 1970s, as a "new" therapy, but in reality, it is an adaptation of the soul management tools that the Bible has advocated for thousands of years. We discussed (in Chapter 3) how the Bible teaches us to bring our thoughts captive, to renew our minds, and to fix our thoughts on good things. A counselor trained in CBT can help us to positively reframe our thoughts if we are unable to do this on our own.

Interpersonal Therapy (IPT)

Another kind of counseling therapy that doctors, psychiatrists, and psychologists use is called interpersonal therapy (IPT). IPT helps patients understand how their relationships have affected their emotions. With this therapy, patients are assisted in developing insight into how their spouse, parents, children, siblings, colleagues, and/or friends might be subconsciously affecting their self-esteem and their moods.

The therapeutic goal of IPT is to help the patient take personal control over their emotions instead of letting others control their feelings. This therapy helps the patient to understand that no one else can *make* them feel angry or anxious or discouraged—that *they* themselves choose these emotional reactions and responses. The patient is counseled on how to choose different reactions and responses to the negative behavior of others. The patient can then learn not to fall into the same old traps. The sled can find a different route down the snowy hill instead of traveling the same old path!

We do not have to be co-dependent on the moods of others. We do not have to accept or believe what they say about us. We can refuse to give them the power to press our buttons or light our fuses. We can take back the power to control our own thoughts and feelings. By taking this power into our own hands, we are less likely to become depressed about relationship issues.

The main premises of IPT are generally consistent with what the Bible teaches and what is advocated in this book.

God's Help

God is, of course, ready and willing to help us overcome depression. When we are weak, God shows Himself to be strong. We can talk to Him about our depression. We simply cannot carry this kind of heavy burden alone. And there are times when human help is not enough.

God is more powerful than depression. He is more powerful than all the antidepressants, doctors, psychologists, psychiatrists, and pastors in the entire world put together.

God loves us, even when we are depressed. God is in control of our lives, even when they feel out of control. God can assure us of His present help—and of His promises to provide, heal, uplift, deliver, sustain—if we are willing to listen. He can remind us that all our troubles are temporal and that we have eternal life to look forward to. He can remind us that our story will have a wonderful ending. One day, we *will* live happily ever after with Him in glory.

The person who knows God is never alone. We may *feel* alone and isolated sometimes. But God has promised to fill us with the Holy Spirit—also called our Comforter and our Helper. The Spirit is always with us, whether we *feel* His presence or not. In the darkness, we are not alone. We can invite the Light into the darkness. We are not hopeless and helpless.

Let's look at the lives of a few contemporary Christians who have battled depression with God's help.

Barbara Johnson

Author Barbara Johnson became angry when she first learned that one of her adult sons was living in a gay lifestyle. Her anger turned into bitterness and then eventually into depression—a depression which dragged on for months, causing her to isolate herself from others.

One day, she felt weary of being so different from her former self. Unable in her own strength to unburden her heavy heart, she decided that she had to totally, absolutely, unreservedly turn her pain and her depression over to God. She could not control her son's choices. She could not fix herself. She could not resolve her own pain.[267]

In response, God did help her. Over time, her anger ended and her depression lifted. Eventually, even her relationship with her son was restored.

Stormie Omartian

Years ago, highly acclaimed author Stormie Omartian was an actress, dancer, and singer in Hollywood. She worked with stars like Jack Benny, George Burns, Dean Martin, Jerry Lewis, Stevie Wonder, Ray Charles, and many others.

Stormie had grown up in an abusive home. As a young adult, she did not deal with the emotional fall-out from her childhood. Instead, she stuffed it down deep inside her soul. Over time, her unresolved buried pain caused her to become chronically depressed. When she woke up every morning, she would ask herself: should she kill herself then or could she make it through another day?[268]

In those early adult years, she was not a Christian. She turned to her career and to alcohol and drugs to relieve her pain. She found some temporary, superficial relief through those means.

But neither the excitement of her career, nor the euphoria of alcohol and drugs was enough to overcome her depression. She went into black periods in which she could hardly function. She would lie in her bed, not even able to read or watch TV. Some

---

[267] Barbara Johnson, *Splashes of Joy*, pg. 57.
[268] Omartian, pg. 22.

days, she managed to drag herself out of bed, barely able to perform the most rudimentary requirements of life.

Marriage did not improve her emotional state. When her first marriage resulted in much stress, anger, and bitterness, she sank into the worst depression of her life. She started to think more seriously about suicide and even began to form a plan.

Here is how she described her life, at the age of twenty-eight, to a psychiatrist. On the outside, her life looked successful. On the inside, there was incredible, non-stop pain. She confided to her therapist that she lived in continual vague fear, not even knowing what she was afraid of. Although surrounded by people, she suffered from great loneliness. Her debilitating depression was compounded by anxiety attacks.

Her psychiatrist was able to give her some insight into the roots of her depression as he led her on a journey back into her childhood. Stormie had been verbally abused by a mother who always seemed angry at her. Sometimes, her mother had forced her to stay inside a dark closet.

Her mother had further battered Stormie's self-esteem by telling her that she was stupid, ugly, and would never amount to anything. By her teens, the degrading language her mother used to address her, and the slaps on the face that were doled out for no reason, had become increasingly emotionally painful.

Stormie spent those years feeling helpless, hopeless, rejected, abandoned, sad, and fearful. She was lonely and felt that she never fit in socially.

The insight provided by her psychiatrist was not enough to help Stormie. At the age of twenty-eight, although successful on the surface, she still felt ugly and unacceptable inside. Stormie continued to think that suicide was the only way out. Traveling back to her childhood had stirred up the pain, had given her insight into it, but had not provided enough relief.

Fortunately, Omartian became a Christian before she carried out her plan to take her own life. In the early weeks of attending church, Stormie began to encounter the love, the peace, and the hope of God. But *some* of the old feelings still dragged her down.

Stormie had to go through years of prayer, counseling, Bible study, learning how to trust God, and fellowshipping with other Christians before she was able to get some control over her depression.[269]

Stormie's many best-selling books on subjects such as prayer bear testimony to God's ability to finally set one of His children free from very dark and deep depression.

Sandi Patti

At the height of her celebrity as a successful Christian singer, Sandi Patti's marriage broke down. She became involved in an affair with a married man that eventually became public. As her life spiraled downward, she fell into depression.

She felt particularly miserable one night at an airport, in the middle of a winter storm. When she realized that it was not possible to fly home to celebrate the birthday of her twin children, she was so distraught that she curled up on the floor and began to cry. At first, she was just crying about not being able to get home for the twins' birthday. As the night wore on, she realized that she was actually crying about everything. She realized she had been crying on the inside for a year. She was full of grief, guilt, and loss. She felt like she was a failure on every front—as a mother, as a wife, and as a Christian.[270]

A broken marriage—and a career suffering from public reaction to both her affair and her subsequent divorce—caused immense inner pain. As she struggled with deep depression, Sandi decided that, first and foremost, she had to get right with God. She had to seek His forgiveness, mercy, grace, and love. She was a mature enough Christian to know that *He* was her only way out of her dark pit.[271]

As with Stormie, her depression did not lift in an instant. Life is not like that. It took a period of time—pursuing ongoing

---

[269] Ibid., especially pages 25, 39, 40, 44, 62, 104.
[270] Sandi Patti, *Broken on the Back Row*, pgs. 90–91.
[271] Ibid. pg. 99.

right-standing with God, praying, seeking support from mature Christians, apologizing to the Christian public she had let down, and receiving counseling—to get her life back on track and her joy restored.

Sandi was eventually able to overcome her depression, to remarry, and to resume her singing career.

Sheila Walsh

From 1988 until 1992, Sheila Walsh was the co-host of the popular CBN television program "The 700 Club." To her admiring public, she seemed poised and successful. Sheila has candidly admitted, however, that her life *beneath* the celebrity veneer was quite different. On the *surface*, she looked fine and acted as if she was fine—but in fact she was severely depressed.

During those years, she had trouble eating and sleeping. She lost twenty pounds. She frequently felt like crying. Other times, she felt emotionally numb. The rest of the time she felt hopeless and unbearably sad. Some days, she lost her concentration to the point that she forgot who she was interviewing on her program and why. She managed to conceal all of this for a while but, in 1992, her life imploded.[272] Unable to manage her depression on her own anymore, she checked herself into a Christian psychiatric hospital.

Her story is an important one for the Christian community. Sheila has demonstrated that it is acceptable to seek psychiatric help when depression gets out of control. There is no shame in reaching out for professional help. Sheila hopes that her story will encourage others to admit their problem and to seek help if the depression is unmanageable.[273] Ignoring the depression will only make it worse.

With therapy, Sheila was able to understand the roots of her severe depression. When she was just four years old, her previously happy and loving father developed a brain thrombosis.

---

[272] Sheila Walsh, *Honestly*, pg. 16.
[273] Ibid. pg. 63.

This condition affected his moods and changed his personality. He became very angry a lot of the time. She was convinced that all of this somehow happened because she was a "bad" little girl. She did not know how else to explain his sudden, unusual anger at her. She suffered from his anger, and her confused inner pain, for a year. Her father died of the blood clot when she was five.

Throughout the rest of her childhood, and then into her adult life, Sheila was aware she had a problem but had no idea what to do. Emotionally, she felt like she had fallen down a deep well and had no way to climb back out.

Sheila stayed in that dark well for many years, until she finally sought professional help. After being treated in the Christian psychiatric facility, Sheila was able to emerge from that deep well of depression and start her life again. With God's help, and the help of caring people, Sheila has become an influential Christian woman again. Presently, she is widely respected as an author and speaker who knows how to be emotionally authentic.

One of Sheila's main pieces of advice about dealing with depression is this: the suffering person should never pretend it does not exist. Suppressing the depression just intensifies it. Wearing a mask in public just deepens the inner pain and turmoil. Running away from the uncomfortable feelings does not make them go away. Instead, the feelings just linger in the shadows. Depression must be brought out into the light. Honesty, with our inner selves and with others, is critical.[274]

Hope for Us All

It is my hope that the stories of historical giants like David, Job, Martin Luther, and C. S. Lewis—and courageous women like Barbara Johnson, Stormie Omartian, Sandi Patti, and Sheila Walsh who have dared to openly tell the truth about their depression— will encourage Christians who battle with depression. There is

---

[274] Ibid., especially pgs. 33; 42;43;46; 57; 62; 63; 87; 200.

hope for all of us, whenever and however we suffer depression. Depression does not have to crush, destroy, or sideline any of us.

Why am I discouraged? Why is my heart so sad?
I will put my hope in God!
I will praise him again—my Savior and my God!
Psalm 43:5 (NLT)

In my anguish I cried to the Lord, and he answered
by setting me free.
Psalm 118:5 (NIV)

17
HOPE
Safely Anchored

Blessed is he whose help is the God of Jacob,
whose hope is in the Lord his God,
the Maker of heaven and earth, the sea,
and everything in them...
Psalm 146:5–6 (NIV)

O Lord, you alone are my hope
...I will keep on expecting you to help me.
Psalm 71:5, 14a

The Lord delights in those who fear him,
who put their hope in his unfailing love.
Psalm 147:11 (NIV)

OVER A DECADE ago, I was defence counsel in a lawsuit that involved multiple plaintiffs, many defendants, and about four dozen lawyers. It was complex litigation. We had already deposed witnesses (for over twelve weeks) when all counsel finally agreed to a three-day pretrial conference, to be presided over by the case management judge. This was our last serious opportunity to settle the litigation. A four-month trial was scheduled to proceed within weeks if the parties could not settle.

The prospects of settling this matter looked grim. Can you imagine trying to get four dozen lawyers to agree to a settlement—especially when a few of them were being quite unreasonable? On top of that, some of the clients were also being unreasonable, refusing to ante up the kind of settlement contribution their potential liability positions called for. Furthermore, some of the lawyers were too deeply immersed in other trials to really put their minds to the settlement of this case.

A four-month trial out of town is difficult for any trial lawyer. It would have been especially difficult in my circumstances. I was the mother of two young children. Most of the year, my firm graciously allowed me to work on a reduced-hours basis. I was usually able to come into the office a few days each week and work at home on the other days. On my office days, I could still be home by the supper hour *most* of the time. On my days at home, I normally closed my files when my children came home from school. It was a perfect arrangement about eighty percent of the time.

Occasionally, however, lengthy depositions and trials turned our family life upside down! We had to lean heavily on our support system: our part-time nanny, extended family, neighbors, friends, and other car-pool parents. Somehow we managed to make those stressful times work, but it was never easy and it was often exhausting.

The prospect of a four-month trial out of town was, therefore, very daunting. It was in my personal interests to settle this litigation, provided (of course) that I was able to negotiate a fair, appropriate deal for my client that did not compromise *their* interests. In the days before the pretrial conference, I began to work the phones, send the faxes and e-mails, and fine-tune proposal after proposal. I will never forget how most of the lawyers just laughed when they answered yet another phone call from me. They told me that the prospect of a settlement, under all of the prevailing circumstances, was *hopeless*. They admired my patience and persistence, but lawyer after lawyer told me I was pursuing a lost cause. They advised me to gear up for trial.

Along with my human effort, I was praying! I remember how I felt the night before the three-day pretrial conference was scheduled to commence. I was alone in my hotel room and feeling pretty blue. I tried to cheer up by reading my Bible. Even that felt burdensome, until I came across this magnificent verse from Romans 15:13: "So I pray...that God who gives you hope will keep you happy and full of peace as you believe in him. I pray that God will help you overflow with hope in him through the Holy Spirit's power within you."

My hope had almost run dry by that point. It was incredibly life-giving to read that God wanted to *give* me hope—hope of such extravagant measure that I would *overflow* with it.

My circumstances were not the least bit hopeful. But I was reminded that God was still able to give me hope—hope that was based on Him alone—on His love, His grace, His mercy, and His power. As I let that Bible passage permeate my soul, meditating on it over and over, I actually felt the heavy pressure lifting off of my shoulders, my back, and my chest.

Have you ever prayed, eyes closed, aware of the darkness and stillness—and then felt light flow behind your closed eyelids? That was how I felt that night in my hotel room. Even with my eyes closed, I was aware of warm, cheerful, soothing light filling my mind. I kept focusing on the word hope—the *promise* of hope—the *choice* between hope and despair—hope as a *reality* quite separate from present circumstances.

I embraced those first warm rays of hope and then dared to ask God to help me have more hope. I was not satisfied with a little hope. I wanted my hope to overflow, as the Bible verse promised. I had a deep desire to understand the power of hope on a whole new level—to grasp what Romans 15:13 was talking about. I did not stop praying and meditating until I felt hope infusing my soul even more powerfully.

Amazingly, the lawsuit did settle that week and the trial was called off. I had learned a valuable lesson about *persevering in hope* regardless of the circumstances or the doom and gloom of others. I had learned that faint hope can transform into overflowing hope.

All of us experience times in life when we feel like we are at the end of our own rope, when we feel helpless and hopeless. In those times, discouragement, despair, and depression weigh us down until we wonder if we will be able to carry on.

As a Christian, I am deeply grateful that there is something called hope. Even when we least *feel* like it, we *can* choose hope. We can *choose* to believe that there is a God watching over our lives. That He loves us. That He will hear our prayers and respond to our faith, however small it is. That He will help us. That the night always ends and morning always comes. Each day *does* promise a whole new beginning. Each new hour *is* the first hour of the rest of our lives.

The word "hope" appears about 150 times in the Bible. It is a repeated theme and promise. In the famous passage of 1 Corinthians 13, Paul wrote that these three things abide in the Christian life: faith, hope, and love. In Hebrews 6:19, Paul described our hope in God as a "...strong and trustworthy anchor for our souls, connecting us with God himself"—an anchor secure enough to keep us safe in any storm, no matter how vicious the waves. Hope has nothing to do with the stability of our circumstances. Hope has everything to do with the stability of our souls as they hold firmly onto God.

David

We talked much about David in the chapters on discouragement, despair, and depression. He was no stranger to these dark emotions. Yet David was still able to say to God: "My *only hope* is in your love and faithfulness."[275] On another occasion, he said: "Be merciful, O Lord, for I am looking up to you in *constant* hope."[276]

It is easy to skim over these words. But stop for a moment to think of David's circumstances during the years he hid out in caves, fearing for his life. He must surely have endured scorching heat by day and bone-chilling desert cold at night. He no doubt slept on the dirty ground without the protection of a locked door or a security alarm. He had no cup of coffee to perk him up in the morning, no corner grocery store to pick up some food, no microwave, and no refrigerator for the meat he probably hunted down. He had no bathroom, no shower, no medical help, and often no company. It is in *these* circumstances that David was still able to speak of his hope in God—his constant hope.

---

[275] Psalm 40:11b.
[276] Psalm 86:3.

Job

Having lost his children, home, health, and wealth, Job had sunk about as low as a person can sink. In his worst moments, he lamented that he felt utterly hopeless. At one point, for example, he wrote about sitting in sackcloth (the cloth of mourning), having "...laid all hope in the dust."[277]

Yet, even in his miserable circumstances, Job was able to muster enough strength, at other moments, to say: "Though he slay me, *yet* will I hope in him..."[278] This is a verse I memorized years ago. In my toughest hours, it has been a short, easy-to-remember verse to focus on.

Jeremiah

The prophet Jeremiah also knew what it felt like to sit in the dust, shunned by men, battling depression and despair. Listen to the picture he paints with his own words about what he *felt* God was doing to him: "He buried me in dark places, like those long dead. He has walled me in; I cannot escape; he has fastened me with heavy chains....I have forgotten what enjoyment is. All hope is gone..."[279]

Jeremiah also moaned about: afflictions; deepest darkness; anguish and distress; bitterness; deepest sorrows; utter shame; anger; fear; streams of tears; feeling trapped, desolate and destroyed; and the heavy weight of sin and its consequences.[280]

Even so, it was this prophet who penned these beloved lines: "*Yet there is one ray of hope: his compassion never ends.* It is only the Lord's mercies that have kept us from complete destruction. Great is his faithfulness; his lovingkindness begins afresh each day. My soul claims the Lord as my inheritance; *therefore I will hope in him.* The Lord is wonderfully good to those who wait for

---

[277] Job 16:15.
[278] Job 13:15 (NIV).
[279] Lamentations 3: 6–7, 17b, 18.
[280] Words are excerpted from chapter 3 of Lamentations.

him, to those who seek for him. It is good both to hope and wait quietly for the salvation of the Lord."[281] Jeremiah showed us that there can be hope even in the midst of the most crushing anguish.

Paul

Paul endured numerous woes: imprisonments, beatings, shipwrecks, illness, and many other problems. Yet Paul was still able to write this to Timothy: "…we have put our hope in the living God…"[282]

In Hebrews 10:23, Paul wrote: "Let us *hold unswervingly* to the hope we profess, for he who promised is faithful. (NIV)" In Philippians 3:7, Paul stated: "But all these things that I once thought very worthwhile—now I've thrown them all away so that I can put my trust and hope in Christ alone."

Words Can Impart Hope

I strongly encourage you to underline and memorize the Bible passages that talk about hope. Read them, soak in them, cling to them—these words can generate hope in our lives, no matter what circumstances we find ourselves in.

King Solomon promised: "There is *surely* a future hope for you, and your hope will not be cut off."[283] The present may be gloomy, but the present time *will* end. Good things pass, but so do negative situations.

King Solomon further observed: "Anyone who is among the living has hope…"[284] Hope is available to everyone, all of the time. It just has to be reached for.

The prophet Isaiah knew that hope in God is difficult when circumstances seem very bleak. Sometimes, God does not seem all that interested in our problems. Yet Isaiah chose to hope

---

[281] Lamentations 3:21–26.

[282] 1 Timothy 4:10 (NIV).

[283] Proverbs 23:18 (NIV).

[284] Ecclesiastes 9:4 (NIV).

anyway. He said: "I will wait for the Lord to help us, *though He is hiding now. My only hope is in him.*"[285] Isaiah later painted this inspiring picture: "...those who hope in the Lord will renew their strength. They will soar on wings like eagles; they will run and not grow weary, they will walk and not be faint."[286]

At any point in time, there are probably a few reasons to feel discouraged. There are also a few reasons to feel hope—at a minimum, we always have the promises of God to hope in! In our tough times, let's more carefully choose what we fix our thoughts on.

The Object of Our Hope

Hope is not the same as wishful thinking. Even as a child, I figured out pretty fast that wishing on a star never changed anything. Hope is also not very solid if it is merely anchored in another person, in medicine, in money, in statistics, or in the limited power of positive thinking. It is certainly easier to have hope if someone is encouraging us, if medical science promises to cure us, if we have an optimistic worldview, if the statistics are on our side, and if we choose to see the cup half full. But true, *sustainable* hope must be anchored in God.

Only God is fully reliable and fully able to help. Other people can too easily let us down or tire of supporting us over time. Medical science does not know the cure for *so many* diseases. The stock market is notoriously fickle. Optimism is tough to maintain in the face of a serious cancer diagnosis, the loss of a job, a major financial setback, or the painful behavior of a wayward spouse or child.

The psalmist who wrote Psalm 119 well understood that his faith and hope had to rest in God alone. In that long Psalm, we find many pertinent verses such as: "May I never forget your words; for they are my only hope....Never forget your promises to me your servant, for they are my only hope. They give me

---

[285] Isaiah 8:17.
[286] Isaiah 40:31 (NIV).

strength in all my troubles; how they refresh and revive me!...I expect your help, for you have promised it....You are my refuge and my shield, and your promises are my only source of hope."[287]

Sometimes God allows our hope in other people, other resources, and in our own strength and ability to be shattered. When the bottom falls out of our lives, when others fail us, when *our* strength and ability end, then we realize the importance and the necessity of putting our hope *in God*. God promises to be with us over the long haul—cradle to grave.

God Imparts Hope

In our discouragement, despair and depression, we often feel very feeble. If we try to do our part to choose to hope in God, (however poor and humble our efforts), God imparts *His* hope. In Psalm 94:19, the psalmist prayed this: "Lord, when doubts fill my mind, when my heart is in turmoil, *quiet* me and *give me* renewed hope and cheer."

Paul wrote: "I pray also that the eyes of your heart may be enlightened in order that you may know the *hope* to which he has called you...and his incomparably great power for us who believe."[288] God supplies whatever extra power we need to hope. He knows that we will rarely have all of the power we need in our limited human strength.

Peter wrote: "In his great mercy, he has *given us* new birth into a living hope..."[289] From the very moment we first become Christians, we have enormous reason to hope!

Although God often directly imparts hope to us, He will sometimes use other people to impart hope and encouragement. A good example of this can be found in 1 Samuel 23:16, where Jonathan encouraged David. David was running for his life from

---

[287] Psalm 119:43, 49–50, 81, 114.
[288] Ephesians 1:18–19a (NIV).
[289] 1 Peter 1:3b (NIV).

King Saul, Jonathan's father. Jonathan inspired hope in David during this very dark chapter in David's life.

Paul often exhorted his fellow Christians to encourage one another—to kindle hope and faith in each other.[290] May we all become bearers of hope, sowing seeds of hope in others. We will need such favors returned!

Eric Liddell

Eric Liddell was one of the gifted athletes on the British team in the 1924 Olympics in Paris. Many Christians are familiar with the story of how Liddell refused, on principle, to run a qualifying heat for the 100-meter event on a Sunday. Because of his refusal to run that Sunday heat, Liddell had to instead try to qualify for the 440-meter race on another day. This was not his preferred distance, nor had he been properly trained for it. Under those circumstances, Liddell would have been foolish to put his faith and hope in his own strength and ability. He knew he was pitted against the finest and fastest runners in the world, all of whom were better trained in that particular distance.

In the qualifying race, Liddell was doing well until another racer cut abruptly in front of him, knocking Liddell over. Suddenly he found himself in last place. Many other men would have given up at that point and finished the race with half-hearted pace. But Liddell refused to abandon hope. He got up, continued the race from the very back of the pack, and went on to actually win the race.[291] Are the odds against you? Has someone knocked you down? Don't give up!

Gladys Aylward

We have talked about how missionary Gladys Aylward bravely escorted over one hundred orphans across the mountains of

---

[290] See, for example, 1 Thessalonians 5:11, Hebrews 3:13 and Hebrews 10:25.

[291] Ellen Caughey, *Eric Liddell*, see pgs. 7–9.

China during war-time all by herself. She was full of faith, trust, and hope, even in dire circumstances.

Gladys later became known for her work with a community of lepers in China. These lepers were understandably very hopeless. They were weary and depressed, shut away in an isolated village. Aylward spent time with these dejected social outcasts, imparting her unquenchable hope to them.

Remarkably, the leper colony actually became a joyful place, where many encountered the love of God and an *eternal* hope in a better life one day.

Corrie ten Boom

As we have seen, Corrie was able to overcome anger, resentment, bitterness, hatred, fear, and many other negative feelings that she experienced in a Nazi concentration camp in World War II. Just as Corrie learned to choose love and forgiveness, faith and trust, she also learned to *hope*. Her barracks at Ravensbruck became known as "the crazy place" — crazy because it was where prisoners audaciously hoped.[292]

Lisa Beamer

We have also talked about Lisa Beamer's various emotional battles after her husband died in a hijacked plane on 9/11. She suddenly found herself as a single mother and widow, caring for two young children and pregnant with a third child. Amidst the firestorm of emotions that assaulted her, she was asked to be one of the key speakers at a Women of Faith Conference that November. She accepted the invitation to speak, knowing that she would have to get up in front of thousands of women, only a few months after her husband's death.

At the Conference, Lisa spoke about how she had chosen, since 9/11, to *not* focus on her loss—but to focus instead on the blessings that still remained. She reminded her audience of the

---

[292] Ten Boom, *Tramp for the Lord*, pg. 18.

sage old adage that everyone has a choice as to whether circumstances will make them bitter or better. She declared that she was choosing to live in hope. Her hope was based on her knowledge that God was in control of everything that was happening in her life—and she knew that God loved her. She did not deny her pain. She acknowledged that the pain was very real, but then reminded her audience that hope is real too.[293] Hope has substance.

Heather Mercer and Dayna Curry

Heather Mercer and Dayna Curry, American prisoners in Afghanistan around the time of 9/11, struggled with fear and despair. I cannot imagine what it must have felt like to be in prison in Kabul, hearing the American planes droning overhead, bombing the city—and wondering all the while if they would soon face execution for their alleged crimes of trying to convert Afghan families they knew.

Yet, in the midst of their ordeal, these two young women found some hope. (In fact, Heather and Dayna later chose to title their book *Prisoners of Hope*.) While they were still imprisoned, family members, friends, lawyers, and diplomats were all trying to help Heather and Dayna. But the two women realized that they could not place all their hope in mere human beings—the circumstances they faced were too impossible. Only hope in God was strong enough to overcome their suffocating fear.

These two women chose hope without any guarantee that they would survive their ordeal. They had no way of knowing that they would be dramatically rescued, reunited with family and friends, honored as guests of the American President, and able to tell their stories on prime time TV. They chose, while still living in the darkest hours, to hope in the loving God who held their futures in His hands.

---

[293] Lisa Beamer, pgs. 276, 296, 297, 301.

The Health Benefits of Hope

Dr. Armand Nicholi Jr. (a member of the Harvard Faculty of Medicine for at least three decades) has said that psychiatrists have suspected for years that hope promotes health on both the physical and emotional levels. He has also noted the growing body of medical evidence documenting the negative effect that *lack* of hope and depression have on a person's health. Hopelessness feeds organic disease. In contrast, hope assists healing.[294]

Over his decades of medical practice, Dr. Sam has observed that choosing hope *is* important for physical, mental, emotional, and spiritual well-being. Patients who have hope in a positive outcome usually fare much better and recover faster from illness than those who feel depressed and hopeless.

The healing power of hope has been proven innumerable times by what is known as the placebo effect. In clinical drug trials, some patients are given the real medicine that is being studied and others are given sugar pills called placebos. None of the patients know whether they are taking the actual medication or the placebos. Remarkably, in most clinical trials, the health situation of a significant percentage (as much as 35–45%) of the patients who are taking the placebo pills improves. The healing effect of the placebos is credited to the power of the patients' expectations that the pills are helping them.[295] Hope has incredible intrinsic power!

Research has also explored the impact of optimism on physical health and healing (aside from the use of placebos). Optimism (expecting a positive outcome) is very similar to faith and hope. Well-controlled studies have shown that optimists fare better following a variety of medical interventions. A growing body of literature documents the benefits of optimism on mental

---

[294] Monroe (ed.), *Finding God at Harvard*, pg. 117, 119.
[295] Dr. Beauregard, pg. 141, 144.

health, coping skills, health-related quality of life, health-related behaviors, physical health outcomes, and longevity.[296]

Our Ultimate Hope

At a certain point, we all face the reality that *some* things will never change in this lifetime. We cannot change our relatives, our race, our gene pool, the timing of our birth in history, and so many other circumstances of our lives. We cannot change our past and we are certainly not in total control of our present or our future.

There are times when we have to get an *eternal* perspective on our lives. In this life, there will be wars, economic downturns, illnesses, injuries, hurts, insults, oppression, persecution, and many other forms of pain. Not all pain will subside. Our bodies will not, in this world, remain completely healthy and youthful. We will age, we will suffer sometimes, and at some point we will die.

Our ultimate hope does not lie in *this* world or in *this* time. Our true hope—our highest hope, our brightest hope—is in the next life. Jesus promised us eternal life if we choose to believe in Him.

I used to love fairy tale endings, where the hero and the heroine lived "happily ever after." Many say that, as we grow up, we have to realize that life is not a fairy tale. I disagree! In fact, for Christians there *will be* a fairy-tale ending. Pain will one day cease. All tears will be wiped from our faces. Sickness, conflict, and death will no longer exist. We shall see Him, face to face. I guess that is why the Bible is my favorite book. The fiery arrows and fierce demons don't win in the end! We *will* live happily ever after, for all of eternity.

While enduring his terrible trials, Job reminded himself of this: "If a man dies, shall he live again? *This thought gives me hope,* so that in all my anguish I eagerly await sweet death!....But as

---

[296] See articles by: Matthews et al., pg. 640, 643; Danner et al., pg. 809.

for me, I know that my Redeemer lives, and that he will stand upon the earth at last. And I know that after this body has decayed, this body shall see God!...Yes, I shall see him, not as a stranger, but as a friend! What a glorious hope!"[297]

We need not fear death. We need not dread it. We can embrace it, knowing that the best is truly yet to come. That is why Paul could write these powerful words: "...'Death is swallowed up in victory.' O death, where then your victory? Where then your sting?"[298] Hope is more powerful than even death.

King Solomon wisely wrote: "The hope of good men is eternal happiness..."[299] When all is dark and gloomy in this life, the promise of better days ahead *remains*, helping us to tough out the hardest hours.

Above all, Jesus came to give us hope in life everlasting. Matthew 12:21 rejoices that "his name will be the hope of all the world."[300] Jesus endured the darkness of His crucifixion on Good Friday so that we might have the hope of Easter Sunday morning. Easter morning is not just about the resurrection of Jesus. It is about *our* promised resurrection too!

...Those who hope in me will not be disappointed.
Isaiah 49:23c (NIV)

We have this hope as an anchor for the soul, firm and secure.
Hebrews 6:19a (NIV)

Let us hold unswervingly to the hope we profess...
Hebrews 10:23 (NIV)

---

[297] Job 14:14; 19:25–26; 19:27bc.
[298] 1 Corinthians 15:54–55ab.
[299] Proverbs 10:28.
[300] NLT translation.

Pardon for sin and a peace that endureth,
Thine own dear presence to cheer and to guide;
Strength for today and bright hope for tomorrow,
Blessings all mine, with ten thousand beside![301]

---

[301] From "Great is Thy Faithfulness," words by Thomas O. Chisholm, (Public Domain).

18
GRUMBLING
AND
COMPLAINING
The Discontented Soul

Don't grumble about each other...
James 5:9a

These men are constant gripers, never satisfied...
Jude 1:16

G EORGE BERNARD SHAW once wrote: "This is the true joy in life—the being used for a purpose recognized by yourself as a mighty one...instead of [being] a feverish, selfish little clod of ailments and grievances, complaining that the world will not devote itself to making you happy."[302]

No one likes to be around us when we grumble and complain—when we self-centeredly dwell on the cup half-empty, magnify our problems, and tell anyone who will listen how unfair life has been to us. Everyone needs to be careful not to fall into this habit; it is one of the defining characteristics of human nature!

Canada and the U.S. ranked fourth and fifth (out of a long list of countries) in an international study measuring which nationalities grumble and complain the most often.[303] These rankings are quite shocking, considering these are two of the wealthiest nations in the world.

---

[302] George Bernard Shaw, *Man and Superman*, (1903, Public Domain).
[303] From a *Toronto Star* article by Patrick Evans, August 26, 2005.

The Israelites

The Israelites, at the time of Moses, were champion grumblers and complainers.[304] Soon after God had dramatically rescued them from their oppressive slavery under Pharaoh, they started to gripe about everything. They did not like the food in the desert they were journeying through and kept wishing for the garlic and leeks of Egypt. They wanted more ample water. Even when God provided them with manna from heaven and water in the wilderness, they found new reason to complain—they wanted meat.

They found reason to grumble about each other. Their grumbling became so common that we read in Exodus 18:13: "...Moses sat as usual to hear the people's complaints against each other, from morning to evening."

One of the things we can learn from the story of the Israelites is that God really dislikes grumbling and complaining. According to Numbers 11:1: "The people were soon complaining about all their misfortunes, and the Lord heard them. His anger flared out against them because of their complaints..."

In response to their ingratitude, God allowed them to struggle and suffer in various ways as they made their way to the Promised Land. In Deuteronomy 1 (verses 1–4, 26–27) we learn that it should only have taken the Israelites eleven days to travel from Mount Horeb to the Promised Land—instead, they wandered in circles for forty years in that wilderness!

Through it all, they constantly rebelled, disobeyed, and complained. God became so sick and tired of their attitude that He decided this: the adult generation He had freed from slavery in Egypt would not be allowed to enter the Promised Land.[305] Not even Moses was allowed to enter in. God gave a fresh chance to the next generation. There is surely a sobering lesson in this story.

---

[304] You can read about this in the books of Exodus, Numbers, and Deuteronomy.

[305] Numbers 14:29–30.

Better Role Models

Other Bible characters stand out because, no matter how difficult their circumstances became, they remarkably did *not* grumble and complain. Particularly notable examples include Joseph, Daniel, Ruth, and Mary (the mother of Jesus). They accepted their lot in life even though it was not easy at times. They shone in their darkest hours: Joseph in prison, Daniel in the lion's den, Ruth in her early widowhood, and Mary in her time of public disgrace as an unmarried, pregnant young woman. They prove that, with God's help, human nature can rise above its ignoble tendency to gripe and grumble.

Developing a Discontented Spirit

Complaining eventually breeds a spirit of discontentment. The more we grumble and complain about our marriages (or our singlehood), our jobs (or lack thereof), our neighbors (or our isolation), our parenthood (or our fertility issues), the more miserable we feel and the deeper our discontentment.

The discontented heart is prone to daydreaming and fantasy. Single people fantasize about marriage—and waste some precious years of freedom. Many married people ponder what it would feel like to find a new mate. No wonder pornography, adultery, and divorce are so rampant in our society!

Fed by the media images that so constantly bombard us, people daydream about a fancy car or a bigger, more luxurious house—assuming that these acquisitions would bring greater contentment. It is no surprise that our society is so steeped in materialism and workaholism.

Paying attention to the frequency of our flights into inner fantasy will tell us something about ourselves—it will show us the measure of our discontentment. Perhaps it will also show us something about the deficit of love we are feeling. Whenever we spend time lying on the couch imagining a life *different* from our real life we need to face up to the fact that we have become discontented.

Why face that fact? Because the fantasy life will eventually wear thin and fail to satisfy. Daydreamers wake up one day and realize that they are no longer living *real* lives. It is easy to waste hours of the day or the night spending too much energy on empty unreality. When the nothingness of it hits, some risk turning to drink or drugs as another way to escape reality. Others become so discontented (with both the reality of their lives *and* the fruitless unreality they have tried to camp out in) that they pack their bags and leave their spouse, their home, or their job—in search of a *new* reality. Sadly, our personal propensity for grumbling, complaining, and seeing the cup half-empty travels with us wherever we go.

Discontentment is a dangerous road to travel down. Change can be healthy at times, but not when it is made in a spirit of grumbling ingratitude.

A Litany of Complaints

What do we grumble about? Teenagers love to grumble about parents, curfews, teachers, and homework. In college, there are many new woes to whine about: the "mystery meat" in the student cafeteria, huge classes, long treks between lecture halls, weird professors, shortage of spending money, and an even greater volume of work.

Young adults gather in after-hours watering holes to grumble about demanding bosses, impossible dead-lines, and tax deductions from their hard-earned paychecks. New parents gripe about lack of sleep, endless diaper changes, loss of freedom, and mounds of laundry. On and on it goes! Old age offers no respite—there are too many aches and pains—and "mystery meat" gets served in the old folks' homes too.

And, at every age, if there is nothing else to complain about, one can always complain about the weather.

A Personal Challenge

To become a lawyer in my Canadian province used to require a Bar Admission Course that was six months long during which we had to pass ten difficult exams in a variety of practice areas. Brutal. In between exams, there were daily classes to attend and massive amounts of dry, technical reading matter. How fun do you think it is digesting the intricacies of corporate tax law or the tedious procedural side of civil and criminal law?

At least we had coffee breaks and meal breaks to punctuate the daily class time. Unfortunately, most of the prospective lawyers spent those breaks grumbling and complaining about the Bar Admission process, the amount of reading material, how hard the exams were, and how boring some of the instructors were. The complaints were underscored by the fact that, in the year that I wrote the Bar exams, the job market was tough— many of my classmates did not have jobs lined up and were nervous about the future.

Very early in this six-month period, I knew that I had a critical choice to make. I was either going to succumb to this prevailing disgruntled attitude or I was going to have to *somehow* rise above it. The studying was going to be difficult enough—but the thought of being surrounded by (or participating in) the constant griping and groaning seemed even more unbearable. I was determined *not* to get sucked into the prevailing mood.

I won't pretend that it was easy to sustain a positive attitude for the entire six months. Some of the instructors *were* boring; some of the texts *were* really thick; some of the exams *were* tough. But it was worth the effort! Crazy as it sounds, I actually began to enjoy the process of writing those exams—to embrace the surge of adrenaline at the moment we were allowed to turn over our questions papers. I began to genuinely appreciate the value of all that I was learning.

In those six months, did I overcome my own propensity to grumble and complain? Unfortunately, the answer is no. Each time I have entered a season of unique challenge and difficulty (going through pregnancies, the newborn phase of child-rearing, the process of moving, and crunch times in my career), I have had to struggle afresh with my own human tendency to gripe, grumble, and complain. It is the default setting for most of us. But whatever efforts I have made in each season to *not* whine and complain have always been worth it.

Dr. Sam's Observations

Grumblers and complainers tend to be pessimists, and pessimists are generally more prone to depression. Always thinking about the negatives in life is bound to make one depressed. Pessimists are also more prone to anxiety and worry for the same reason—they are focusing on what is wrong with their world, not what is right. This also fosters a state of chronic stress or fear, which in time will negatively impact one's health.

Pessimists are full of aches and pains that often have no medically-detectable cause. They are more likely to complain of a vague fatigue and lethargy, often unaware of the link between what occupies their thoughts and how they feel physically. Even when something specific is actually diagnosed, pessimists are more likely not to recover as well as optimists from either illness or surgery. This correlation between mental outlook and physical outcome has been repeatedly confirmed in numerous studies on healing and recovery.

Grumbling and complaining will block positive feelings such as joy, peace, hope, or faith—and rob the individual of the health benefits those emotions can bring.

The Spill-Over Effect

Grumbling and complaining do not just corrode our bodies and souls. The discontented person damages many of their relationships, especially close relationships like marriage. King Solomon had a few choice things to say about this:

It is better to live in the corner of an attic than with a crabby woman in a lovely home. (Proverbs 21:9)

Better to live in the desert than with a quarrelsome, complaining woman. (Proverbs 21:19)

A constant dripping on a rainy day and a cranky woman are much alike! You can no more stop her complaints than you can stop the wind or hold onto anything with oil-slick hands. (Proverbs 27:15–16)

For the record, grumbling and complaining men are not much fun either!

Constructive Communication

At times we *do* have to discuss some negative aspects of life. This can be done productively, if the goal is to find a practical solution or to figure out how to improve the situation. Legitimate complaints made in a spirit of courtesy, love, and respect have their proper place.

This mindful search for ways to make things better needs to be contrasted with needless whining, droning self-pity, and self-centered irritability that accomplishes nothing but annoying the people around us, perhaps dragging down their moods along with our own.

The Onward Challenge

Habitual grumbling and complaining, with no constructive, goal-oriented purpose, is as harmful to us as it was to the Israelites in the days of Moses. I challenge each one of us, no matter what kind of atmosphere we are living in right now, to see the cup half-full (or even full and running over!) as often as we can. Let's begin each day focusing on our blessings and opportunities, not our pressures and problems.

19
JEALOUSY
Competing and Comparing

...jealousy and selfishness are not God's kind of wisdom.
Such things are earthly, unspiritual, inspired by the devil.
For wherever there is jealousy or selfish ambition,
there will be disorder and every other kind of evil.
James 3:15–16

A RECENT HARVARD study, involving tens of thousands of subjects over three decades, revealed how common it is for individuals to compare themselves with others.[306] Instead of busying themselves with their *own* lives, many consciously choose to focus on someone else's life. "The grass is always greener on the other side of the fence" mentality seems more prevalent today than ever.

Jealousy has afflicted humankind from the beginning of time. Cain's jealousy of Abel was so strong that it led Cain to murder his brother. All of us encounter jealousy at one time or another, for one reason or another.

Even the noblest of missionaries admit to struggling with a jealous heart. Helen Roseveare, for example, a medical missionary to the Congo, had to deal with jealousy. After she came home on her first furlough (after five years in the Congo), she had time to think about her various struggles, problems, and personal issues. One issue was her singlehood. She began to envy other missionaries who were married and to wonder why she wasn't. She went through a season of wrestling with this tough issue.[307]

---

[306] From an article in the *Toronto Star*, November 23, 2006, by Craig and Marc Kielburger.
[307] Helen Roseveare, *Give Me This Mountain*, page 118.

Competing and Comparing

A sure sign of the presence of jealousy is the tendency to constantly compete and compare. On a certain level, a competitive instinct is natural. People are usually competitive in a tennis match or hockey game. That kind of competitive instinct is normal. But when the competitive drive is *so* fierce that the game stops being fun and winning becomes everything, the competitive instinct has gone off the rails.

We are most inclined to compete with, and to compare ourselves against, siblings, classmates, friends, work colleagues, and spouses. When any of these people tell you about some success, achievement, or acquisition, are you happy for them — or do you immediately start to measure their success, achievement, and acquisition against what *you* have done or attained? When someone else gets promoted, rewarded, or recognized, does that make you feel great—or does it simply grate on you? Does that spur you on to want the same attention? When someone you know buys a new home or car or goes on a fabulous vacation, do you automatically begin to compare these things with the blessings in your own life (or maybe lacking from your life)?

Obsessive competing and comparing are not healthy. These kinds of thoughts usually only feel good when we are ahead in the race. But we can't realistically win every race. Competing and comparing are rooted in self-esteem that is built on wrong footings. Whether we are brave enough to label it rightly or not, constant competing and comparing are manifestations of jealousy.

In those seasons of life when we do not feel like we are leading the pack, we are more likely to feel jealousy. A jealous mindset can lead to anger, bitterness, anxiety, discouragement, depression, grumbling, and a spirit of discontentment. James 3:16 points out that wherever there is jealousy there will be "...every other kind of evil." Jealousy often gets tangled up with pride, selfish ambition, and an egocentric perspective. Jealousy creates heartburn of the soul, a chronic inner discomfort not easily soothed.

Jealousy Is Futile

What is the point of being jealous? Jealousy never diminishes the blessings of its object. If we are jealous of someone else because they are attractive, gifted, wealthy, or loved, our jealousy does not have the slightest effect on that person's looks, talents, riches, or relationships with others.

Of course, the exception to this is when jealousy escalates into theft, vandalism, assault, or murder. In these cases, the more the jealous person tries to harm the object of the jealousy, the more they eventually end up hurting themselves.

Jealousy might motivate some people to strive for worldly success. Those who compete and compare often work *very* hard to get ahead. Deep down, they feel a painful ache. They yearn for their fair share of approval, affirmation, attention, affection, and applause from the world around them. So they push themselves to excel and stand out. Some become insatiable *over*achievers. Solomon commented on this in Ecclesiastes 4:4: "Then I observed that the basic motive for success is the driving force of envy and jealousy! But this, too, is foolishness, chasing the wind."

A suitable verse to quote alongside Solomon's observation is Jesus' question: what does it profit a person if they gain the whole world but lose their own soul?[308] Jealous straining and striving does not lead to *true* significance or success from God's perspective.

Paul's Advice About Competing and Comparing

Paul had to warn some of the early Christians about their tendency to compete and compare. In Galatians 6:4 Paul wisely provided this antidote to jealousy: "Pay careful attention to your

---

[308] Luke 9:25.

own work, for then you will get the satisfaction of a job well done, and you won't need to compare yourself to anyone else." (NLT)

If we focus on our own opportunities, blessings, privileges, and challenges, we will be far less inclined to be jealous of others. It is when we put our focus on someone else's opportunities, blessings, privileges, and challenges that the ugly seeds of jealousy are sown. Each one of us can find out what God wants *us* to do—our own unique, special, significant assignments in life. If we get caught up in God's purposes for our *own* lives, we will be so busy, energized, enthused, and fulfilled that we won't have time or inclination to compete or compare with anyone else. When we do think of others, we can then be genuinely happy for them as we watch them run their own personal races in life.

One Common Origin of Jealousy

I have read over the years that jealousy often begins in the family of origin, during a person's childhood. Most people go through some measure of jealousy towards their siblings.

Because parents are only human (and often too busy to think every parenting decision right through) they don't always equally divide their time, energy, attention, affection, affirmation, money, or other resources between their children. In many cases, the inequality is unintentional. Sometimes it is the most gifted child who receives the most attention. Other times it is the child with the sunniest disposition. In some families, it is the first-born child who is doted on; in others, it is the youngest child who is spoiled and indulged. Or maybe it is the sick or disabled or otherwise disadvantaged child. One way or another, most people have grown up with *some* degree of sibling jealousy and rivalry arising from unequal parental treatment. In our own parenting, my husband and I *tried* to treat our children equally, but circumstances, opportunities, and challenges beyond our control did not always cooperate with our best intentions.

If a child feels they are not getting their fair share of parental love, approval, time, and resources, they set themselves up for a lifetime of jealousy—beginning with jealousy of one or more siblings, progressing to jealousy of friends, and later to jealousy of their spouse and colleagues.

Sibling rivalry can also stem from being surrounded by brothers and sisters who get affirmative attention from teachers, peers, coaches, and others. I grew up with three siblings who were high achievers. One brother went to medical school. My other brother earned an MBA from Harvard Business School. My sister traveled all over the world in connection with her film career and is presently recognized for her humanitarian work in Afghanistan. Over the years, I developed the habit of competing and comparing with my siblings. In my twenties, I married a very accomplished husband and worked alongside some outstanding legal colleagues, which only sharpened my competitive drive. On a certain level, the competition felt harmless, sometimes even fun.

One day, many years ago, I made the decision to stop competing and comparing with anyone. It had finally dawned on me that this energy-wasting habit was never going to make me feel better about my lot in life. Instead, it sometimes fueled feelings of ambition, pride, or discontentment.

Like any other mental habit, I could not change my thought patterns overnight. But I was determined to eradicate this particular habit. I can now say that I am usually genuinely happy for other people when they are the center of attention. Immense inner freedom and enhanced contentment have accompanied this change in my thought patterns. Like any other mental and emotional discipline, however, I will need to remain vigilant—the tendency to be jealous is so deeply ingrained in human nature!

Joseph's Brothers

Joseph's eleven brothers developed jealousy in their family of origin. These brothers were initially jealous because their father treated Joseph as the obviously favorite son. You will recall that

Joseph was the only one to receive a special, multi-colored coat from his father. No one likes to grow up in a family where one or more siblings are the favorites.

The fires of jealousy were further stoked when Joseph began to have dreams about his brothers bowing down to him.[309]

How did the brothers handle this? They wanted to kill Joseph. Jealousy can be that strong an emotion. Ultimately, they sold him to a caravan of traders passing by, then lied to their father about Joseph being mauled by a wild animal. Jealousy always brings out the worst in people.

Rachel and Leah

Sisters Rachel and Leah are further examples of siblings who competed and compared. Their story is told in Genesis 30. Both of them were wives of Jacob. Leah, the least favorite wife, began to bear children first. Rachel was distraught at her own seemingly barren womb and became jealous of Leah.

Although God eventually blessed Rachel with a few of her own sons, the two women were in an ongoing competition to bear the most sons, using even their maids to help bear children for them. At one point, Rachel had the attitude: "...I am in a fierce contest with my sister and I am winning!"[310] How very human.

Saul and David

Jealousy is certainly not restricted to sibling relationships. The Bible records how King Saul was insanely jealous of David. Once powerful and popular in his own right, King Saul became jealous of David when he saw how much the people admired David. As the citizens of the realm joyfully danced because of David's victories on the battlefield, they chanted that King Saul

---

[309] Genesis 37:11.
[310] Genesis 30:8.

had killed his thousands, but warrior David had slain *tens* of thousands.[311]

And so began Saul's murderous intent to kill David. For many years, David was forced to be a fugitive on the run, hiding in faraway places from the dangerous jealousy of Saul. Saul developed a "tormenting spirit"[312] that troubled him to the grave. His obsessive jealousy was, no doubt, a part of that torment.

New Testament Examples

Two thousand years ago, the religious leaders in Jerusalem were jealous of the crowds who adoringly followed Jesus by the end of His ministry. This jealousy was so fierce that it set the ball in motion for the Roman crucifixion of Jesus. Later, the religious leaders were jealous of the crowds who came to hear Paul preach about Jesus. They cursed and argued against whatever Paul said.[313]

A Serious Command

The Ten Commandments contain great insight into what God considers important. Right up there with worshipping other gods, murder, and adultery, God condemns the practice of coveting anything our neighbor has—whether his or her property, spouse, or servants. God takes the related mindsets of envy, coveting, and jealousy very seriously.

It is interesting that God allows Himself to be jealous. In many places in Scripture, God describes Himself as a jealous God.[314] He does not want humankind to worship any other gods. He calls Himself the only true God. God's jealous character is one dimension of His character that He does not want human-kind to imitate. (It is not the only such character attribute.

---

[311] See the full story at 1 Samuel 18.

[312] 1 Samuel 18:10.

[313] Acts 13:45.

[314] See, for example, Exodus 20:5.

Another is God's exclusive right to avenge an injustice. We are told not to seek vengeance when we are wrongly treated. God says that vengeance is His as the ultimate judge and ruler over all humankind.)

Some Further Warnings About Jealousy

In Psalm 37:7b King David cautioned: "Don't be envious of evil men who prosper." In Psalm 73:3 he admitted that he himself had once struggled with envying the apparent prosperity of the proud and the wicked. At some point, all of us can relate to that struggle. I encourage you to study that whole Psalm. David ultimately concluded that there was no reason to envy the success of the wicked—he had come to understand the nature of their final destiny.

In Proverbs 27:4, King Solomon observed that jealousy is even more dangerous and more cruel than anger. King Solomon also understood the negative impact of jealousy on a person's body. One translation of Proverbs 14:30b states that "envy rots the bones"; another translation asserts that jealousy "rots" life away; yet a third translation notes that "jealousy is like cancer in the bones."[315] Jealousy is bad news no matter which translation you prefer.

In the New Testament, Paul affirmed that jealousy is a serious sin. In Galatians 5:19–20, in his list of the obvious fruits of the sinful nature, he includes jealousy and envy. Similarly, in Romans 13:13–14, Paul counseled: "...Don't spend your time in wild parties and getting drunk or in adultery and lust, or fighting, or jealousy. But ask the Lord Jesus Christ to help you live as you should..." I invite you to notice the kind of sins that jealousy is equated with.

---

[315] NIV; TLB; NLT.

Jealousy and Love

Let's briefly revisit a few principles we talked about in the chapter on love. We talked about how much God loves each one of us. Once we realize how much God loves us, we are able to love ourselves. Only then can we truly love others.

A person who deeply receives God's love and who has consequently been able to love themselves in a healthy manner will have no need to be jealous of anyone else. In fact, they will be able to graciously and generously love others. Loving others means *not* being envious of them (see 1 Corinthians 13:4)—true love always wants what is best for the beloved. This healthy love for others is only possible when a person has healthy self-esteem, primarily rooted in their deep acceptance of God's love for them.

In addition, those who authentically love others are careful not to provoke jealousy in the other person. Do you remember, in your teenage years, how common it was for a girl or guy to try to make their partner jealous by flirting with other members of the opposite sex? They wrongly believed that this would make their boyfriend or girlfriend desire them all the more. This has nothing to do with real love—and everything to do with immature ego. Real love neither entertains nor provokes jealousy.

Carol Kent

Author Carol Kent has shared about many of the raw feelings that have emerged in her life since the day her twenty-five-year-old only son was arrested for the murder of his wife's ex-husband. He had been a model son. At the time of the murder, he was a navy officer who had graduated from the prestigious U.S. Naval Academy in Annapolis. Carol's son was eventually convicted of first degree murder and received a life sentence in prison with no chance of parole.

After the conviction was upheld by the appeal court, Carol realized that her family would never again celebrate Christmas outside of prison walls. Understandably, she struggled with jealousy toward other families who could gather each year around a Christmas tree and share a turkey feast.[316] When life throws any of us an unexpected and unthinkable curve ball, it is only natural to be jealous of everyone around us and their seemingly normal lives.

As she progressed in her emotional journey, Carol learned much about displacing her jealousy with gratitude for what still remained in her life. On a broader level, Carol has had an astounding emotional journey since her son's arrest for murder. She bears amazing witness to how God's power can help a Christian cope with a devastating array of raw, painful human emotions.

Brother Yun

I love one of the stories in the book *The Heavenly Man,* by Brother Yun, about his years as a well-known Christian leader in modern China. At one point in his life, Brother Yun was grieved about the incredible jealousy between various Chinese house churches and their leaders. He knew that this was not right. He saw how such jealousy had also morphed into bitterness, even hatred.

His solution? He gathered the leaders together and had them wash one another's feet, just as Jesus taught His disciples to do. This humble exercise of love began to melt the vicious competition between the men involved, initiating a new era of brotherhood, unity, and partnership between the different churches.[317]

What do you think would happen if we tried to love, serve, and bless the people we are jealous of? If we could bring ourselves to wash their feet (even if only metaphorically)?

Divine Help

God does not want us to be jealous. Instead, He wants us to feel extravagantly loved. He wants us to know that we are special,

---

[316] Carol Kent, *A New Kind of Normal,* see page 10–13.
[317] Brother Yun, *The Heavenly Man,* pages 237–238.

we are valued, we are treasured, we are esteemed. We do not ever have to compete with anyone else for *His* love.

It need not depend on whether our parents (or siblings or peers or spouse) love us, love us *equally* alongside others, or love us *enough*. It is a waste of energy to strain or strive for more of the love, approval, affection, attention, time, or resources of the people we are close to. Instead, we can choose to focus on the incomparable abundant love of God—the great, unfailing, all-surpassing love of God, so freely available for all of us.

Besides pouring out His love on us, God will provide other people to love us beyond those who might have failed us, marginalized us, neglected us, or hurt us in the past. When we feel deeply, truly loved—by God and by these others that He provides—we are enabled to cut loose all childhood and other relational roots of jealousy.

God wants to embrace us and to tell each one of us how significant we are in *His* estimation. He can help us run our own challenging personal races with our eyes firmly fixed on our very own worthy goals, not distracted by the races being run by others.

Anger is cruel and fury overwhelming,
but who can stand before jealousy?
Proverbs 27:4 (NIV)

No matter how much we see, we are never satisfied.
No matter how much we hear, we are not content.
Ecclesiastes 1:8b (NLT)

20
GRATITUDE
AND
CONTENTMENT
The Cheerful Soul

Thank the Lord for all the glorious things he does...
Psalm 105:1

...I will keep on thanking you forever!
Psalm 30:12b

No matter what happens, always be thankful,
for this is God's will for you who belong to Christ Jesus.
1 Thessalonians 5:18

W E HAVE ALL been told that it is beneficial to develop an "attitude of gratitude." Yet I know that I am not alone in struggling to be grateful from day to day. It is one thing to be grateful to the people who bless our lives. It is another matter to be grateful to God. In our prayer lives, it is so easy to get caught up in asking God for this or that when we should be regularly spending some of that time thanking Him for what He has already done for us.

Gratitude in the Good Times

God wants us to express our gratitude to Him in the *good times* of life. That is why, for example, in the Old Testament times, the Israelites were commanded to have a special festival a week after the harvest. This was to be "...a time of deep thanksgiving to the

Lord..."[318] for blessing them with an abundant harvest and in various other ways. God wanted His people to take the time and make the effort to say thank you for His goodness and provision.

Gratitude in the Tough Times

God also wants us to express our gratitude to Him in the *tough* times of life. Perhaps this is when it matters most.

David once wrote: "Go through his open gates with great thanksgiving; enter his courts with praise. Give thanks to him and bless his name. For the Lord is *always* good. He is *always* loving and kind..."[319]

Did David have a problem-free life? Absolutely not. David suffered greatly: running from the murderous pursuit of King Saul; hiding in caves and desert places; enduring fierce military battles; losing several of his children; facing his guilt and the punishment of God for his own wrong-doing; receiving contempt from some of his wives and betrayal from some of his sons.

Yet David penned the above words, declaring that God is "*always* good" and "*always* loving and kind." David realized that he needed to count his blessings—and to see the ways in which God was still bestowing some measure of goodness and loving-kindness in his life—even during his times of loneliness, sickness, grief, pain, and struggle.

Here's the deal: each day has its burden of problems and sorrows, headaches and hassles, but each day *also* has some blessings and benefits, privileges and opportunities. We can choose to consciously look for the evidence of God's daily goodness.

Journaling

Some years ago, I stopped journaling about anything that would fuel anger, bitterness, resentment, unforgiveness, despair, grumbling, and discontentment if I read it again at a later date. What

---

[318] Deuteronomy 16:15b.
[319] Psalm 100:4–5.

was the point of writing about life's negatives? Why re-live the unpleasant and painful experiences of life?

Instead, I decided that I would generally only journal about what would later generate thoughts and feelings of love, peace, hope, faith, joy, and *gratitude*. This was quite easy on the golden days, when the sun shone and the skies were blue and health, strength, and prosperity were available in good measure, but of course, not every day is golden.

Did this mean ignoring the tough trials I went through? No, I could journal about those times too. I was just very careful and very deliberate regarding how I wrote about the difficult times. On even my worst days, during my most depressing circumstances, I decided that I would find *something* to be grateful for, *something* that stirred up thankful praise to God, *something* that I would enjoy reading about years later.

A recent study has shown that such basic mental exercises as making a list of three good things that happen each day can increase positive feelings, instill a sense of satisfaction, and decrease symptoms of depression.[320] So begin to think or journal about those three good things every day!

I love Paul's timeless advice: "…whatever is true, whatever is noble, whatever is right, whatever is pure, whatever is lovely, whatever is admirable—if anything is excellent or praiseworthy—think about such things."[321]

Sincere Thanks

God does not want us to just go through the motions of saying thanks. Psalm 50:14 reveals: "What I want from you is your *true* thanks…" From the deepest levels of our souls, He wants us to genuinely and sincerely thank Him—for His goodness, His love, His blessings, His provision, His healing, His deliverance, His forgiveness, His mercy, even His discipline and, most of all, for the gift of Himself.

---

[320] See articles by: Flannery Dean; Emmons and McCullough M.E.
[321] Philippians 4:8 (NIV).

God also wants us to remember to thank Him for answered prayer. In Colossians 4:2 we are instructed: "Don't be weary in prayer; keep at it; watch for God's answers and remember to be thankful when they come."

Paul's Thankful Heart

Like David, Paul did not have smooth sailing most of his life. Paul endured many hardships and trials. Yet it was Paul who wrote words such as: "Since we have a Kingdom nothing can destroy, let us please God by serving him with thankful hearts..."[322]

In Ephesians 5:20 he exhorted: "Always give thanks for everything..." In Colossians 1:11–12 Paul reminded his fellow Christians to always be thankful to God, "no matter what happens."

In Philippians 4:6–7 Paul scribed the famous passage: "Do not be anxious about anything, but in everything, by prayer and petition, *with thanksgiving*, present your requests to God. And the peace of God, which transcends all understanding, will guard your hearts and minds in Christ Jesus. (NIV)"

Paul learned that a constant attitude of gratitude in *all* circumstances helped to offset anxiety and to promote deep inner peace.

Corrie and Her Sisters

Let's look at two more brief snapshots from the lives of Corrie and her sisters. You will recall that this family courageously hid Jews in their Dutch home during the Nazi genocide of Jews in World War II.

One terrible day, prior to her own imprisonment, Corrie had to stand by and watch as her beloved sister Nollie was arrested by the Nazis. While Corrie safely stood outside, she could hear music coming from a window of her home—Nollie's son had chosen to play a beautiful Bach hymn as the Nazis led his mother away. Even in the horror of the immediate situation,

---

[322] Hebrews 12:28.

Corrie paused to thank God for using that hymn to remind her that He had Nollie in His hands.[323]

During a later period of the war, when both Corrie and another sister Betsie were in the Ravensbruck concentration camp, Betsie decided to deliberately thank God for the fleas that infested their living quarters. Because of the prevalence of these fleas, the German guards did not like to enter their dormitory. This allowed the sisters to freely read the Bible aloud to their suffering room-mates, to worship, and to pray without fear or restraint.[324]

Contentment

Those who learn to maintain an attitude of gratitude, no matter what they go through, become deeply contented people. True contentment has little to do with circumstances; it has everything to do with the set of the soul.

We have noted that the apostle Paul modeled a constantly thankful heart throughout a difficult life. It should come as no surprise that he developed continual contentment. Paul penned these magnificent statements while he was under house arrest, chained to a Roman guard: "...I have learned to be content *whatever* the circumstances. I know what it is to be in need, and I know what it is to have plenty. I have learned the secret of being content in any and every situation, whether well fed or hungry, whether living in plenty or in want."[325] I personally find this one of the most inspiring and challenging passages in all of Scripture. Is it *really* possible to live in this dimension?

Paul could even be content as he faced the likelihood of imminent death. In 2 Corinthians 5:8, Paul said: "And we are not afraid, but are quite content to die, for then we will be at home with the Lord." This is quite the opposite of the well-known poem by Dylan Thomas that tells us not to go gentle into that

---

[323] Carole Carlson, *Corrie Ten Boom: Her Life, Her Faith*, pg. 78.

[324] Ibid. page 108.

[325] Philippians 4:11–12 (NIV).

good night but to instead rage against the dying of the light. Christians *can* go gentle into that good night, knowing that it is not a dying of the light, but actually an embracing of life eternal.

Paul is believed to have been brutally beheaded by Roman soldiers just outside of Rome during the reign of the Emperor Nero—not long after penning his words about being content in all circumstances.

Contentment Cannot Co-Exist with Grumbling, Complaining, or Jealousy

It is probably trite to point this out, but sometimes we need to remind ourselves that contentment cannot exist side by side with grumbling, complaining, or jealousy. These negative attitudes focus on what others have (and we don't) and on what we think we are entitled to. In contrast, contentment wisely focuses on the blessings, opportunities, and privileges *we* have. The contented person has stopped competing and comparing. They have discovered the futility of stressing, straining, and striving to get ahead of the pack. The contented person knows how to *savor* all that is already good in their own life.

Contentment Embraces Simplicity

We can learn to be content with a simple life. In 1 Timothy 6 Paul encouraged us to learn to be content with food, shelter, and clothing. He warned about the snares of wanting to be rich.

In similar vein, Solomon observed in Ecclesiastes 5:10: "He who loves money shall never have enough. The foolishness of thinking that wealth brings happiness!" If we are constantly craving more (bigger, newer, better), we will never be content.

The Challenge: Accepting Our Personal Lot in Life

Solomon wrote in Ecclesiastes 5:19b-20: "…To enjoy your work and to accept your lot in life—that is indeed a gift from God…" We waste a lot of emotional energy wishing we could be someone else or have what they have. God wants us to accept our lot in life with gratitude and contentment—to be thankful for where He has placed us and with what He has given us. A contented person can go through each day enjoying every meal, enjoying their work, enjoying people along the way, enjoying time spent with God, then enjoying a good night's sleep.

Accepting our personal lot does not mean that we never seek change or improvement or a higher level of excellence. As we seek to improve any aspect of our lives, we can do so with a continual spirit of thanksgiving for whatever point we are at in our journey instead of resenting the fact that we have not yet arrived at our destination. We can cultivate contentment while we are still studying, still single, and still renting, even if we dream and aspire to some day complete a degree, earn a regular paycheck, find a life partner, have children, and own a home. We can be content through life's journey, enjoying each phase whether or not we ever reach our original goals or destinations.

Solomon queried in Ecclesiastes 6:6: "Though a man lives a thousand years twice over, but doesn't find contentment—well, what's the use?"

Good question!

Come before him with thankful hearts.
Psalm 95:2a

It is good to say, "Thank you" to the Lord,
to sing praises to the God who is above all gods.
Every morning tell him, "Thank you for your kindness,"
and every evening rejoice in all his faithfulness.
Psalm 92:1–2

And always be thankful.
Colossians 3:15b

21

JOY
Exquisite

...oh, the joys of those who put their trust in him!
Psalm 2:12c

Joy rises in my heart until I burst out
in songs of praise to him.
Psalm 28:7c

A FEW YEARS ago, I had dinner with Janice, the beautiful and wealthy wife of the owner of an NFL football team. She was clearly distraught. Notwithstanding having the homes, cars, vacations, and clothes of their dreams, this couple's marriage was on the skids. Her husband had become an abusive alcoholic. Janice's health was deteriorating and her sanity hung by a thread. For her own safety, she had recently separated from her husband. Although she felt like her marriage was painfully spiralling downward, she told me that she still held onto one source of inner joy—she had found Christ and was discovering immense joy in her relationship with Him. She affirmed what I had known for years—the most profound joy in life comes from a personal relationship with God.

Chuck Colson

I was struck by Chuck Colson's interesting depiction of the night that President Richard Nixon was re-elected in 1972. In the hours after a landslide victory (in which Nixon captured a record-breaking forty-nine of the fifty states), one would imagine that Nixon and his closest staff (including Colson) would have been ecstatic, excited, energized, and caught up in happy celebration.

The scene Colson paints is unexpected. Nixon was *not* in a good mood—he grumbled and complained as he thought of words to say to his opponent on that eve of his victory. Nixon's chief of staff was also in a foul mood. Colson himself just sat there in a numb fog.

The next day was no more joyous. An atmosphere of continued negativity, anger, and griping prevailed. In fact, for the next few months Colson described himself as a miserable man, unable to find happiness even in the White House.[326]

Here were men at the pinnacle of worldly power, status, and success, finding that happiness was as elusive as ever. Colson claims that he did not find true happiness until he committed his life to Christ—when his outer world was in shambles after the Watergate scandal brought Nixon and his administration down.[327]

Soon after becoming a Christian, Colson spent some time in prison. He went through many difficult days, going from the privileges of the White House to living behind bars. Near the end of his time in prison, he was dealt a further blow. He learned that his son had been arrested for possession of narcotics.

At that low point, Colson could do nothing but surrender his pain to God. As he did so, he noticed renewed joy flowing through him. In the hours after turning this fresh crisis over to God, he began to feel stronger than ever. He was later to write that this surrender of his pain to God was his personal mountaintop experience—the world all around him seemed full of love, joy, and beauty in a way it never had in his White House years. Strangely, but wonderfully, this mountaintop experience with God came when his circumstances were so dismal.[328]

Hockey Hero Paul Henderson

Canadian hockey hero Paul Henderson is well-known for his winning goal in the fiercely contested 1972 hockey series between

---

[326] Charles Colson, *Born Again*, pgs. 17–19.

[327] Ibid., pg. 75.

[328] Ibid., pg. 340.

Canada and Russia. The photographs of him raising his hockey stick in gleeful victory are still being shown in the media all these years later.

In the days and months following that famous goal, Henderson began to notice that he was not really happy. Despite all the accolades, he did not feel the way he expected he would feel, nor the way the whole country assumed he would feel. He recalls wondering: if that momentous goal, watched by millions of wildly cheering fans, could not make him truly happy, what hope was there? He slowly began to realize that no amount of celebrity or success could erase the anger and other negative feelings that rumbled in his heart.

Henderson's realization that lasting happiness would never lie in worldly achievement was a crucial factor in Henderson later committing his life to Christ.[329] In the years following his Christian commitment, Henderson has found a lot of joy in knowing and serving God. After leaving the world of professional hockey, Henderson became well known for his ministry with Christian business leaders. Next to the joy he has found in his relationship with God, Paul loves to talk about the joy that he has experienced as husband, father, and grandfather.

So Many More

I could tell story after story of how many people—even the rich, the powerful, the talented, the beautiful—have given up looking for happiness in worldly stature and gain and have instead found real joy in Christ. Many of the world's best and brightest have not been genuinely happy or at peace until they have found Christ.

Are Happiness and Joy the Same Thing?

Many Christians debate whether happiness is the same thing as joy. The words are sometimes used interchangeably in different

---

[329] Facts from various public talks Paul Henderson has given in the Greater Toronto area.

Bible translations. Neither word can be precisely defined—after all, there is a strong personal and subjective element to what happiness and joy look like in each individual life.

When happiness is described in modern media and secular literature, it is often connected with whatever pleasure, self-fulfillment, possessions, entertainment, or relationships make people "feel good." There is an emphasis on self and a dependence on good circumstances. Worldly happiness supposedly emanates from a shiny new car, a picture-perfect Christmas, size 4 designer jeans, a flawlessly decorated home, a yacht in the Caribbean, or a trip to Disney World. There is nothing wrong with any of these things, but I challenge you to find a Bible verse that links any of them with joy—or a human soul who will honestly say that deep, lasting, true happiness has been generated by any of these things.

Biblical joy, on the other hand, really has *nothing* to do with self or with surrounding circumstances. The truly joyful Christian is focused as much on God and on their fellow human beings as they are on their own interests. Furthermore, true joy can bubble up in the Christian even during the worst storms of life. All of us can learn to understand what the apostle Paul meant when he said that we can rejoice even "...when we run into problems and trials..."[330]

Sources of Joy

Lasting joy is not found in material goods or self-centered pleasure-seeking. The Bible tells us that true and lasting joy is only found in living life in Christ. But where exactly can we find this joy in the Christian life? Let's briefly examine some of the sources of joy described in the Bible.

---

[330] Romans 5:3.

God Himself

I love what Charles Finney (the lawyer who became a great American evangelist) wrote about the early days of his relationship with God: "No words can describe the wonderful love that was shed abroad in my heart. I wept aloud with joy....When I awoke in the morning the sun had risen and was pouring a clear light in my room. Words cannot express the impression that this sunlight made upon me....I arose upon my knees in the bed, and wept aloud with joy..."[331]

It is only joy at its most supreme that makes a grown man weep at something as simple as the presence of sunlight—*this* kind of joy exemplifies the quality of inner being in those who truly know God.

David expressed his delight in his relationship with God with equal emotion: "Heart, body, and soul are filled with joy....You have let me experience the joys of life and the exquisite pleasures of your own eternal presence."[332] Another Psalm declares: "All who seek for God shall live in joy."[333]

The early Christians knew this same incredible joy. Peter wrote to them: "Though you have not seen him, you love him; and even though you do not see him now, you believe in him and are filled with an inexpressible and glorious joy..."[334]

Leo Tolstoy, the brilliant Russian novelist, had this to say about entering into personal relationship with God: "Five years ago I came to believe in Christ's teaching, and my life suddenly changed....I heard the words of Christ and understood them...I experienced happiness and joy of life."

Truly my most joyful moments are found in the hour I spend each day in communion with God. I crave that time and place more than I crave anything else. The joy of being in God's

---

[331] Bonnie Harvey, *Charles Finney*, quoting Finney on pgs. 42, 45.

[332] Psalm 16: 9, 11.

[333] Psalm 69:32c.

[334] 1 Peter 1:8 (NIV).

presence (praying, reading His word, listening to His Spirit) transcends any other joy I find during the rest of the day.

One of the reasons we can be so joyful in God's presence stems from the fact that God has agreed to forgive all of our sins if we choose to confess them. God's grace and mercy remove those sins forever. David once wrote: "What happiness for those whose guilt has been forgiven! What joys when sins are covered over! What relief for those who have confessed their sins and God has cleared their record."[335]

Our Eternal Destiny

Peter recognized that life on this earth will have many problems and pressures, perhaps even seasons of persecution. And so, he told Christians to never forget where they are ultimately heading. We are on our way to a much better place—to an eternal destiny immeasurably superior to this life. Peter wrote to his fellow believers: "So be truly glad! There is wonderful joy ahead, even though the going is rough for a while down here."[336]

Paul echoed this same encouragement in 2 Corinthians 4:18: "So we do not look at what we can see right now, the troubles all around us, but we look forward to the joys in heaven which we have not yet seen. The troubles will soon be over, but the joys to come will last forever." Fire, flood, theft, disease—even death— cannot rob us of this ultimate joy.

We can experience this same joy when we ponder the eternal destiny of loved ones who have known God. Less than a week after 9/11, Lisa Beamer went to the site where her husband, Todd, and other brave passengers lost their lives when their hijacked Washington-bound plane crashed. Standing in that bleak field with other mourning families, Lisa should have been overwhelmed with shock, grief, anger, bitterness, or pain. Instead, Lisa chose to focus on the words of "It is Well with My Soul," the hymn written by a father soon

---

[335] Psalm 32:1–2.
[336] 1 Peter 1:6.

after his four daughters drowned at sea. When Lisa reminded herself that Todd was not *in* that crash site—that he was heaven-bound—she felt an immediate peace and a surprising joy.[337] She *knew* his eternal destiny, and she knew that she will share it with him some day.

Our Fellowship with Other Christians

John wrote that, as Christians, we can "...have wonderful fellowship and joy with each other..."[338] Paul wrote often about the joy he received from other believers even when he was not present with them but was simply receiving news about them.[339]

One of my favorite summer destinations is a place called Muskoka Woods, where my husband is a camp doctor for one week each year. The place is breath-takingly beautiful, but that is not the primary reason I love going there. I love the fellowship of the many Christian friends there that I have known for years—in some cases for decades.

I have found the same kind of rich joy in various church communities that I have been a part of over the years (including my present church!), and in other gatherings of Christian friends. The joy is especially sweet when someone I know has just accepted Christ, or has been healed, or has achieved some spiritual victory, or has some fresh story to share about God's work and blessing in their lives. This kind of joy far surpasses the temporary and somewhat shallow happiness I feel when I buy something new or immerse myself in some form of entertainment.

I am blessed that everyone in my family has embraced Christian faith, so fellowship is always close at hand. Particularly deep joy has flowed from these relationships—joy that is precious beyond words.

---

[337] Lisa Beamer, pg. 311.

[338] 1 John 1:7.

[339] See, for example, 1 Thessalonians 2:19–20 and 3:9.

Our Enjoyment of God's Creation

God wants us to enjoy His creation. Nature is one of His special gifts to us—a gift that is often totally free, if we are willing to stop in the mad rush of our days to notice the clouds, the sky, the stars, the sunset, the birds, the flowers, the butterflies, or whatever aspect of nature is around us. I won't even begin to list the many Psalms that rhapsodize about the joys of nature.

Meaningful Work

King Solomon tried to experience everything that he could in life, in order to discover what was *truly* satisfying and meaningful. He was healthy, wealthy, and wise, but for some years he was disenchanted with life—nothing seemed inherently meaningful. Ultimately, Solomon realized that only a relationship with God was of lasting value, but along the way he also had this to say: "So I saw that there is nothing better for men than that they should be happy in their work, for that is what they are here for..."[340]

Next to our relationships with God and with others, we are intended to find great pleasure in our everyday work.

This same truth was conveyed centuries before to the Israelites at the time of Moses. They were told that "the Lord your God will bless you in all your harvest and in all the work of your hands, and your joy will be complete."[341]

I really enjoyed my twenty years of practicing law. At this point in my life, I am finding even greater joy in developing Christian ministries. I *choose* to work in various ministries (primarily writing, speaking, and serving on Boards) because this kind of work brings me enormous joy. There is a particular kind of joy in working for God. The psalmist understood this when he wrote: "Those who sow tears shall reap joy. Yes, they go out weeping, carrying seed for sowing, and return singing,

---

[340] Ecclesiastes 3:22.
[341] Deuteronomy 16:15b (NIV).

carrying their sheaves."[342] Working for God is not always easy or painless, but it always results in joy in the end.

The Pursuit of Wisdom

Solomon asserted, in Proverbs 2:10: "...wisdom and truth will enter the very center of your being, filling your life with joy." In Proverbs 3:13, Solomon said: "Joyful is the person who finds wisdom, the one who gains understanding." (NLT)

Is it not truly joyful to discover some fresh insight, a new layer of knowledge, a tough truth finally grasped? The author of Psalm 119:54 certainly thought so when he declared that "...these laws of yours have been my source of joy and singing through all these years of my earthly pilgrimage."

Persecution and Suffering

So transcendent is Christian joy that Jesus assured His followers that they could have joy even when they are being reviled and persecuted.[343] This strongly underscores the biblical truth that real happiness or joy has nothing to do with circumstances and everything to do with knowing, loving, and serving God and His people.

Obedience to God

Joy is the reward of obedience to God. Solomon observed the happiness of all those who followed God's instructions.[344] Psalm 84:5 similarly asserts: "Happy are those who are strong in the Lord, who want above all else to follow your steps." Psalm 106:3 further comments: "Happiness comes to those who are fair to others and are always just and good." Psalm 119:93 states: "I will never lay aside your laws, for you have used them to restore my

---

[342] Psalm 126:5–6.
[343] Matthew 5:11.
[344] Proverbs 8:32.

joy and health." There is a direct link between obeying God by living right and possessing joy.

The Promise of Joy

For the person who has entered into a personal relationship with God, joy is clearly promised. Here are some further verses that declare this promise:

> Weeping may go on all night, but in the morning there is joy. (Psalm 30:5b)
>
> The prospect of the righteous is joy... (Proverbs 10:28a, NIV)
>
> The good man can look forward to happiness... (Proverbs 11:23)
>
> Ask and you will receive, and your joy will be complete. (John 16:24b, NIV)
>
> ...I say these things while I am still in the world, so that they may have the full measure of my joy within them. (John 17:13, NIV)

Exquisite Joy in the Midst of Exquisite Pain

The most amazing dimension of Christian joy is that it can come to us even in the midst of incredible pain. I experienced a particularly difficult time earlier in my adult life during a sustained crisis. At times, I felt overwhelmed with fear, despair, anger, confusion, sorrow, and bitterness. My world seemed to be crumbling around me. Images of worst-case scenarios robbed me of sleep.

I turned to prayer and also started saturating myself with uplifting Bible verses. It was during this time that I first began to really understand the concept of soul management from a biblical perspective. I was praying earnestly for God to restore my joy and my peace, my hope and my faith. I was also praying for Him to change my circumstances! Eventually God did both, but first He taught me some valuable lessons.

It was during this time of anguished prayer, petition, and meditation on God's Word that I started to understand that God was far more interested in my *reaction* to my circumstances than He was in my actual circumstances. He was interested in my *character*. And my character was being formed by the accumulation of the choices I was making in response to all of my unfolding circumstances. It became very clear to me that we cannot always choose or change our circumstances. Nor can we compel God to change our circumstances. All we can truly control is our reaction to the circumstances we encounter. These were not original insights. This was simply the point in my life when those timeless truths deeply penetrated my inner being.

I still remember one particular morning in that season of my life. I woke up feeling like I was drowning in despair, worry, and pain and I decided that I did not like feeling that way. I decided that, instead, I was going to *enjoy* that day. I was going to really notice my cup of coffee—how good it tasted, how energizing it was—and to be thankful for the quiet moments I had to savor it. I was going to notice how blue the sky was that day. (It actually surprised me to notice that it was remarkably blue, because, when I first opened my eyes, I had somehow perceived the day as quite dreary and grey.) I chose to notice that the sun was shining and sparkling magnificently on freshly fallen snow. I decided to take a few moments to make my favorite breakfast—which at that time was home-made banana and pecan pancakes.

And so went the rest of that day. My overall circumstances had not changed one bit. But I was learning that I could deliberately choose what I was going to think about (and what I was *not* going to think about), and the amazing thing was that by the end of that day I actually felt quite light-hearted. While I still had to honestly acknowledge my difficult circumstances (and my initial human tendency to respond with negative thoughts and emotions), I realized I did not have to indulge those negative thoughts and emotions. In fact, I had the power to cast them right out of my life.

In the following days, I chose, moment by moment, to deliberately notice the birdsong, the stars at night, the taste of my food, the smiles of strangers, and the laughter of children. I began to experientially understand that one can find *exquisite joy* even in the midst of *exquisite pain*. I learned that if I focused on the joy, it could become stronger than the pain.

Long before my circumstances changed, my soul changed. Even more importantly, I felt the power and presence of the Holy Spirit in my life more than ever before. I began to experience deep peace, bubbling joy, unshakable faith, and certain hope in the midst of the same circumstances that had seemed so impossibly bleak.

Further Lessons

The lessons I learned in that season of life were to later serve me well. Some years further down the road, a loved one was in the hospital with a serious illness. One day, feeling tired and stressed, I decided to leave the hospital to get some fresh air. It was spring and refreshingly cool outside. As I walked, I prayed. I asked for God to show me: was it possible to feel even a moment of joy that day, in the midst of my heart-wrenching pain?

While walking through a university campus near the hospital, I came across a long row of large pink rosebushes at the zenith of their bloom. A gentle breeze began to stir as I passed those bushes. Thousands of rose petals floated upward in the air all around me, creating a fragrant, surreal spiral of rose petals so thick I could not see beyond them. It was achingly beautiful. The presence of God was so real—and with His presence came the joy I had been asking for. I wanted the moment to go on forever. While, in fact, the moment probably lasted only a few minutes, I felt transported to this other pink-petalled world for a suspended period of time. In the midst of those dizzily spinning petals, the exquisite pain I had been feeling became bearable. God was there with me. God cared.

A few years later, my husband, Sam, had to have a serious operation. The day we drove to the hospital together, I remembered that day years before when God had lovingly surrounded me with His joy in a tunnel of rose petals. And I dared to ask, once again, for God to show me His joy in the midst of the present pain.

I decided to actively look for little moments of joy with each passing minute. The first thing I noticed that morning, as we drove onto the highway leading into the city, was a perfectly round, scarlet-red sun lighting up the early morning sky. I focused on that with every fiber of my being. At the hospital, we were placed in a room where we were expected to wait for some pre-op procedures. Along came a volunteer—a cheery man who had gone through a similar surgery himself and was there to help us pass the time. I found out that he was a good friend of my sister. Before I knew it, I was caught up in an interesting conversation. And more time flew by—moments I chose to enjoy.

Then, while in the room outside the operating theater, an old classmate of Sam's from medical school walked by. He was a surgeon in that hospital. His eyes grew wide as saucers when he saw Sam in the pre-op bed. This friend sat by the bedside and talked for a while. Imagine both of us finding some measure of enjoyment just *minutes* before Sam was put under for his operation. Once again, it was surreal.

So on and so forth went the day. John, a family friend, was waiting for me as I said good-bye to Sam and walked tearfully into the corridor. John had come to keep me company and to pray with me. As we walked along, we ran into Patty, a friend from my church—she relayed to me how a large group from my church had prayed together for Sam's surgery the night before.[345] This also lifted my spirits.

Of course, a part of me was scared, anxious, tense, sad, and shaky. But God showed me, once again, how I could find joy in

---

[345] Thank you, Cedarview Community Church.

even the most unusual circumstances, when joy was least expected from a human perspective. All through that day, I found joy — in small but sustaining doses.

More Tales of Exquisite Joy

The ability to experience joy while still in the midst of pain has been described by many Christians. Lisa Beamer wrote about an occasion less than half a year after her husband's death. She was celebrating her son David's fourth birthday. She realized that she could very easily start to think about her late husband Todd. She could feel sorry for herself. She could feel sorry for her son. She could spend the day grieving. But instead, she chose to notice the joy of her children. Her children were enjoying the occasion, living in the moment. She realized that she could too.[346]

I have also been impacted by the great love story of C. S. Lewis and Joy Davidman. Soon after their marriage, they learned that Joy had cancer. It was devastating news. Much physical agony awaited her. Yet, in the midst of the physical and emotional pain, Joy actually found herself experiencing a strange sort of ecstasy. Their last year together was surprisingly quite a joyful year.[347]

And what about Hannah Whitall Smith, beloved author of *The Christian's Secret of a Happy Life*? What kind of a life do you imagine this author lived? Let me share just a few facts about this remarkable woman. Four of her children died. Her husband went through bankruptcy and a nervous breakdown. And then he cheated on her. One of her daughters married an atheist.

Hannah's life was crammed full of pain and problems. Yet her words are undeniably some of the finest words written by a Christian author. She had learned the secret of a happy life. She was authentically joyful in the cruelest of life circumstances.

A few years ago, I heard world figure skating champion Barbara Underhill speak about the tragedy of her little daughter

---

[346] Lisa Beamer, pg. 285.
[347] Petersen, pgs. 196–197.

drowning in her backyard swimming pool. Even though Barbara was a Christian at that time, she felt she would never be able to experience joy again. She lived through some tough years. And then one day, she was walking along a beach and joy broke through into the depths of her spirit. The pain was still there—perhaps in some measure it will always be—but she realized that it did not have to rob her of feeling joyful for the rest of her life.[348]

I was once privileged to help facilitate an Alpha Bible study with an amazing group of eighteen women in a nearby town. One evening we were discussing joy. A young Christian in the group shared about how joyful she felt in her newly-found faith. One of the seekers in the group, not yet convinced about the reality of God or His Son, skeptically commented that this joy would soon disappear if a calamity happened, such as her house burning down. Without missing a beat, the new Christian shared that *in actual fact* her house had recently burned down—but God was giving her joy day by day anyway. (Not surprisingly, the skeptic was later to embrace Christian faith!)

I invite you to consciously internalize this truth: we can experience exquisite joy in the midst of exquisite pain. Our task is to find that joy. Each one of us can understand the paradox Paul spoke about in 2 Corinthians 6:10a: "Our hearts ache, but at the same time we have the joy of the Lord." He repeats that paradox in 2 Corinthians 7:4b: "...you have made me so happy in spite of all my suffering."

This incredible paradox, lived out in real lives, continues to persuade me of both the reality and the relevance of life in Christ.

The Choice to Rejoice

Clinical psychologist Richard Dobbins has asserted that a person's happiness is mostly determined by how they *choose* to

---

[348] From Barbara Underhill's talk at *The National Conference of Leading Women*, Toronto, Canada, 2004.

think and feel about themselves, their circumstances, their relationships, and the events that happen throughout their lives. Circumstances need not determine anyone's happiness or lack of it. Dobbins noted that it is the lens through which a person chooses to look at their circumstances, not the actual circumstances themselves, that determines whether or not a person is happy.[349]

The Bible shows us that joy is a choice. We do not get magically zapped with joy just because we have become Christian believers. For some, there is initial euphoria when we encounter Christ, but joy over the long haul partially comes from the daily inner choices we make.

The noun joy is connected to two action verbs: rejoice and enjoy. The following verses demonstrate the onus that is on *us* to make this *choice* to rejoice:

> Rejoice before the Lord your God in everything you do. (Deuteronomy 12:18c)

> This is the day the Lord has made. We will rejoice and be glad in it. (Psalm 118:24)

> So rejoice in him, all those who are his…(Psalm 32:11)

> I lie awake at night thinking of you…I rejoice through the night beneath the protecting shadow of your wings. (Psalm 63:6–7)

> I delight greatly in the Lord; my soul rejoices in my God. (Isaiah 61:10a, NIV)

> Now we rejoice in our wonderful new relationship with God… (Romans 5:11)

> …I will continue to rejoice… (Philippians 1:18, NLT)

> Rejoice in the Lord always. I will say it again: Rejoice! (Philippians 4:4, NIV)

We know that the world can be a dark, difficult, even dangerous place—full of sin, sickness, evil, pain, pressures, and problems.

---

[349] Dobbins, pgs. 43–46.

Yet, even though we are beset by these perils and ills, we can still choose to rejoice. To this day, I do not fully comprehend how joy can co-exist with pain, grief, or loss—I simply know, from personal experience and observation, that it can. Sorrow and sighing will only fully disappear in heaven. Until then, we must choose joy while still living in a broken world, as imperfect souls, surrounded by six billion other imperfect human beings.

Expressing Our Joy

Worship, Praise, Singing

The psalmist encouraged us to sing and praise: "Shout with joy before the Lord, O earth! Obey him gladly; come before him, singing with joy."[350] Many other Psalms repeat these kinds of instructions. Praise and singing are integral to the Christian way of life and form a vital part of church worship.

Of course we can easily sing when all is well. But God wants us to learn how to worship, praise, and sing at *all* times. The apostle Paul, in prison and in chains, freshly beaten, chose to sing in the midnight hour *before* God delivered him from his circumstances.[351] And that song must have been especially sweet.

God wants every one of us to learn to sing *in the midnight hour*. In the darkness. In the gloom. He wants all of us to learn how to express joy in the midst of our trials.

Smiles and Laughter

Just as we can sing in the midnight hour, we can laugh in our tough times. Former American President Ronald Reagan knew how to do this. Moments after an assassination attempt on his life when a bullet struck his body perilously close to his heart, he turned to his wife and joked: "Honey, I forgot to duck."[352]

---

[350] Psalm 100: 1–2.

[351] Acts 16:25.

[352] Ronald Reagan, *Ronald Reagan: An American Life*, pg. 329.

Barbara Johnson is one of the most humorous Christian writers I have read. She writes with such light-hearted good cheer that I found it almost beyond my comprehension to learn that she had lost two of her sons under tragic circumstances. We have talked earlier about her estrangement from another one of her sons. Barbara could have crumbled under the weight of her difficult circumstances. Instead of developing sustained anger at God, or bitterness, or cynicism, Barbara developed the ability to smile and laugh—and to help others smile and laugh their way through life's troubles. Barbara has so wisely observed that we can either count our blessings or we can count our calamities.[353] If you are looking for a fresh dose of smiles and laughter in your life, pick up one of Barbara's books.

Life provides a lot of its own spontaneous entertainment if we are willing to look for it. We can choose to smile or to laugh anytime, anywhere. Let me briefly share two funny stories, both of which happened to me during particularly tiring, stressful, problematic periods in my law career.

One morning, I was riding the subway to work. The subway car was really hot, crowded, and smelly. I was not having fun. For some reason, the subway car seemed to be jarring and jolting more than normal, causing me to almost lose my balance several times as I stood, in high-heeled shoes, jockeying to hold onto the precious few inches of the vertical handrail nearest me. Suddenly, the subway train braked abruptly at one station and I lurched forward into the man in front of me. My bright red lipstick left a perfect lip-shaped mark on the back of his suit jacket. Before I could tell him about it, he dashed out of the train—this was his stop. I chuckled off and on throughout that day—in the midst of some stressful work—as I thought of that poor (probably bewildered) guy explaining the lipstick to his officemates and perhaps to a wife at home that night.

Another morning, I was standing out on the street corner with my two kids, and several other parents and their kids,

---

[353] Barbara Johnson, pg. 15.

waiting for the school bus. The neighbor I was chatting with started to laugh and point at my feet. Hanging from the bottom of my stylish black pants was a piece of underwear. Her laughter attracted the attention of all the other moms and dads. In my embarrassment, I mumbled that at least the underwear was clean. I had just taken those dress pants out of the dryer minutes before, and I was obviously the victim of some static cling between the pair of pants and the underwear it had been laundered with! After the immediate humiliation of the moment, I had to admit this was pretty funny—and once again I had reason to chuckle as I later recalled the incident throughout that hectic day at the office.

Behind my back (or to my face), no one would likely link my name and the word comic in the same sentence. If anything, I've been accused of taking life too seriously. (This used to bother me until I realized that serious birds catch some good worms.) Having said that, I am trying to lighten up and laugh more. This remains one of my perennial personal challenges!

Actively Enjoying Each Hour

Many Christians say that it is impossible to be joyful every hour. They say that this would deny the realities of life. On occasion, I have come close to agreeing with this—and then God reminds me of verses such as: "*Always* be joyful."[354] These kinds of verses freshly challenge me to look . . . to look again . . . to look harder for the joy that can accompany the problems, the pressures, and the pain of everyday living. If we are told to always be joyful, it must be possible.

Proverbs 15:15 teaches that "the cheerful heart has a *continual* feast."[355] This sounds pretty attractive to me.

Solomon told the people to accept their lot in life and to be "occupied with gladness of heart." He further instructed them: "Go, eat your food with gladness, and drink your wine with a

---

[354] 1 Thessalonians 5:16.
[355] NIV translation.

joyful heart...."; "However many years a man may live, let him enjoy them *all*..."[356]

When we have trouble enjoying routine everyday tasks and pleasures, it is worthwhile spending time in the book of Ecclesiastes. King Solomon reminds us that we are meant to enjoy our day from the time we get up until the time we go to bed—every meal, every drink, every moment of work, everything that comprises our personal lot in life.

We can choose to listen to joyful music (even if it is just playing inside our head). We can get outside for a walk. We can sit down for a moment with a cup of hot tea or a glass of cold water. We can write or speak some cheery words to a friend. We can feel the warmth of the sun, watch the clouds pass overhead, or listen to the rhythm of the rain. We can hug a loved one or smile at a stranger. We can think about some special memories. Most of these kinds of moments are free—or they cost very little. And they all inspire joy.

The Body-Soul Connection

Obviously, it is hard to be joyful if we are tired, run-down, malnourished, out of shape, sick, or depleted of energy. Dr. Sam advises that if we neglect our health and make poor choices regarding sleep, nutrition, and exercise, we are sitting ducks for mental/emotional problems such as depression or anxiety, along with a host of sicknesses and diseases. Poor care of our physical health can steal our joy, even when our circumstances are actually positive.

In contrast, if we take good care of ourselves, we are more likely to have a sense of well-being. Good health facilitates joy.

The flip side of this is that choosing joy promotes good mental and physical health. It is a virtuous cycle. According to Dr. Sam, the fields of medical science and psychology have become increasingly interested in studying the link between positive

---

[356] Ecclesiastes 5:20; 9:7; 11:8a (all NIV).

emotions and good health. Some research indicates that joy helps to foster vitality (a positive state associated with energy and enthusiasm), the ability to concentrate and problem solve, improved intellectual performance, and greater social skill and motivation.[357] Other research has explored the correlation between positive emotions and post-operative healing, the health of the immune system, and cardiovascular fitness.[358]

Take, for example, the well-known story of Norman Cousins, a man who suffered from the chronic pain and disability of ankylosing spondylitis. Instead of feeling sorry for himself, Cousins decided to immerse himself in humor—in anything that made him laugh—and to cultivate emotions such as love, hope, and faith. Cousins actually recovered from his terrible disease. His remarkable story about the healing effects of laughter and other positive emotions was published in the prestigious *New England Journal of Medicine*.[359]

Canadian psychiatrist Stephen Stokl has noted: "...humour helps to lower blood pressure, decrease levels of stress hormones such as adrenaline, and boost immunity by raising levels of anti-bodies such as T-cells....Laughter releases endorphins, the body's natural pain killer; increases oxygen in the blood, and relaxes the muscles, and strengthens the immune system."[360]

Thousands of years ago, the prophet Nehemiah asserted that the joy of the Lord is our strength.[361] The connection between joy and strength was also made by Paul in Colossians 1:11: "We are praying...that you will be filled with his mighty, glorious strength so that you can keep going no matter what happens—always full of the joy of the Lord..." Joy fosters tremendous strength and energy on every level—spiritual, emotional, mental, and physical.

---

[357] See articles by: Rozanski and Kubzansky, pg. S 48; Fredrickson, pg. 305.

[358] See articles by: Fredrickson and Levenson; Fredrickson.

[359] Article by W. Cousins.

[360] Dr. Stokl, pg. 6; also see article by Berk et al, regarding the biochemical changes caused by laughter.

[361] Nehemiah 8:10.

Beyond Human Joy

True joy is not purely the result of human effort, choice, or will-power. Isaiah understood this when he said that "...the joy of the Lord shall fill you full..." and when he later transcribed God's words: "I, even I, am he who comforts you and gives you all this joy."[362]

In the New Testament, joy is sometimes described as a blessing bestowed by the Holy Spirit. In Galatians 5:22, Paul affirms that joy is indeed a fruit of the Spirit.

Even Jesus received His joy from the Holy Spirit. In Luke 10:21a, for example, we are told that Jesus was "full of joy through the Holy Spirit" (NIV). If *He* needed the Holy Spirit to fill Him with joy, how much more do we?

Jesus Himself said that He would give us joy if we remain in relationship with Him. He said to His followers: "I have told you this so that my joy may be in you and that your joy may be complete"; "...Now is your time of grief, but I will see you again and you will rejoice, and no one will take away your joy....Ask and you will receive, and your joy will be complete."[363]

Paul commented on the kind of supernatural joy that was present in the early church: "...in spite of severe suffering, you welcomed the message with joy *given* by the Holy Spirit."[364]

Paul, commenting on the synergy between our own efforts and the empowerment of the Holy Spirit, stated in Romans 14:17 that "...the important thing for us as Christians is not what we eat or drink but stirring up goodness and peace and joy from the Holy Spirit." We *stir up* joy—and somehow, in that process, a divine measure of joy is granted by the Holy Spirit.

Centuries before, in his reflections on the meaning and purpose of life, King Solomon alluded to this same synergy. Remember we just talked about enjoying our food and drink and

---

[362] Isaiah 41:16 and Isaiah 51:12a.

[363] John 15:11; 16:22, 24b (NIV).

[364] 1 Thessalonians 1:6 (NIV).

work? Listen to the connection that Solomon made between our human decision to do so and God's part in the process: "So I decided that there was nothing better for a man to do than to enjoy his food and drink, and his job. Then I realized that even this pleasure is from the hand of God. For who can eat or enjoy apart from him? For God *gives* those who please him wisdom, knowledge, and joy..."[365]

I sing because I'm happy. I sing because I'm free.
For His eye is on the sparrow, and I know He watches me.[366]

So cheer up! Take courage if you are depending on the Lord.
Psalm 31:24

A cheerful heart is good medicine...
Proverbs 17:22 (NIV)

At last I shall be fully satisfied; I will praise you with great joy.
Psalm 63:5

Rejoice in the Lord always. I will say it again: Rejoice!
Philippians 4:4 (NIV)

---

[365] Ecclesiastes 2:24–25; also note similar statement in Ecclesiastes 3:12–13.
[366] From the song "His Eye is on the Sparrow" by Civilla D. Martin and Charles H. Gabriel (Public Domain).

22
PAINFUL MEMORIES
Deleting, Editing, or Redeeming Them

O Lord, you have examined my heart
and know everything about me.
Psalm 139:1

MANAGING OUR THOUGHTS and emotions would be a lot simpler if we did not have to deal with our painful memories of past events. It is tough enough to get a grip on our reactions to the circumstances unfolding in our *present* moments. Our minds, however, are prone to sometimes dwell on the *past*, which is fine when the memories are delightful, but burdensome when the memories are distressing.

The Biochemical Nature of Our Memories

On a biochemical level, our brains do not care whether a memory is about something that happened yesterday or something that occurred decades ago. Once the mind focuses on a specific memory, the body responds to the emotional component of the memory with a set of biochemical reactions. When we revisit painful events in our minds, our bodies react just as if the events were occurring in the present. As a result, our bodies are called upon to bear the brunt of the pain of death, divorce, abuse, hurtful words, *over and over*—as often as we choose to remember those painful circumstances.[367] Rekindled *memories* can generate current anger, resentment, fear, anxiety, or despair that can do as much damage to our bodies as the *actual events* that triggered those emotions in the past.

---

[367] Dr. Colbert, pg. 24.

Neuroscientist Dr. Beauregard believes that, when an individual remembers and re-experiences an event, the brain returns to the same pathways that were traveled when the person originally experienced the event.[368]

It has also been shown that the more often we remember something, the sharper and more deeply entrenched that memory becomes. In effect, the neural pathways become more deeply rutted. Our strongest memories are those which are steeped in emotion and those which are most frequently revisited.

In light of this, we need to be careful about what we choose to remember. In most cases, we do not have to remember any painful event. We can instead choose to delete (or at least edit) some of our unpleasant memories, just as we so frequently delete unwanted material stored in our computers. We should only choose to remember painful events if recalling them is beneficial to us or others. I will explain this in more detail below.

Divinely Deleting or Editing our Memories

Ecclesiastes 3:6 tells us that there is "a time to keep and a time to throw away..." (NLT) Of course we want to keep our wonderful memories! We can treasure those memories the rest of our lives. In contrast, we can choose to throw out most of our negative memories. We have the freedom to refuse to entertain any hurtful memory. Every time an unwanted memory tries to resurface, we can press the "delete" or the "edit" button in our mind.

Joseph did this. In his youth, his brothers had been jealous of him. You will recall that they hated him so much that they threw him in a pit and soon after sold him to a passing caravan of traders. For many years, Joseph lived as a servant in a foreign land, far from his family.

In his mind, Joseph could have bitterly relived the cruel actions of his brothers over and over again. If he had done that,

---

[368] Dr. Beauregard, pg. 266.

his soul would have been filled with anger, resentment, hatred, and unforgiveness by the time his brothers sought his help years later. Instead, Joseph was able to forgive his brothers. With God's help, he made the *choice* to *forget* their hurtful conduct. How do we know this? At a time when names given to a child were of great significance, Joseph named one of his sons Manasseh, which meant to forget. Joseph deliberately chose this name "because God has made me forget all my trouble and all my father's household".[369]

I have heard many pastors and speakers compare our memories of specific events to DVDs or videotapes in our minds. We can choose to throw out a DVD we don't like. Or we can keep popping it into the DVD player, replaying it over and over.

Do you watch a terrible movie twice? If you didn't like it the first time around, why see it again? If it made you feel anxious, depressed, or upset, why on earth would you ever want to see it a second time? Or a third or fourth time? We can treat our memories of painful events the same way we treat the movies we have seen. With God's help, we can refuse to re-experience what is not worth re-experiencing!

When it comes to our entire life stories, we do not need to destroy the whole "movie." In the process of making a movie, every scene is acted out and "takes" are filmed. After all the "takes" have been filmed, the director and editor decide what is to be kept and what is to be edited out.

The actual scenes of our past can be handled just like these "takes." We cannot undo the past. In the present, however, we have the power to *cut out* whatever scenes we do not like. We can keep whatever scenes we want to keep. We are in control of the "movie" of our life that presently plays in our mind. We have that power.

I am not suggesting that we alter the truth. I am simply saying that we do not have to constantly *retrieve* and *replay* memories that are painful to us. We cannot rewrite the

---

[369] Genesis 41:51 (NIV).

unpleasant scenes, but we can leave them behind on the cutting room floor.

Redeeming Our Negative Memories

Should we choose to delete or edit *all* of our painful memories? My personal view is that we should leave most of them behind, unless God has helped us to *redeem* them. In some cases, God teaches us something from the pain of our past circumstances. God sometimes shows us how He has used what appeared to be a negative situation and turned it into something positive.

I have shared about how traumatic it was for me to speak in front of even a few people when I was a child. I could choose to never think about this (let alone write about it), but the truth is these memories are no longer painful for me. Instead, these memories of what was once painful now generate joy and gratitude in me because of how much God has transformed me in this area. Memories of what was once negative now stir up positive emotions in me and I enjoy telling others about what God has done for me in this area of my life.

If we can positively reframe our negative memories, they can become beneficial to us and others. We can do this by *seeing* how God has used our painful experiences to bring about transformation in us. Perhaps what we went through has helped us to develop more faith, compassion, empathy, wisdom, or understanding. Or perhaps we can see how God has used our pain for some purpose outside of ourselves. Christian psychologist Dr. Dobbins has asserted that the facts of our life history will always remain fixed—we cannot change the facts of our past, but we can control how we choose to think and feel about those facts.[370]

To the extent that Joseph remembered his painful past at all, he was able to see it in this *positive light*: what his brothers had meant for evil, God had intended for good. God used the cruelty of Joseph's brothers to bring Joseph to Egypt, where he

---

[370] Dr. Dobbins, pg. 172.

eventually rose to be second in command to Pharaoh. He was able to help his family when the years of famine came. At that time, Joseph was able to say to his brothers: "You intended to harm me, but God intended it for good to accomplish what is now being done, the saving of many lives."[371] Joseph had reframed the past. He no longer remembered the details of his pain, but instead focused on God's positive purposes. He redeemed the hurt of his past by being able to see it all from God's point of view.

If, in the present, we can joyfully testify about what God has done for us (or through us) because of some difficult circumstances we have endured, then we can keep the memories alive. These redeemed memories will bless us and others.

If memories simply stir up old wounds, old anger, or old resentment—if they fan the flames of unforgiveness or generate fresh anxiety—if we cannot redeem them by finding a way to positively reframe them by seeing God's purpose in them, then we can choose to leave yesterday in yesterday. The past is *over* and does not need to *ever* be relived. As we learn to selectively forget, we can develop "divine dementia."[372]

Journaling

In my teen and early adult years, I sometimes journalled (in excruciating detail) about my anger, my angst, and other negative feelings. I used to think that this was a healthy way to process feelings such as anger. In the immediate moment, it was. Journaling helped me to understand myself and what pushed my buttons. It helped me to gather my thoughts. It helped me to constructively spend the surge of biochemical energy that accompanied some of my negative feelings.

One obvious danger of journaling about emotions such as our anger is that our words might fall into the hands of others at

---

[371] Genesis 50:20 (NIV).

[372] I heard this expression in a sermon by Pastor Kent Griffin, in August of 2007.

some point, hurting or inflaming them. Just as dangerous, however, is our *own* future reading of what we have written. This can re-open a healing (or healed) wound, making the wound fresh again. This can also further imbed the incident even deeper in the memory.

If you decide to write out your anger or other negative feelings, I recommend that you plan to toss the paper in the fire sooner rather than later—or be very cautious about if and when you ever re-read your words. I have kept a shredder busy in recent years, destroying old journal entries that recorded various negative feelings (and unnecessarily re-ignited them years later). What a catharsis all that shredding has been! How wonderful I have felt leaving bags of shredded anger and angst at the end of my driveway on garbage pick-up days!

I no longer journal much about negative emotions. Earlier I shared about how I now only write about what will help me both in the present *and* when I re-read my journal later. I write about nice words someone has spoken to me; a kind act that has brightened my day; answers to prayer; what God is teaching me; a helpful insight; a joyful moment worth remembering; life's daily victories and blessings; and whatever else prompts gratitude, inspires faith, or generates love for God, myself, or others.

Words bring either life or death. I have learned to be careful not to write down words that have the potential to bring "death" to the soul.

Earlier, I told you about a serious operation that Sam had to undergo. What did I focus on and write about on the actual day of the surgery? In the last chapter, I shared about the scarlet red sun at daybreak, warming the eastern horizon as we drove to the hospital; the kind volunteer; how God sent us one of Sam's former medical school classmates to talk with us just before the surgery; how God then sent two friends across my path, just after Sam was wheeled into the OR; and various other positive moments punctuating the stress and the pain. *These* are the details I chose to journal about. I could have written about my fears, or about one particularly rude, cantankerous nurse, or about how hot, crowded, and noisy one of the waiting rooms was. I chose not to write about any of these details. I trust that, in time, the memory of the unpleasant details will fade if I choose not to imbed them deeper.

When I re-read my journal entry for the day of my husband's surgery, it does not bring back negative memories. Instead, my soul is uplifted as I dwell on gratitude to God, thanking Him for the mercies and blessings woven through that difficult day.

Praying for Emotional Healing

Psalm 34:18 tells us: "The Lord is close to the brokenhearted and saves those who are crushed in spirit."[373] Psalm 147:3 promises: "He heals the brokenhearted and binds up their wounds."[374] In Luke 4:18, Jesus proclaimed that He was sent "...to heal the broken-hearted..."

We can pray for God to heal our broken hearts, to bind up our emotional wounds, and to restore our crushed spirits. How much God wants to heal our hurts!

We can pray, in general, for God to heal all of our past hurts and wounds. Or, if we can bear it, we can deliberately and prayerfully travel back to specific painful memories and ask for emotional healing. The inner healing won't usually happen right away. In the meantime, we can consider what to do with the specific memories. We can ask God for help with either deleting the memories or finding some redemptive, positive purpose to keep the memories alive.

Many years ago, Sam and I helped a pastor collect and organize some materials on the subject of emotional healing. At that time, I decided to spend an hour or so in prayer every day, mentally traveling back into my past one year at a time. I had just turned thirty, so the process took a full month. As I deliberately summoned up painful memories, I prayed just as I have suggested. With each memory, God helped me to decide

---

[373] NIV translation.
[374] NIV translation.

whether to edit the memory (and to thereafter refuse to entertain it ever again) or to remember it with a fresh perspective. That process was incredibly healing. There are so many memories I have since refused to replay. Other memories have made great examples in my talks and books—God has shown me how these examples can help others who personally identify with them.

Counseling

Unfortunately, the process of emotional healing is not so simple for those with very traumatic memories of rape, abuse, war, divorce, major illness, the death of loved ones, serious accidents, or other pain-filled life events. For those unable to deal with their memories—and those who do not feel that they can pray about the past on their own—Dr. Sam recommends counseling. With serious life trauma, the emotional wounds tend to be rooted deeply and layered over with defensive, adaptive mechanisms and behaviors that allow the hurting individual to function despite the constant pain these memories cause. Those who need help dealing with a painful past can turn to the counsel of a mature, trusted Christian friend, a pastor, a trained layperson in the church, or a professional such as a doctor, psychologist, or psychiatrist.

Sandi Patti, Stormie Omartian, Sheila Walsh, and many others referred to in this book have all benefited from seeking counseling to help them break free from their painful pasts.

In some circumstances, cognitive behavioral therapy (CBT) can be used to help a person deal with a painful past. A therapist can help a person assign a fresh, more positive meaning to each hurtful experience.

Freedom

I believe that God wants all of us to live free from the painful, difficult burdens of the past. We cannot change our past. But we can choose to leave it behind us or to see it in a new light. The more freedom we find from the negative emotions of the past, the stronger we will be as we deal with fresh emotional battles in the present.

...where the Spirit of the Lord is, there is freedom.
2 Corinthians 3:17 (NIV)

...whatever is true, whatever is noble,
whatever is right, whatever is pure,
whatever is lovely, whatever is admirable—
if anything is excellent or praiseworthy—
think about such things.
Philippians 4:8 (NIV)

23
MORE OF
THE SPIRIT
The Empowered Soul

...the Holy Spirit has been at work in your hearts,
cleansing you with the blood of Jesus Christ
and making you to please him.
1 Peter 1:2b

A T THE AGE of nineteen, after backpacking around Europe for almost a year, I committed my life to Christ. In the following days, I began to read the Bible and to pray that I would meet some other Christians who could answer the numerous questions that were swirling around in my mind.

God answered my prayer swiftly. A month later, I was invited to stay for a while on the southern coast of Spain at a villa owned by an ex-alcoholic named Barb. It was a gorgeous white-washed villa, surrounded by sun-dappled green gardens on a hillside above the Mediterranean. Barb had become a Christian the year before and had opened her marvelous spacious home to more than a dozen young people. We were all attending an international church in the nearby town and were being deeply discipled by the pastor and other church leaders.

The other young guys and girls staying at Barb's villa had also been backpacking around Europe. Some had been sleeping on beaches and had been desperate enough to sell their own blood to a donor bank each day to pay for their next meal. Others had been hooked on heroin or cocaine. Most had been partying and drinking as they drifted from place to place. One of them had fled Canada to escape his alcoholic father who, in drunken rages, had tried to kill him a few times. This young man had fled in fear—not from fear of his father, but fear that he himself, now a strapping six-footer, might be the one to land the fatal punch in the next angry encounter with his father. Whatever our personal stories, all of us had been spiritually searching, had recently become Christians, and by God's mercy had ended up in this same incredible place.

Night after night, we shared dinners together at the long table in Barb's villa. On some nights, we gathered by her fireplace, read our Bibles, immersed ourselves in great Christian books, talked together, prayed, or sang while someone strummed a guitar. We were a rather ragged group of former hippies, dressed alike in patched and faded jeans, radiant in our newly found faith.

What I remember most about my nights at Barb's villa is this—love, joy, and peace were *so* visibly present in people's eyes and smiles. Everyone around me seemed even more aglow than the fire in the hearth. I had never before encountered the Holy Spirit as I encountered Him in that place. The Spirit was truly palpable. At first, I wondered if they were all just faking it. Time taught me otherwise. As weeks passed, and as I saw such dramatic transformations in the lives of these young people around me, I hungered to get to know the Spirit on a deeper level. I was not in a rush to leave that place.

Do you remember the conversation I told you about at the beginning of the book—the conversation at a lakeside cottage with an older woman who wanted to know how to find love, joy, and peace in her Christian life? That encounter happened just months after my experiences in Spain. I did not know how to formulate a clear, Scripture-based answer for the older woman at that time, but I did know *this* much then—love, joy, and peace *were* real and available and they had something to do with the Holy Spirit.

One decade later, Sam and I had the privilege of visiting that same church in southern Spain and some of the same young people I had known in the '70s. The further maturation of those who had remained in that church community as leaders impacted me all over again. They had not lost their love, joy, and peace—instead, these fruits of the Spirit had grown even more.

I am still hungry, many years later, to know the Spirit with an ever-increasing intimacy. My experiences in Spain set me off on a life-long quest, seeking to understand the various roles that the Holy Spirit is meant to play in our lives.

The Holy Spirit and Jesus

Shortly before Jesus began His public ministry, John the Baptist stated that he himself could only baptize with water, but that Jesus would baptize them with the Holy Spirit and with fire.[375] From my earliest days as a Christian, I wanted to know what John meant by that.

John baptized Jesus with water. After he did this, the Holy Spirit descended on Jesus.[376] Soon after, Jesus was led by the Spirit into the desert,[377] where He faced, and overcame, some temptations. According to Luke 4:14, Jesus then returned to Galilee in the power of the Spirit.

These events marked the beginning of Jesus' three years of public ministry, during which He healed and delivered people and performed many other miracles. If *Jesus* needed the power of the Spirit during his life here on earth, how much *more*so do we?

The Promise that *We* Will Receive the Holy Spirit

Jesus made this invitation to His followers: "...If anyone is thirsty, let him come to me and drink. Whoever believes in me, as the Scripture has said, streams of living water will flow from within him."[378]

---

[375] Matthew 3:11 (also see John 1:33).

[376] Matthew 3:16; Luke 3:21–22; John 1:32).

[377] Matthew 4:1 (also see Luke 4:1).

[378] John 7:37–38 (NIV).

John later explained what Jesus was referring to: "By this he meant the Spirit, whom those who believed in him were later to receive. Up to that time the Spirit had not been given, since Jesus had not yet been glorified."[379]

Jesus promised, not long before his death, that His Father would send the Holy Spirit to those who believed in Him. Jesus explained: "...the Holy Spirit, whom the Father will send in my name, will teach you all things and will remind you of everything I have said to you."[380] After He finished speaking, Jesus prayed and told the Father that He was praying, not only for his followers at that present time, but also "for those who *will* believe in me through their message."[381]

"On one occasion," Luke recorded, "while he [Jesus] was eating with them, he gave them this command: 'Do not leave Jerusalem, but wait for the gift my Father promised, which you have heard me speak about. For John baptized with water, but in a few days you will be baptized with the Holy Spirit...you will receive power when the Holy Spirit comes on you...'"[382]

Acts 2 tells the world-changing story of how the Holy Spirit did in fact come upon many of the followers of Jesus shortly after His death and resurrection: "When the day of Pentecost came, they were all together in one place. Suddenly a sound like the blowing of a violent wind came from heaven and filled the whole house where they were sitting. They saw what seemed to be tongues of fire that separated and came to rest on each of them. All of them were filled with the Holy Spirit..."[383]

The Book of Acts tells numerous stories of people being filled with the Spirit. In Acts 2:38b-39, after Peter told a crowd of people to repent of their sins and be baptized, he said: "And you will receive the gift of the Holy Spirit. The promise is for you *and*

---

[379] John 7:39 (NIV).

[380] John 14:26 (NIV).

[381] John 17:20 (NIV).

[382] Acts 1:4–5, 8 (NIV).

[383] Acts 2:1–4 (NIV).

your children *and* all who are far off—for *all* whom the Lord our God will call. (NIV)"

Paul was filled with the Spirit and taught that we are also to be filled with the Spirit. Paul explained that "by faith we might receive the promise of the Spirit."[384] In Galatians 5:25, Paul further taught: "If we are living by the Holy Spirit's power, let us follow the Holy Spirit's leading in every part of our lives." In his other letters, Paul encouraged his fellow Christians to seek the presence, the fruits, and the gifts of the Spirit.

More of the Spirit

Paul warned us: "Do not put out the Spirit's fire."[385] Why? Because we need this fire to empower every facet of our Christian lives. As we mature in our Christian faith, we all need to nurture our relationship with the Holy Spirit with as much effort as we nurture our relationship with God the Father and Jesus the Son.

We can each seek to receive more of the Holy Spirit. The Holy Spirit indwells each one of us, in some measure, as soon as we become Christians. There does not have to be any specific or immediate outward manifestation of this, nor do we have to belong to a particular denomination. Paul wrote about this quite simply in Galatians 3:2b: "…the Holy Spirit came upon you…after you heard about Christ and trusted him to save you."

We can thereafter invite the Spirit to indwell us in *greater* measure, and He will do so more and more as we set sin and self-centeredness aside to make greater room for Him. He will begin to occupy every area we surrender to Him.

If you want more of the power of the Holy Spirit in your life, I encourage you to begin praying to receive *a fuller measure* of the Spirit. Perhaps you have not consciously nurtured your relationship with the Spirit since becoming a Christian. You can begin today.

---

[384] Galatians 3:14 (NIV).
[385] 1 Thessalonians 5:19 (NIV).

After the crucifixion and resurrection, Jesus appeared a few times to some of His disciples. On one occasion, Jesus "breathed" on His disciples and said: "Receive the Holy Spirit."[386] Those same disciples were later "filled with the Holy Spirit" on the day of Pentecost.[387] Being "filled" with the Spirit does not happen on just one single occasion, but is instead an incremental process.

In my prayers, I ask God every day for a fresh infilling of the Holy Spirit. I want my life to be as full as possible with the presence and the power of the Holy Spirit. Jesus described the Holy Spirit as "streams of living water"[388] that would flow within us. Why be satisfied with a tiny rivulet of water when we can ask for a mighty river to flow through our lives? If your spiritual life feels dry (perhaps it feels like nothing more than intellectual knowledge or religious ritual), pray for the streams of living water to begin to flow within. And remember that, at the same time, you must be prepared to set sinful inclinations and self-centeredness aside.

In 1 Corinthians 4:20 the apostle Paul taught this: "The Kingdom is God is not just talking; it is living by God's power."

Six Roles of the Spirit

The Spirit wants to play many roles in our yielded lives. I will briefly mention six of the roles that are pertinent to this book. In various scriptures, the Spirit is described as our Conscience, our Companion, our Comforter, our Counselor, our Intercessor, and our Helper.

(1) If we are harboring anger, bitterness, hatred, or unforgiveness, the Spirit as our Conscience will prompt us to deal with these kinds of thoughts and emotions (and, of course, with any wrong words or actions flowing from them). The Spirit will not give us peace until we deal with wrong thoughts and emotions.

---

[386] John 20:22 (NIV).

[387] Acts 2:4 (NIV).

[388] John 7:38 (NIV).

(2) The Holy Spirit wants to be our constant Companion in life. In 2 Corinthians 13:14b, for example, Paul wrote: "May God's love and the Holy Spirit's *friendship* be yours." We are not just meant to encounter the Spirit on isolated occasions. We are meant to have a *relationship* with Him.

(3) If we are hurting or grieving, the Spirit will be a Comforter to us,[389] closer than any other person can possibly be.

(4) If we need guidance as to how we should deal with troublesome thoughts and emotions, the Spirit can be our Counselor.[390] God has been with us since the very moment of our birth. He fully understands all of the events, circumstances, and relationships that have shaped us. That is why He is so able to guide us into understanding the roots of our painful or destructive emotions. He knows precisely how we got ourselves *into* various emotional messes, and He knows how to get us *out* of them. The Spirit is infinitely and perfectly insightful, superior to any human counselor.

Author Stormie Omartian grew up with severe emotional abuse and, as a result, began her adult life with panic attacks, depression, substance abuse, and suicidal thoughts. After she became a Christian, she sought counseling to deal with her emotional issues. The counseling was useful, but eventually she realized that it is not possible to *live* in a counselor's office. She realized that the time had come for her to rely on the Holy Spirit as her ongoing Counselor.[391] She learned, over time, how wonderful it was to deal with her pain by praying about it. The Spirit showed her how to find emotional healing.

(5) Sometimes we don't know how to pray about our emotional pain. Romans 8:26 tells us that on those occasions when we don't know what to pray, the Holy Spirit will be our Intercessor, praying to God the Father on our behalf.

---

[389] John 14:26.
[390] John 14:26 (NIV).
[391] Omartian, pg. 145, 159.

(6) As we struggle with difficult emotions, the Spirit will be our Helper. Catherine Marshall wrote one of the best books I have ever read about the Holy Spirit, so aptly and simply called *The Helper*.[392]

As we battle troublesome emotions, our intellectual beliefs, our dogma, our "religion," our morals, and our values won't be enough to bring us to victory. We need to invite the Spirit to play these six vital roles in our lives. The Spirit will empower us to do our part in taking appropriate control over our thoughts and emotions.

...all of us as Christians can have the promised Holy Spirit...
Galatians 3:14

But you have received the Holy Spirit
and he lives within you, in your hearts...
1 John 2:27a

After starting your Christian lives in the Spirit,
why are you now trying to become perfect
by your own human effort?
Galatians 3:3 (NLT)

---

[392] Reprinted by Chosen in 2001.

24
THE
RESHAPED
SOUL
Rest At Last

Let my soul be at rest again...
Psalm 116:7a (NLT)

...Christ has made us free.
Galatians 5:1a

L ESLIE HASKIN, ONE of the survivors of the 9/11 attack on the World Trade Center, suffered enormous emotional trauma on that day and in the years that followed.[393] In graphic detail, she has written a book about the sheer horror of 9/11 and the rubble it left in her life.

Those of us who saw 9/11 unfold on CNN have disturbing mental images of what happened on the *outside* of the World Trade Center on that day. Most of us have seen the video-stream of hijacked planes crashing into the twin towers and the balls of fire and smoke that followed. None of us will easily forget the shocking television coverage of the two towers later imploding and crumbling to the ground as if made of dust. In disbelief, we watched millions of sheets of paper floating in the air, layers of ash raining down on everything, chaos in the streets, and the burning rubble of the Ground Zero site.

---

[393] The details of Leslie's story come from the advance reading copy of her book *Between Heaven and Ground Zero*.

Leslie has struggled with even *worse* memories of what transpired that day. An executive of an insurance firm located in the World Trade Center, she had just started her workday when the first tower was hit. With many others, she made the slow, agonizing trek down a crowded stairwell from the 36th floor. Along the way, she saw decapitated bodies—heads had been disconnected from torsos by giant slabs of razor-sharp bloodied glass. Powerless to help, she listened to the screams of people trapped in elevators. As she stepped around blown-apart limbs and charred flesh, she smelled the urine and excrement expelled from bladders and bowels that had not been able to bear the sudden panic and terror of it all. Acrid jet fuel, mixed with blood, dripped down on them from floors above.

The horror did not end when she finally reached the collapsing concourse at ground level. She saw the huge revolving glass doors leading out of the towers, chunks of glass missing, with bloodied pieces of human flesh impaled on the jagged edges. Once outside, she looked into the living faces of the bodies falling from the sky above, then saw their bodies brutally mangled as they smashed onto the concrete right beside her. Men and women ran by her, some in flames, some screaming and cursing. Others in her path were curled on the floor in shock, huddled in the fetal position.

Until I read Leslie's book, I had not fully imagined the scenes of suffering and carnage that unfolded for those who had to make their way through the *inside* of the towers on that day.

I also could not imagine the magnitude of the emotional trauma *within the souls* of the survivors that occurred that day. Thoughts of human excrement, spilled blood, charred flesh, and severed heads are sickening enough. But what about the anger, fear, hatred, anxiety, grief, and depression that threatened to implode the souls of those who endured that day?

For Leslie, the emotional wreckage remained for some time. Just as Ground Zero could not be cleaned up overnight, her shrapnelled soul and life could not be dealt with in a short time. Added to the trauma of experiencing that day, Leslie had to cope with the sudden loss of her job and the ensuing loss of her car and her home. After living homeless for four months with her teenage son, she suffered through three further years of financial struggle.

Leslie's story does not end here. Leslie encountered God in this tragedy. She cried out to Him in her darkest hours and He responded.

She had been raised by a Christian mother. As a child, she had embraced the Christian faith to some extent, but the lure of money, power, and success had drawn her away from her Christian roots and into a prestigious office in the World Trade Center. She was caught up in the fast-paced excitement of Manhattan. The events of 9/11 shook the foundations of her life—and brought her back into the loving arms of God.

Even after her return to Christian faith, her emotional recovery was neither instant nor easy. Dealing with flashbacks, nightmares, and severe post-traumatic stress syndrome, Leslie struggled for a long time. But God brought her through. Just as He had helped her out of the World Trade Center, He faithfully helped her out of her financial problems and her emotional rubble.

Today, Leslie has a ministry with homeless women and children who have been the victims of domestic violence. She has embarked on a whole new life—a happier, more meaningful life than the Manhattan glitz and glamor she left behind. Having come into unspeakable encounters with anger, fear, pain, and loss, she has emerged with a fresh awareness of the love, joy, and peace that are possible for the Christian. Her level of inner healing is beyond what modern medicine has to offer the emotionally afflicted.

Thankfully, most of us will not go through what Leslie went through (or what Lisa Beamer, Corrie ten Boom, the Lang family, John Harper, Helen Roseveare, Kim Phuc, and so many others in this book went through). I tell Leslie's story and the stories of these others to help lift our faith by showing that even at these *extreme edges* of horrific life circumstances, God is present—He is real and He is relevant and He is ready to help each one of us, no matter how grave the trouble we are in or how troublesome the emotions that beset us. With God's help, we can overcome *any* level of anger, unforgiveness, hatred, anxiety, despair, and depression. Some measure of trauma and drama will happen in all of our lives sooner or later, knocking the wind out of us. But, as Leslie's story so powerfully testifies, just as the land where Ground Zero stood is being restored, the debilitated soul can be restored. For the Christian, a better life can rise up out of the ashes of any tragedy or trial.

Finally Finding Love, Joy, and Peace

While writing this book, I spent one evening watching Gracia Burnham being interviewed on television. Gracia and her husband, Martin, had worked with the New Tribes Mission in the Philippines for fifteen years. In the spring of 2001, they were kidnapped by Muslim extremists and held hostage for over one year. Their captors hid them deep in the jungle. For months, Gracia and her husband literally slept on the jungle floor, some-times chained to a tree. They were exposed to the elements, often soaked by torrential rains, and tormented by insects. They went for days at a time without food and suffered wretched intestinal viruses. Not surprisingly, Gracia felt herself slipping deeper into depression, despair, and mounting frustration.

She asked herself, as the months dragged on, questions such as: Where is God in this ordeal? And where are the love, joy, and peace He promised? How could she find hope and faith? This part of her television interview caught my attention. These are the very questions that this book has attempted to address.

Gracia decided to stop merely *asking* those questions. Gracia and her husband asked God to help them find love, joy, peace, faith, and hope, even in their extreme circumstances. Gracia and Martin had reached a place in their mental, emotional, and spiritual journey where they wanted to stop feeling depression, frustration, bitterness, and other negative emotions. They wanted to start living in a more joyful, peace-filled, hopeful way. It was tough enough being held physically hostage. They no longer wanted to be held emotionally hostage.

God faithfully responded to the desire of this couple for love, joy, and peace in the very midst of their crisis. In the final months of their hostage situation, Gracia said they began to feel love for their captors—to listen to their stories, trying to understand why they had committed this radical act of kidnapping foreigners. In those latter months, this remarkable couple began to feel a much greater measure of joy and peace, hope and faith as they focused on trusting that God was in control of their long journey through the jungle.

After more than a year, the Philippine military found the Muslim extremists and their hostages. In an unfortunate shoot-out between the military and the terrorists, Gracia was shot in her right leg and her husband was fatally wounded. As Martin lay dying on the hillside beside her, Gracia knew that she had a vital choice to make. Was she going to be bitter that it was all ending this way? Or would she yet again seek God's peace, even as she watched her husband die? She made the choice then and there—God reaching down to help her—to resist bitterness even as she stared death in the face. And God gave her a transcendent peace—not days, months, or years later, but even as the tragic events unfolded.[394]

As I listened to Gracia's tearful interview on the television broadcast, I knew that I had found a powerful story with which to end this book. Here was yet another witness able to give first-hand testimony of the biblical principles and promises that form the foundation for all that I have been writing about. These principles and promises are *true* and *real*—Gracia's story, lived

---

[394] Facts taken from: Lorna Dueck's interview of Gracia Burnham on *Listen Up*, broadcast during the week of March 4, 2007; Gracia's website, www.graciaburnham.org; and from Gracia Burnham's book, *In The Presence of My Enemies*.

out in one of the most difficult and desperate of human situations, bears witness to their truth and reality.

Where are the love, joy, and peace that the Bible promises? As Gracia discovered, they are very near to us. Moment by moment, they are one choice away. The partnership between a Christian who is prepared to diligently make healthy emotional choices and the Spirit, who is always willing to help, is full of supernatural synergy.

I encourage you to read *more* about the individuals I have highlighted throughout this book. You will be greatly enriched and edified by digging deeper into the lives of the great men and women you have met in previous pages. I have been especially blessed by those who have written autobiographies, in which the writers have shared candidly, transparently, and authentically about their personal emotional struggles. The stories of all of my "witnesses" have a rich depth and dimension that are difficult to capture in the brief references I have made to their lives. It is a great tribute to these men and women that even such *brief* references have the power to inspire and encourage us all. I pray that I have not sacrificed the poignancy of their stories on the altar of brevity.

Establishing Good Pathways

I wrote my first book on the subject of finding the best pathways to take in our lives.[395] That book deals primarily with the *external* paths we follow as we make decisions about education, career, marriage, family, ministry, and other such matters. This present book has considered the *inner* pathways we establish for our lives—the choices we make at soul level regarding our thoughts and emotions.

We briefly discussed how some neuroscientists are researching how our most habitual thoughts and emotions create neural pathways in our brains—pathways that either become

---

[395] Karen Henein, *Counsel of the Most High: Receiving God's Guidance for Life's Decisions* (Winnipeg, Canada: Word Alive Press, 2007).

more deeply entrenched over time or which disappear if they remain untraveled again. My hope and prayer for each one of us is that we deliberately choose the *best* of *inner* pathways to follow—hour by hour, day by day—and that we have the strength and wisdom to abandon the paths that have caused us so much inner turmoil, tempest, discomfort, and pain.

In partnership with God, we *will* be able to find those best inner pathways and all of the love, joy, and peace that we have been looking for.

---

*...let us strip off anything that slows us down
or holds us back...*
Hebrews 12:1

...God is greater than our feelings...
1 John 3:20 (NLT)

March on, my soul; be strong!
Judges 5:21 (NIV)

APPENDIX A

A PRAYER

I f you would like to become a Christian, you can pray this prayer today:

Father, I believe that You exist and that Jesus Christ is Your Son. I believe that He died on the Cross to pay the penalty for the sins of all men and women. I believe that He has risen and is now seated at Your right hand.

I confess that I am a sinner. I confess all known sins and I desire to turn from them. I confess that my greatest sin has been ignoring You and rebelling against Your sovereignty in my life. I ask You to forgive all of my sins, on the basis of what Jesus did on the Cross for me. Create in me a clean heart! Please remove my sins as far as the east is from the west, as You promised You would. Please give me a fresh, new start in my life.

I ask that You would now live in me by Your Spirit, empowering me to live as I should. I give my life to You. May I be aware of Your loving Presence every day. Thank You!

I pray in faith, in the name of Jesus Christ, Amen.

If you have prayed this prayer, you have made a new beginning in your life! The Enemy of your soul will start to attack you with doubts and discouraging thoughts over coming days. Do not listen to him! I encourage you to get a Bible and begin to read it every day, especially the New Testament. I also encourage you to pray each day, talking to God as you would talk to a valued friend. If you spend even ten minutes a day developing your relationship with God, you will become more aware of the Holy Spirit who now lives within you. Finding a Bible-believing church and making Christian friends will also help you to grow spiritually.

You are beginning a journey that will bring you life, light, love, joy, peace, and all of the other wonderful inner treasures that we have been discussing in this book. Welcome to the family of God and to the fellowship of His people. I am praying for you!

SELECTED BIBLIOGRAPHY OF BOOKS, ARTICLES, AND OTHER SOURCES

Books

Adams, Moody. *The Titanic's Last Hero*. South Carolina: The Olive Press, 1997.

Anderson, Neil T. and Dave Park. *Stomping Out the Darkness*. California: Regal Books, 1993.

Arterburn, Stephen. *Healing Is A Choice*. Nashville, Tennessee: Nelson Books, 2005.

Beamer, Lisa. *Let's Roll!* Wheaton, Illinois: Tyndale, 2002.

Beauregard, Dr. Mario and Denyse O'Leary. *The Spiritual Brain: A Neuroscientist's Case for the Existence of the Soul*. New York: HarperCollins, 2007.

Bordon Books. *Mothers of Influence*. Colorado Springs, Colorado: Honor Books, 2005.

Brother Andrew. *Light Force*. Grand Rapids, Michigan: Fleming H. Revell, 2004.

Brother Yun. *The Heavenly Man*. Grand Rapids, Michigan: Monarch, 2002.

Bunyan, John. *The Pilgrim's Progress*. (Public Domain)

Burnham, Gracia. *In the Presence of My Enemies*. Wheaton, Illinois: Tyndale, 2004.

Carlson, Carole. *Corrie ten Boom: Her Life, Her Faith*. New York: Jove, 1984.

Caughey, Ellen. *Eric Liddell*. Ohio: Barbour, 2000.

Chong, Denise. *The Girl in the Picture*. Toronto, Canada: Viking, 1999.

Colbert, Dr. Don. *Deadly Emotions*. Nashville, Tennessee: Thomas Nelson, 2003.

Colson, Charles. *Born Again*. New Jersey: Fleming H. Revell, 1977.

Crabb, Dr. Larry and Dr. Dan Allender. *Hope When You're Hurting.* Michigan: Zondervan, 1996.

Curry, Dayna and Heather Mercer. *Prisoners of Hope.* New York: Doubleday, 2002.

Dobbins, Dr. Richard. *Your Feelings...Friend or Foe?* Ohio: Totally Alive Publications, 1994.

Dobson, Dr. James C. *Emotions: Can You Trust Them?* California: Regal Books, 1980.

Doidge, Dr. Norman. *The Brain that Changes Itself.* New York: The Penguin Group, 2007.

Elliot, Elisabeth. *Through Gates of Splendour.* London, U.K.: Hodder and Stoughton, 1968.

Gerhart, Ann. *The Perfect Wife: The Life and Choices of Laura Bush.* New York: Simon & Schuster, 2004.

Grubb, Norman. *Rees Howells Intercessor.* Fort Washington, Penn.: CLC Publications, 1952.

Harvey, Bonnie. *Charles Finney.* Ohio: Barbour Publishing Inc., 1999.

Haskin, Leslie. *Between Heaven and Ground Zero.* Minnesota: Bethany House, 2006.

Johnson, Barbara. *Splashes of Joy in the Cesspools of Life.* Nashville, Tennessee: Thomas Nelson, 1992.

Kent, Carol. *A New Kind of Normal.* Nashville, Tennessee: Thomas Nelson, 2007.

Lewis, C. S. *A Grief Observed.* New York: HarperCollins, 2001 new edition.

Lewis, C. S. *The Four Loves.* Glasgow, Scotland: William Collins Sons, 1981.

Lotz, Ann Graham. *The Vision of His Glory.* U.S.: W Publishing Group, 1996.

Mangalwadi, Vishal and Ruth. *The Legacy of William Carey.* Wheaton: Crossway Books, 1999.

Monroe, Kelly Ed.. *Finding God at Harvard*. Michigan: Zondervan, 1996.

Mullen, Dr. Grant. *Emotionally Free*. Chosen, 2003.

Newton, John. *John Newton: His Autobiography*. Chicago, Illinois: Moody Press.

Norton, Howard and Bob Slosser. *The Miracle of Jimmy Carter*. New Jersey: Logos, 1976.

Omartian, Stormie. *Stormie*. Oregon: Harvest House, 1986.

Pascal, Blaise. *Pensées*. 1669, Public Domain.

Patti, Sandi. *Broken on the Back Row*. Louisiana: Howard Publishing Co., 2005.

Petersen, William J. *25 Surprising Marriages*. Grand Rapids, Michigan: Baker Books, 1997.

Reagan, Ronald. *Ronald Reagan: An American Life*. New York: Pocket Books, 1990.

Roseveare, Dr. Helen. *Give Me This Mountain*. Intervarsity Press: 1995.

Rustin, Michael and Sharon. *The One Year Christian History*. Illinois: Tyndale, 2003.

Seamands, David. *Healing for Damaged Emotions*. Wheaton, Illinois: Victor Books, 1981.

Smith, Hannah Whitall. *The Christian's Secret of a Happy Life*. Public Domain. Republished in Ohio: Barbour Publishing, 1998.

Stokl, Dr. Stephen. *Mentally Speaking*. Canada, 2006.

Swindoll, Charles R. *Paul*. Nashville, Tennessee: The W Publishing Group, 2002.

Ten Boom, Corrie. with J. and E. Sherill. *The Hiding Place*. New Jersey: Fleming H. Revell Co., 1971.

Ten Boom, Corrie. *Tramp for the Lord*. New Jersey: Fleming H. Revell, 1974.

Walsh, Sheila. *Honestly*. Grand Rapids, Michigan: Zondervan, 1996.

Waters, Ethel. *His Eye is on the Sparrow*. New York: Jove, 1978.

Wellman, Sam. *Amy Carmichael*. Ohio: Barbour, 1998.

Wellman, Sam. *Mary Slessor*. Ohio: Barbour, 1998.

White, Dr. John. *The Masks of Melancholy*. Illinois: InterVarsity Press, 1982.

Wiersbe, Warren. *Victorious Christians You Should Know*. Michigan: Baker, 1984.

Wilkerson, David. *The Cross and the Switchblade*. New York: Jove, 1978.

Articles and Reports

Barsky, A. J., G. Wyshak, and G. L. Klerman. (1986). "Medical and psychiatric determinants of outpatient medical utilization." *Medical Care* 2, 548–560.

Berk, L., et al. "Neuroendocrine and stress hormone changes during mirthful laughter." *The American Journal of the Medical Sciences* 298 (1989): 390–396.

Blair, Kathy. "Langs' pain will always be there." *Anglican Journal*, October 1999.

Cousins, W. "Anatomy of an illness as perceived by the patient." *New England Journal of Medicine* 295 (1976): 1458–1463.

Danner, D. D., D. A. Snowdon, and W. V. Friesen. "Positive emotions in early life and longevity: findings from the nun study." *Journal of Personality and Social Psychology* 80 (2001): 804–813.

Dowsett Johnston, Ann. "Stalking a Silent Killer." *Macleans*, November 14, 2005.

Emmons R.A. & M. E. McCullough. "Counting blessings vs. burdens: an experimental investigation of gratitude and subjective well-being in daily life." *Journal of Personality and Social Psychology* 84 (2003): 377–389.

Evans, Patrick. "I can't believe this is running on page 3: Canadians fourth worst grumblers in the world." *Toronto Star*, August 26, 2005.

Everson, et al. "Hostility and increased risk of mortality and acute myocardial infarction: the mediating role of behavioral risk factors." *American Journal of Epidemiology* 146, no. 2 (1997): 142–152.

Fieguth, Debra. "Father Draws Jesus into Shooting Tragedy." *Anglican Journal*, June 1999.

Dean, Flannery. "Think Yourself Happy." *Chatelaine*, April, 2007.

Fredrickson, B.L. "What good are positive emotions?" *Review of General Psychology* 2 (1998): 300–319.

Fredrickson, B.L. and R. W. Levenson. "Positive emotions speed recovery from the cardiovascular sequelae of negative emotions." *Cognition and Emotion* 12 (1998): 191–220.

Friedman, H. S., and S. Booth-Kewley. "The disease-prone personality: A meta-analytic view of the construct." *American Psychologist* 42 (1987): 539–555.

Gordon, Andrea. "Working with Depression." *Toronto Star*, November 20, 2007.

Gulli, Cathy. "A Lawn to Die For." *Macleans*, April 3, 2006.

Harvey, Robin. "Reframing Sad Thoughts." *Toronto Star*, September 8, 2006.

Heinen, Tom. "Of Forgiveness and Friendship." *Milwaukee Journal Sentinel*, January 7, 2006.

Herrald, M. M., and J. Tomaka. "Patterns of emotion-specific appraisal, coping, and cardiovascular reactivity during an ongoing emotional episode." *Journal of Personality and Social Psychology* 83 (2002): 434–450.

Johnstone, Meg. "The 'girl in the picture' is flying." www.canadianchristianity.com (accessed 1/10/2006).

Kawachi, Ichiro. "Anger and hostility linked to coronary heart disease." *Lancet* 355 (2000): 1621.

Kiecolt-Glaser, J. K., I. McGuire, T. F. Robles, and R. Glaser. "Emotions, morbidity, and mortality: New perspectives from psychoneuroimmunology." *Annual Review of Psychology* 53 (2002): 83–107.

Kielburger, Craig and Marc. "No purchase necessary to find real fulfillment." *Toronto Star*, November 23, 2006.

Kneip, R. C., A. M. Delamater, T. Ismond, C. Milford, L. Salvia, and D. Schwartz. "Self and spouse ratings of anger and hostility as predictors of coronary heart disease." *Health Psychology* 12 (1993): 301–307.

Kubzansky, L.D., I. Kawachi, A. Spiro III, S. T. Weiss, P. S. Vokonas, and D. Sparrow. "Is worrying bad for your heart? A prospective study of worry and coronary heart disease in the Normative Aging Study." *Circulation* 95 (1997): 818–824.

Lawler, K.A., J. W. Younger, R. L. Piferi, E. Billington, R. Jobe, K. Edmondson, and W. H. Jones. "A change of heart: cardiovascular correlates of forgiveness in response to interpersonal conflict." *Journal of Behavioral Medicine* 26 (2003): 373–393.

Lemonick, Michael. "The Flavor of Memories." *TIME,* Canadian edition, January 29, 2007.

Luskin, Dr. Frederic. "The art and science of forgiveness." *Stanford Medicine* 16, no. 4 (1999), accessed online at http://stanmed.stanford.edu/1999 summer/forgiveness.html on 11/6/2007.

Matthews K.A., K. Raikkonen, K. Sutton-Tyrrell, and L. H. Kuller. "Optimistic attitudes protect against progression of carotid atherosclerosis in healthy middle-aged women." *Psychosomatic Medicine* 66 (2004): 640–644.

Mayo Foundation for Medical Education and Research. "Healthy Marriage: Why love is good for you." www.mayoclinic.com, accessed February 6, 2006.

McKeen, Nancy A. et al. "A longitudinal analysis of discrete negative emotions and health-services use in elderly individuals." *Journal of Aging and Health.* 16, no. 2 (April 2004): 204–227.

Mittleman, M. A., M. Manclure, J. B. Sherwood, et al. "Triggering of acute myocardial infarction onset by episodes of anger." *Circulation* 92 (1995): 1720–1725.

Moussavi, Saba MPH, Dr. Somnath Chatterji, et al. "Depression, chronic diseases, and decrements in health: results from the World Health surveys." *Lancet* 370 (2007): 851–858.

Puchalski, Dr. Christina. "Forgiveness: Spiritual and Medical Implications." *The Yale Journal for Humanities in Medicine,* September 17, 2002.

Raikonen, K., K. A. Matthew, J. D. Flory, and J. F. Owens. "Effects of hostility on ambulatory blood pressure and mood during daily living in healthy adults." *Health Psychology* 18 (1999): 44–53.

Rowan, P. J., K. Davidson, J. A. Campbell, D. G. Dobrez, and D. R. MacLean. "Depressive symptoms predict medical care utilization in a population-based sample." *Psychological Medicine*, 32, (2002): 903–908.

Rozanski, Dr. A., and Dr. Laura D. Kubzansky. "Psychologic functioning and physical health: A paradigm of flexibility." *Psychosomatic Medicine* 67 (2005): S1:S47–S53

Smith, Brooke. "Defeating Depression." *Canadian Health*, March/April 2007.

Van Biema, David. "Her Agony." *TIME*, Canadian edition, September 3, 2007.

"World Drug Report 2006." New York: United Nations Office on Drugs and Crime, 2006.

Poems and Hymns

Chisholm, Thomas O. "Great is Thy Faithfulness." Public Domain.

Crosby, Fanny. From an unnamed childhood poem. Public Domain.

Henley, W.E. "Invictus." 1875, Public Domain.

Martin, Civilla D. and Gabriel, Charles H. "His Eye is on the Sparrow." Public Domain.

Scriven, Joseph. "What a Friend We Have in Jesus." 1855, Public Domain.

Spafford, Horatio. "It is Well with My Soul." 1873, Public Domain.

CONTACTING THE AUTHOR

The author would love to hear from you. She can be contacted by mail at the publisher's address or by e-mail at khenein@rogers.com.

The author is available for speaking engagements on the topic of emotions and on other topics of interest to Christians.

The author wishes to thank you for reading her book. She prays regularly that each reader will find and express increasing measures of forgiveness, love, faith, peace, hope, contentment, and joy.

ALSO FROM KAREN HENEIN

Counsel of the Most High

Receiving God's Guidance
for Life's Decisions

ISBN # 1-894928-99-7
Word Alive Press, 2007

Do you have clear direction for your life? Do you know where you are heading and why? Do you make life choices with confidence and clarity? Do you find the decision-making process daunting?

God cares about our decisions, both large and small. Counsel of the Most High discusses how we can wisely tackle the "big" decisions—how we can discover God's specific plans and highest purposes for our own individual lives—while also exploring how we can receive God's guidance regarding our more minor everyday choices.

Whether you are a young adult just beginning to make significant decisions regarding education, career and marriage...or you are thinking of starting a family, buying a home, maybe moving across the country...or you are a mid-lifer changing careers and adjusting to an emptying nest...this book can help you find God's guidance regarding the ever-changing landscape of your life. Fresh choices are on the horizon of each one of us!

Discover the privilege of receiving the intimate counsel of the Most High. Direction, confidence and clarity are available to each one of us as we tackle the countless choices and decisions that challenge us at each stage of our lives.